"This lucid and wonderful book provides the reader with a compelling autobiographical account of the intricate life journey of a prominent trauma therapist and his courageous road to healing. Frank Anderson gently shows how his life's work has its roots in his own history—his troubled upbringing, the relatively late emergence of his sexual identity (that clearly led to a vastly heightened capacity for intimacy), and the courageous transition to raising two sons in a two-male-parent household. A passionate, courageous, and inspiring work."

—BESSEL VAN DER KOLK, MD, AUTHOR OF THE #1 *NEW YORK TIMES* BESTSELLER *THE BODY KEEPS THE SCORE*

"Leading trauma expert Frank Anderson gifts us with an intimate and vulnerable glimpse into his personal journey of self-discovery to overcome his own childhood trauma. *To Be Loved* is a beautifully written and empowering story of resilience, healing, and forgiveness that offers hope for all survivors of childhood trauma."

—NICOLE LePERA, PHD, AUTHOR OF THE #1 *NEW YORK TIMES* BESTSELLER *HOW TO BE THE LOVE YOU SEEK* AND *HOW TO DO THE WORK*

"Moving and masterful! Filled with humor, empathy, and candid self-reflection, Frank's story demonstrates the power to heal childhood trauma, develop resilience, and ultimately find love, forgiveness, and restoration."

—LORI GOTTLIEB, *NEW YORK TIMES* BESTSELLING AUTHOR OF *MAYBE YOU SHOULD TALK TO SOMEONE*, TED SPEAKER, CO-HOST OF THE POPULAR *DEAR THERAPISTS* PODCAST, AND "DEAR THERAPIST" COLUMNIST FOR *THE ATLANTIC*

"The courage and care of this powerful memoir invites us to share a journey from childhood trauma and alienation to professional and personal success. Along the way, we are inspired to reflect on how our own minds work and ways to empower ourselves to face challenging relationships with integrity, compassion, and forgiveness. Thank you, Frank Anderson, for the gift of this powerful life reflection!"

—**DANIEL J. SIEGEL, MD,** *NEW YORK TIMES*
BESTSELLING AUTHOR OF *MINDSIGHT, AWARE,*
AND *THE WHOLE-BRAIN CHILD*

"A heartbreaking yet remarkable story of transcending childhood trauma. Through Dr. Anderson's vulnerable exploration of his past, we can all learn how to find forgiveness and become more compassionate and loving caregivers. An inspiring, must-read memoir for anyone who has experienced childhood trauma or has a loved one who has suffered through this ordeal."

—**DR. SHEFALI,** CLINICAL PSYCHOLOGIST AND
NEW YORK TIMES BESTSELLING AUTHOR OF *THE
CONSCIOUS PARENT* AND *THE PARENTING MAP*

"*To Be Loved* is the journey of one of our top trauma experts, Frank Anderson, MD—his personal account of healing, self-acceptance, achievement, and finding long-lasting love. As a film producer with an extensive childhood trauma history, reading Frank's beautifully told story gave me hope that no matter what a person has gone through, it is within reach to create a happy and stable life unencumbered by fear, loneliness, and resentment."

—**ALEXANDRA RYAN,** TWO-TIME EMMY-
NOMINATED FILM AND TELEVISION PRODUCER

"Frank Anderson has been my friend and mentee for many years, and from the beginning I saw the tremendous leadership potential that he is now manifesting. When most leaders reach his level, they write about the epiphanies and glorious victories that got them to where they are. In this compelling and beautifully written book, Frank models for us all a different and far more valuable approach. He has an amazing memory of the details of growing up in a colorful, Mafia-connected Italian family in

Chicago, so it holds your interest like a good novel. But he also shares the traumas of having a physically abusive father, an enmeshed but unprotective mother, and the process of recognizing and owning his gay identity. With courageous disclosure, he also reveals how he repeated dysfunctional patterns from his childhood in his adult relationships and in his parenting. His happy ending is well-earned and his journey is full of lessons for us all."

—RICHARD C. SCHWARTZ, PHD, FOUNDER OF INTERNAL FAMILY SYSTEMS THERAPY AND AUTHOR OF *NO BAD PARTS*

"In *To Be Loved*, Dr. Frank Anderson masterfully weaves together his traumatic childhood story with lessons of resilience, truth, and authenticity. It takes an enormous amount of courage for the expert to show his own vulnerable journey of healing. This book will inspire readers to utilize his hard-won tools for processing their own past and discovering a more hopeful future."

—DAVID KESSLER, RENOWNED GRIEF SPECIALIST AND AUTHOR OF *FINDING MEANING: THE SIXTH STAGE OF GRIEF*

"*To Be Loved* is a unique and deeply personal narrative that stands out in the genre of self-authored trauma histories. Unlike many memoirs that focus solely on the negative aspects of one's story, this book presents a surprisingly warm and honest account, acknowledging both the joyous moments in childhood and the tragedies. Frank's ability to portray even the individuals who caused harm in a human and empathetic light, while still recognizing the impact of their actions, is remarkable. His narrative goes beyond mere storytelling; it's a compelling exploration of the complexities of trauma, the nuances of human relationships, and the journey toward healing and forgiveness. Knowing Frank personally, I can attest to the authenticity and depth he brings to his life's work, making this book an invaluable read for anyone interested in understanding the full spectrum of human emotion and the path to healing."

—MATTHIAS BARKER, LMHC, CEO, TRAUMA INSTITUTE

"Frank Anderson has woven the stories of his life into a book that will both enthrall and uplift you. He writes with wisdom and compassion about the roller coaster of being human, and the result is a vivid picture of how healing and growth actually happen."

"A nationally known expert on trauma, Frank Anderson shares a compelling personal story of his own childhood trauma and his journey to transcendence over fear and prejudice. As a trauma survivor coming out as a gay man in a family and professional culture that could not welcome him, he describes the long, painful journey to self-acceptance and recreation. A deft storyteller, Frank brings an informed perspective to this experience of recovery and resilience, driven by his refusal to give up his dreams of transcending the past by creating a healthy family with his husband and their children. Going beyond traditional trauma processing, he emphasizes the transformative power of extending compassion not only to our abusers but also to the young, wounded parts within ourselves. By sharing his own journey, Frank will inspire others to find hope and determination."

"In *To Be Loved*, trauma recovery expert Frank Anderson offers us an intimate look at his journey in the hope that we can better understand our own. His story highlights the cultural and societal changes that have transformed our understanding of love, family, and mental health—and that have made possible a deeper understanding of what it means to truly belong. Embedded within Frank's story is the vital insight that recovery and resilience come from not only forgiving our perpetrators of trauma and abuse, but also healing the perpetrator within ourselves."

"Trauma therapist and Harvard-trained psychiatrist Frank Anderson's memoir homes in on a universal desire and need: *to be loved*. His book models practicing what he preaches—with his characteristic frankness (no pun intended), humility, vulnerability, courageous self-reflection, and a trauma-informed compassion for his own 'parts' that shines through and inspires the reader to do the same for themselves. Given how rare it is for a man with his level of success and prestige to be this forthcoming about the traumatic 'moments that made him,' he's certain to be an inspiration for anyone who has believed they have to be stoic and invulnerable in order to be loved, only to discover that the truth is just the opposite. A must-read for anyone interested in understanding the heart-opening trauma healing path."

—**LISSA RANKIN, MD,** *NEW YORK TIMES* BESTSELLING AUTHOR OF *MIND OVER MEDICINE*

"Dr. Frank Anderson unfolds a compelling narrative, offering a raw, relatable testimony of what it truly means to overcome intergenerational trauma, family dysfunction, and the systemic limitations of cishet patriarchal societal norms and biases. His profound insight emphasizes the courage required in acknowledging and embracing childhood trauma, to extend compassion not only to external perpetrators but also to the internalized, wounded parts of ourselves. A storyteller armed with scientific evidence as well as lived experience, Frank brings a fresh, authentic perspective to the lifelong journey of loving ourselves toward deep psychospiritual healing."

—**DERAN YOUNG, LCSW, MPA,** FOUNDER OF BLACK THERAPISTS ROCK

"*To Be Loved* is a profound exploration of the human capacity to heal. Through his deeply personal narrative, Dr. Frank Anderson shares his triumphant path from childhood trauma to embracing his authentic self, a journey that deeply touches and inspires. This book is a gift to anyone who has grappled with the shadows of their past, offering a powerful message of hope, resilience, and the transformative power of the human spirit."

—**KATE TRUITT, PhD, MBA,** TRAUMA EXPERT AND AUTHOR OF *HEALING IN YOUR HANDS* AND *KEEP BREATHING*

"*To Be Loved* draws you in from the very first page. By bravely sharing his own story of healing, Frank has given the world the gift of an incredible memoir. But he's done so much more than that. Thanks to Frank's unique expertise in healing trauma, his story provides a blueprint for all of us who are seeking healing, love, and forgiveness."

—**SEANNE WINSLOW,** AWARD-WINNING
WRITER, DIRECTOR, AND PRODUCER

"Frank Anderson understands his patients, not just because he is a brilliant clinician, but because he has lived his own deeply painful childhood experiences and has dedicated his life to healing himself as well as others. His new memoir, *To Be Loved*, is an honest look at what it means to be in a family, to experience generations of trauma, and to be the one who finally wakes up and refuses to pass it on to his children. I read this book in two days; I couldn't put it down. *To Be Loved* is a fascinating story of transformation and will help any reader understand what it means to truly grow up."

—**TAMMY NELSON, PhD,** TEDx SPEAKER, RELATIONSHIP
THERAPIST, AND AUTHOR OF *OPEN MONOGAMY*

"In a world where trauma experts can appear flawless, Dr. Frank Anderson's *To Be Loved* is a breath of fresh air and a testament to the power of authenticity. Dr. Anderson doesn't just preach about trauma healing; he lives it. His profound belief that 'trauma blocks love, and love heals trauma' isn't just a catchphrase—it's a philosophy he embodies, inspiring us all to approach healing trauma with authenticity and love."

—**MASTIN KIPP,** CREATOR OF FUNCTIONAL LIFE COACHING™
AND BESTSELLING AUTHOR OF *CLAIM YOUR POWER*

"Healing from a traumatic childhood often feels like riding a roller coaster naked. In *To Be Loved*, Frank Anderson guides the reader through the ups and downs of his own healing journey, sharing a beautifully textured, deeply relational story. With insight, brutal honesty, and an appreciation for the frailties of human nature, Frank walks the reader along his healing path, where the dichotomies of perpetrator and victim, good and evil, melt away through the power of love and forgiveness. His story of transformation will serve as both a roadmap to healing and a beacon of hope for others struggling with the isolation and alienation of childhood abuse, whose desire to be loved is as basic as the need for air."

—**AMY BANKS, MD,** COAUTHOR OF *FIGHTING TIME* AND *WIRED TO CONNECT* AND FOUNDING SCHOLAR AT THE INTERNATIONAL CENTER FOR GROWTH IN CONNECTION

"I am very impressed by Frank as a teacher, a friend, and a fellow human being. He has a remarkable trauma history—and an even more remarkable history of transcending trauma, transforming his suffering into a profound understanding of humanity, deep love, and a devotion to help people heal from trauma. I encourage everyone who encounters challenges in life to read this book, which will for sure inspire you with courage, wisdom, hope, and most importantly, love."

—**HAILAN GUO, MD, PhD,** FOUNDER OF HAILAN FAMILY WELL-BEING, BEIJING, CHINA

"*To Be Loved* is a unique coming-of-age story that is a powerful read for trauma survivors and LGBTQIA+ readers. Frank shines a spotlight on the forces of family and cultural trauma that shape our understanding of who we are and what we can become. This beautiful story is a beacon of hope for anyone seeking support in the journey toward resilience, forgiveness, and love."

—**PAUL DENNISTON,** CREATOR OF GRIEF YOGA® AND AUTHOR OF *HEALING THROUGH YOGA: TRANSFORM LOSS INTO EMPOWERMENT*

To Be Loved

To Be Loved

A STORY OF TRUTH, TRAUMA, AND TRANSFORMATION

Frank G. Anderson, MD

Bridge City Books

TO BE LOVED
Copyright © 2024 by Frank G. Anderson

Published by
Bridge City Books, an imprint of PESI Publishing, Inc.
3839 White Ave
Eau Claire, WI 54703

Library of Congress Cataloging-in-Publication Data
Subjects: LCSH: Anderson, Frank G. | Psychiatrists—United States—Biography. | Gay
men—United States—Biography. | Psychologically abused children—United States—
Biography. | Coming out (Sexual orientation)—Psychological aspects.
Classification: LCC RC438.6.A387 A3 2024 | DDC 616.890092--dc23/eng/20240205
LC record available at https://lccn.loc.gov/2023058497

Cover design by Martha Kennedy
Interior design by Amy Rubenzer & Emily Dyer
Editing by Chelsea Thompson

ISBN: 9781962305112 (print)
ISBN: 9781962305136 (ePDF)
ISBN: 9781962305129 (ePUB)

Bridge City Books
An Imprint of PESI Publishing

Printed in Canada

To my greatest teachers—my father and my two sons.

TABLE OF CONTENTS

THE JOURNEY

A few months after the release of my second book, *Transcending Trauma*, my publisher reached out to set up a meeting with me. They wanted to talk about the next project; I wanted a break. It had taken four long years to write about the treatment of complex posttraumatic stress disorder (C-PTSD) in a way that integrated current neuroscience knowledge with the Internal Family Systems (IFS) model of therapy for the treatment of relational trauma. Much as I love teaching (and hate disappointing people who have supported me), I came to the meeting ready with a gracious decline.

As it turned out, another teaching book was not what they had in mind either.

"Frank, we think you should write a memoir," said the four smiling faces on the Zoom screen.

Are you crazy? I thought. *I'm not eighty years old. I haven't won a Nobel Peace Prize.* "Why would anyone want to hear my story?" I asked.

"Because you're a Harvard-trained psychiatrist, a well-respected trauma therapist—and you talk openly about your own trauma history during the workshops you teach and in your latest book," they explained. "We think that you're the perfect person to tell this story and show people that healing from trauma is possible."

Their words nudged a memory into my mind—less a memory than a recollection. Just the night before, I'd had a dream that consisted mainly of a single phrase, whispered over and over: "*The moments that made me.*"

As soon as I shared this phrase with my publishing team, pieces instantly started falling into place. I felt chills race throughout my body. In recent years, I'd learned to recognize this sensation as an affirmation, a signpost telling me that I was on the right path.

I got off the call and went for a run. As my feet pounded the pavement, I found my mind wandering back to the last four years of working on *Transcending Trauma*. The hours I spent after work. The nights I didn't go to bed until two o'clock in the morning. The weekends when I was physically present but mentally elsewhere. *My family is going to kill me.*

What had made those years worthwhile? I knew the answer—it was the conviction that *Transcending Trauma* was the culmination of my professional life's work and the hope that it would help people heal from their trauma. But maybe the work wasn't done. My first book, directed mainly at clinicians and therapists, had taught the "how" of healing from trauma, but what good was teaching people how to heal if they didn't believe they could?

Maybe my publishers were right. Maybe there was a story in me that was waiting to be told. My life's work was out there, but now it was time to share the life that led to the work.

"Okay," I said. "I'm going to write a memoir."

* * *

To Be Loved is a brutally honest account of how I spent a lifetime trying to right the wrongs of my childhood, only to realize that I repeated the very thing I tried so hard to get away from. I imagine that parts of my story may be very painful, even activating, for some people; please read with an awareness of and tenderness toward your own history. Moreover, I'm shaken by the thought of how sharing this story will impact members of my own family. To spare them pain or exposure, I've done my best to protect the names and personal details of those mentioned here. The purpose of this book isn't revenge, or even catharsis. It comes from a place of love, a desire to demonstrate that pain and trauma are universal and that healing and forgiveness are attainable.

In many ways, the world is in bad shape right now. Mental health issues including depression, suicidal ideation, substance use, and anxiety are at an all-time high for children, teenagers, and adults alike. While the debate goes on about the impacts of "big T" versus "little t" trauma, I've yet to meet anyone who hasn't gone through something difficult or overwhelming that impacts their life in ways they wish they could change. After twenty-five years in this field, I've never been more sure that now is the right time to bring true healing out of the therapy office and into people's homes, workplaces, families, friendships, and personal lives.

I'm encouraged (and amazed) to see how trauma is a common topic of conversation today. Our culture is awakening to the commonality and the significance of trauma. Athletes, politicians, and celebrities now talk candidly about their struggles with mental health and the experiences that led to them. Our society is actively reckoning with collective trauma through movements like #MeToo and Black Lives Matter. As a global community, we lived through a shared experience of trauma during the COVID-19 pandemic. I believe we're at the beginning stages of a collective shift in consciousness, with many of us finally willing to compassionately view our symptoms, our hardships, and our attempts to cope as our best attempt to fix a problem that was beyond our human capacity to manage at the time. This compassion leads us to forgiveness, the driving force behind healing. When we can forgive our own trauma-informed behavior, knowing it was the best we could do at the time, we can begin to similarly understand and forgive those who perpetrated that trauma in our lives.

I also see the backlash against this collective awakening. Transparency around trauma is difficult for those who don't believe healing or forgiveness is possible. The curtailing of conversations around mental health, trauma recovery, and cycle breaking, the ridicule against people who choose to share their stories—I understand it all as a means to avoid reckoning with their own trauma, hurt, and shame. I understand it precisely because I lived it for so long. What I hope to show in these pages, along with the long-term and widespread impact of traumatic experiences, is the tremendous freedom that results when we stop running from our past and confront the truth of who we are.

* * *

As much as I intend this book to be a gift to the world, it turned out to be a gift to myself. While my work centers on helping people own and process their stories, I somehow never thought that sharing my own narrative would prove to be an incredibly therapeutic process for me. Even after years of therapy, writing about my own trauma brought a deeper level of healing. Long-buried memories came out of the shadows. The meaning I'd made of certain experiences emerged from my subconscious. Connections between long-forgotten events, years apart, fired and fused together like live wires.

This led to something even more surprising: My life started unfolding to support the story. I thought it was supposed to be the other way around, that you write a book about your life, not that your life takes the shape of the book you're writing. But all the work I had done in the past had beautifully prepared me for what would unfold in the present.

The last quarter of the book was written in real time. I would go through something impactful or even overwhelming, pull out my computer, and watch the story reveal itself right before my eyes. I had never experienced anything quite like it before. It was as if the book wrote itself in real time. For months, I found myself getting up at three or four o'clock in the morning to capture new insights. Then, as if on cue, life would offer me a fresh opportunity to put those insights to use. It seemed as though opening myself up to the idea of my traumatic past having a purpose, a meaning bigger than me, empowered me to choose actions and perspectives that would support the story my life needed to tell.

Along with friends, family members, mentors, and clinicians, I've been tremendously supported in my healing journey by the many patients who were willing to vulnerably share their stories of hardship, adversity, and loss with me. Even though our individual experiences are unique, we all can learn from hearing about someone else's journey. My wish is that this book offers you insights and connections to your history and sparks your curiosity and interest in letting go of the experiences that plague you from your past. I hope it gives you permission to choose hope over heartache, beauty over pain, and love over loneliness. Know that whatever you end up choosing, you deserve to be loved.

With gratitude,
Frank

ABOUT THE
TO BE LOVED PLAYLIST

Like many of us, music has always been a big part of my life. It has also been an important component of healing my trauma. Whether it was on an eight-track tape player, a boombox, a Walkman, an iPod nano, or my cell phone, I've listened to songs on repeat to help me identify, verbalize, and process emotions that were at times too intense to feel, while at other times inaccessible or out of my conscious awareness. As you read *To Be Loved*, you will notice that each chapter starts with a song, the artist, and a phrase that depicts what the chapter means to me as well as how I used that particular song to help process that chapter of my life. There is a downloadable playlist available at the end of the book so you can listen to my musical journey as you read the book.

Music touches us all differently and deeply at various stages of our lives. I encourage you to create your own "To Be Loved" playlist—your musical journal—that captures the way you access, name, and process the important experiences in your life. Feel free to share your playlist with me at FrankAndersonMD.com. I would love to hear it.

CHAPTER ONE

"YOU'RE NOT GOING
TO SCHOOL TODAY"

"Kid Fears" | Indigo Girls

My kid fears invaded every cell of my body; they were present with every breath I took. I also had a secret crawlspace where I could run and hide—a place where I could escape to, and one where I desperately wanted to be found.

* * *

I was just six years old when I learned there was something seriously wrong with me. Even though it happened more than fifty years ago, I can still see where I was when it happened, as vividly as a Polaroid snapshot: the carpeted hallway from my bedroom to my parents' room, the king-size bed that swallowed up most of the room, the two dressers that occupied the remainder of the space—Dad's against the far wall, tall and narrow with a wooden box on top that held his cufflinks, and Mom's at the foot of the bed, its wide surface scattered with jewelry boxes, perfume bottles, and their framed wedding picture, all reflected in the big vanity mirror.

I was used to stumbling down this hallway in the mornings and climbing into my parents' bed. Today, however, both my parents were awake already. My dad was perched on the edge of the bed in his Jockey underwear and "dago T" (as we used to call it). At his side was my mom in her lace-edged nightgown, propped up by pillows against the headboard. Though they'd called me in, they looked up when I entered the room as if I'd caught them in a secret conversation.

"You're not going to school today, Frankie," said my father.

For another kid, these words might have brought a moment of pure elation. For me, it was a disappointment; I loved my first-grade class. Moreover, being kept out of it was a clear signal that something strange was happening. Louis and Maggie weren't the sort of parents to have me miss a day of school without a good reason.

It's not the weekend. We're not on summer vacation. I don't feel sick.

"Why not?" I asked.

Their answer was more confusing than the announcement. "We're taking you to a hospital downtown for some tests," said my dad.

Missing school, visiting a hospital in the city rather than our local hospital, my parents' secretive tone—all this could mean only one thing: I must be sick. Very sick.

• • •

My parents drove me to Rush Presbyterian St. Luke's Medical Center, more than an hour away from our house in Oak Lawn, Illinois. The familiar surroundings of our tranquil Midwestern suburb, all modest split-level homes like ours, fell away in the rear window as the road took us into the high-rise canyons of downtown Chicago.

The tests weren't the kind one would expect at a big university hospital. No bright lights, no stethoscopes, no blood work or X-rays. No explanation from my parents, either. I found myself alone in a stark white room with a stranger, trying to answer the questions he asked me while looking at a peculiar array of pictures: a woman gazing forlornly out a window, a little boy playing with a dog, a series of half-finished shapes, a collection of black and white blobs that made no sense to my eyes.

More mysterious than the pictures themselves was the purpose behind it all. I'd never been in a hospital room like this one, never heard of my friends being left alone with a stranger who asked questions like these, never encountered the kind of tone my parents had used in talking to me that morning or to the stranger afterward. Sensing that it wasn't something they wanted to explain to me, I didn't ask. But I could tell that whatever was wrong with me, the hospital visit hadn't made it go away. Deep in the pit of my stomach, I felt what they wouldn't tell me: *There's something in me that needs to be fixed. I'm clearly wrong somehow.* Staring out the car window as the skyscrapers returned to split-levels and manicured lawns, I made my first attempt at what would become a life-long practice: forget what just happened, suppress my feelings about it, and try my best to appear normal.

* * *

That visit set a new routine in place for the next six years. Every Tuesday night, I took a long car ride with one of my parents to a long, low building in the distant suburb of La Grange. Arriving there felt like pulling up to a motel—the entrance to the psychiatry office was one of several doors in the building, and we walked directly from the parking space into the waiting room. I remember reading *Highlights* magazine as I waited for my turn. I remember the big wooden desk in Dr. Dwight's office, which he said was strictly off-limits. I remember two big chests of drawers against the wall and, beyond them, a white desk filled with art supplies.

Dr. Dwight directed me to sit down at the desk and laid out sheets of white paper, crayons, and colored pencils. "Can you draw a picture of your family?"

Dutifully, I sketched representations of my family—my mother; my father; my brother, Ross; our dog, Puggie. I liked to draw and, since he seemed impressed by my work, I added my red house with the front door, several windows, a chimney, and a big tree to the right. I hoped for more drawing assignments; instead, he proceeded to ask me questions about my family. I answered readily, wondering again what this was all about. *Why does a doctor want to know about what color my dog is or what my house looks like or how I play with my brother?*

Despite having no answers, I got used to the routine. Every Tuesday brought another long car ride, another "special meeting" that remained largely a blur. It wasn't until several years later, when I was in the sixth grade, that I remembered Dr. Dwight asking me if I would like to play with some toys. He walked me over to the carpeted area and opened the chests of drawers. My eyes lit up at the things in the first chest—stuffed animals, ribbons and buttons, multicolored beads. But even as I reached for them, Dr. Dwight intervened.

"No, Frankie, we're going to play with *these* toys."

He gestured toward the other chest and instructed me to choose something I would enjoy playing with. I looked inside—construction trucks, the game Battleship, tiny plastic army men. Nothing interested me, but he sat and waited until I finally chose the army men. Dr. Dwight chose a plastic battleship. Together, we lined up the little green figures in rows and pretended to fight, knocking each other's men down, and pushed the boat around the carpeting as if it were the sea, making motor noises with our mouths. Noticing that the tiny men would fall over if I pushed the boat too quickly, I was careful to make it cruise along slowly—if these were the "right" toys to play with, there was probably a right way to play with them.

No one ever asked me what had happened during the hour I spent with Dr. Dwight. Even if they had, I don't know if I'd have been able to answer. I spent the long drive home each week finding other things to think about, things that helped me ignore the uneasy feeling and the unnameable truth behind it. I got so good at ignoring my own questions that by the time I got home, whatever had happened in that day's session had faded into mystery. To this day, I find myself wondering, *What in the hell was I doing in there?*

* * *

During the time I was seeing Dr. Dwight, my parents had a "special meeting" of their own with a marriage and family therapist named Dr. Johnson. As a result of these counseling sessions, a new rule was issued in our house: No more hitting.

I have no memory of telling Dr. Dwight about the hitting. Those memories were as blurry for me as the sessions in his office. What I do remember is the frequent feeling of breathless relief: *I got away. He didn't get me this time.* Just one visual memory is burned into my mind: I'm ducked on the floor with my hands clasped over my head, elbows squeezed tightly together to protect my face. I'm frightened, and my mind is focused. *Don't hit my face. I need to protect my face. It will hurt too much if he gets my face. Hit me on my back. My back is strong. It can handle anything.* I hear the blows—BOOM, BOOM, BOOM—as his fists pound on my back, but I don't feel any pain.

How did I do that? Why didn't I feel anything? Despite the thrill of being apparently invincible, I always hoped for a broken bone or a bruise, some visible mark on my body to prove what just happened. But other than the occasional red handprint that remained on my arm or leg, lasting evidence of my father's physical abuse never materialized.

My dad was the only one who did the hitting, and for some reason, I was the one who got hit most. My younger brother, Ross, despite always getting into trouble for one reason or another, was hit only occasionally. My sister Luna was born six years after me, and Sophia eleven months after that—by the time they were toddlers, the "no hitting" rule was already well established, and so was the habit of acting as if none of it had ever happened at all.

This wasn't the only new rule in our family. My brother was under strict orders not to say anything to anyone about my "special meetings" on Tuesday nights. Those meetings were private, a family secret, and they were to be kept that way. When Ross made fun of me about it or dared to tell someone, he got in trouble for it. It felt nice to be protected by my parents, though the protection had its limits. For instance, the "no hitting" rule didn't put an end to my father cracking me across the face if I said anything to contradict him. Dinnertime offered a prime opportunity for this—our family's seating arrangement made me an easy target because I sat directly to the left of him. A differing opinion, a word in

5

defense of my mom or siblings, even an eye roll at his dictatorial rants, and his hard knuckles met the side of my face. It came too quickly for me to get out of the way; it left my face on fire with pain and humiliation. In the tense silence that followed, I'd soothe my wounded feelings with fantasies of one day being an adult and getting out of this house for good.

The "no hitting" rule also didn't prevent my dad from flying off the handle and chasing me around the house. This is the part of my childhood I remember best—it happened hundreds of times, as easily from a major infraction as from something trivial.

"Frankie, what did you just say?"

"I said I don't want to go to Isabella and Louie's house today. We were there last Sunday."

"Well, we're going, and that's that. I have one day off a week, and Tony invited us over for dinner, so we're going. We're a family and we do things together. End of story. *Capisci*?"

"I'm sick of being in this family!"

I should have known better than to challenge him. It was like I'd thrown a match on a barrel of gasoline.

"What did you just say?"

His voice didn't change but his eyes did. A switch had been flipped, and we were no longer father and son but predator and prey.

"Get over here right now. I'll give you something to be sick about, you son of a bitch."

I started running. Up the basement stairs, into the kitchen, circling the dinner table, into the living room, and around the couch to the next flight of stairs leading to the bedrooms. I took the steps two at a time, hearing him shout behind me, "Get over here, you cocksucker!"

Slamming the bedroom door, I clicked the lock button seconds before his fists rang against the door. My eyes fixed on the rattling hinges as they strained back and forth at every blow. *If those hinges bust open, I'm dead.*

"Open the door, you goddamn paranoid schizophrenic!"

I vaulted from my bed to the top of my dresser, yanked opened a door in the wall that led to a crawlspace, and inched along between the rafters, careful not to fall into the pink insulation. There I waited, wedged between some old suitcases and boxes of baby clothes until, with a few more curses and a final pound on the door, he retreated.

My heartbeat was like an electric current surging through my body. I felt terrified and utterly alone, but at least I was temporarily out of harm's way. Familiar questions raced through my mind. *Why did he leave? Why didn't he keep pounding on the door until it broke open? Was it because he cares about me or was it just because of the "no hitting" rule?*

Time passed—who knows how much—and a shroud of silence fell over the house, broken at last by a gentle knock on the door.

"Honey, it's me. Let me in."

"No!" I cried out, even though I knew to expect her. My mother always came around once my dad's rage subsided. "Leave me alone."

"Please honey," Mom persisted. "I want to talk to you."

"No, go away. He hates me. Can't you see how much he hates me?"

"He doesn't hate you, sweetheart. Please open the door."

"I just want to be alone right now. You're going to tell him."

Mom didn't give up. "No, I won't. I promise I won't say a word. You can tell me anything. Please, Frankie, just let me in."

Desperation finally made me cave in, as it did every time. I needed my mother—I had to believe her.

Through tears of humiliation and anger, I described what he did to me, expressed how much I hated him, told her she should leave him, that he was evil. Saying nothing, she stroked my hair, rubbed my back. Under her gentle touch, rage gave way to exhaustion, and I slowly drifted off to sleep.

The comfort lasted only until my dad let me know, days or even weeks later, that my mom had told him everything I confided in her. "So you think I'm a monster, do you? You think your mother should leave me, do you?" These little jabs, delivered with a smirk, pierced my heart like a knife. My mom had gone back on her promise. He was in charge, and always would be.

Even with my parents and myself regularly attending therapy, this routine went on for years after the "no hitting" rule was established. Anything I said or did could set my dad off; a certain look would come across my father's face, and my body instinctively tensed in protection. As soon as he started swearing, I started running. The chase, the hiding, the straining door—followed by the silence of a funeral home, which left me to tentatively reemerge when it seemed everyone had decided to act as though nothing had happened.

With no one to confirm my experience or validate my pain, the conflict stayed inside me. I did my best to shove it aside, but it eventually made it itself known through a series of fresh new abnormalities: sleepwalking, bedwetting, talking in my sleep. Once, I sleepwalked right into the shower at three o'clock in the morning. My parents found me soaking wet in my pajamas, eyes half-closed, seemingly engaged in a lively conversation with somebody, until they roused me enough to get out of the shower, change my clothes, and go back to bed. Another time, I sleepwalked my way out of the house; my parents found me at the kitchen door, a full garbage bag clutched in my hand.

I had no conscious awareness of these events; they were recounted to me the following morning as though it was all a good joke I had played (or someone had played on me). The bedwetting, however, I was aware of, and I kept it to myself. Whenever I woke up to find myself soaked in pee, I quietly brought the sheets downstairs, put them in the washer, and made up my bed with fresh clean sheets, hoping that nobody would find out. My mom must have known—after all, she did the laundry—but she never said anything to me. I remember seeing a TV film called *The Loneliest Runner*, written and directed by the actor Michael Landon, that shared his personal journey—a troubled childhood, bedwetting, becoming a runner. I couldn't imagine being brave enough to share my story like that, but seeing the similarities between my experiences and his brought some comfort. *At least I'm not the only one.*

. . .

The violence in our home wasn't only between my dad and me. My younger brother and I fought constantly. Everyday scuffles would escalate to him chasing me around the house with anything he could get his hands on—a metal toy truck, a steak knife, a pencil that he lodged so deep into my skin that the tip broke off and left a gray mark in my forearm that remains to this day.

At the suggestion of their therapist, my parents called us into the living room one day for what was supposed to be a final reckoning.

"Okay," my dad said, "since you guys like to fight so much, go ahead. Fight! We're going to watch." He sat back against the orange plaid couch and folded his arms, my mom doing her best to appear comfortable beside him.

What did he just say? Ross and I looked at each other, equally confused and alarmed. Neither of us had any idea how to start a fight from scratch.

I was afraid—my brother was tougher and stronger than I was. *Why are they doing this? This is not what parents are supposed to say.* But there they sat, like theatregoers waiting for the show to begin. Unsure how to proceed, Ross and I started yelling at each other.

"I hate you. You're an idiot."

"You're such a jerk. I hate you too."

We both threw punches, quickly ending up on the floor. Initially, Ross was on top of me. Then I took control; I yelled louder, fought harder. I got on top of Ross, pinned him down, and punched him in the face over and over again. I felt simultaneously drunk with power and terrified of what I was capable of. If Ross had cried out in pain or started to bleed, I might have stopped, but his face showed nothing but the same surprise I felt. It was like I'd been struck by lightning.

Finally, Dad stopped us. "Okay, that's enough." He pulled me off my brother as my mom sat on the couch, her face twisted in distress.

Did that just happen? Sweat dripped down my face as I tried to catch my breath. I was stunned. I was dismayed. Most of all, I was exhilarated. *I won?!* All my life, I'd been the butt-end of every conflict. Today, for the first time, I could look down on someone else and think, *I am strong. I am powerful. I am a man.* I now knew, and so did Ross, that I could beat him up if I wanted to. But how had I done it? Where had that power come from?

After that, our fighting diminished to only the occasional brawl. The verbal violence, however, never let up—we went on taunting and threatening each other as we always had. As a kid, I often hated my brother, sometimes as much as I hated my father. Nevertheless, there was an underlying feeling of love and security, a trauma bond that would sometimes radically reverse into tender care when the chaos and violence of the day turned into one of my regular nightmares. Monsters and firebreathing dragons, as terrifying as my father's rages, came at me while I slept, trying to attack and kill me. But the most chilling dream of all was the one where I was a baby in a crib, crying as a dark figure towered over me. Long after the monsters and dragons had been laid to rest, even into my adult life, this image continued to plague me.

"Help me! Help me! Make them stop! Oh no, they're chasing me. It's tearing my arms off. It's trying to eat me!"

Eventually I'd hear my brother's voice cutting through the fog between dream and reality. I'd open my eyes to find Ross out of bed and at my side, helping bring me back from the edge of oblivion. "You're okay now, Frankie. It was a dream. It's all over now."

I'd say nothing, only try to steady my breathing and hide not only the fear but also the love and gratitude I felt for Ross's kindness in being there for me when I needed him.

Strangely, the worst nightmares were rewarded with the even rarer experience of tenderness from my father. Occasionally, the terror brought screams loud enough to wake up my parents, and both would come running into our bedroom to soothe me. While my mother stood by, my dad sat at my bedside, settling me down with kind and soothing whispers. It was confusing, but it felt so good I didn't question it, nor did I question the hushed words of my mom in the background—"The doctor told us this would happen"—as I gratefully drifted back to sleep.

• • •

A large part of my early childhood was spent trying to figure out why my father treated me so badly. What was wrong with me and what could I do to get him to stop attacking me—to stop hating me? I looked at my brother and wondered, *What does he have that I don't? What is he doing that I'm not?* Only one conclusion made sense: I was defective. Something was wrong with me, and whatever it was, I needed to figure out how to fix it.

My conviction only grew more urgent during one of our big family parties at Auntie Dorothy and Uncle Steve's house. I was in the back room of their basement, looking at a Barbie playhouse that was stashed away in a box of old toys. I was intrigued by all the real-life trappings rendered at doll scale: the miniature couch, table, and chairs, a tiny brush and comb, even a toilet with a seat that moved up and down. Drawn in by the tantalizing details of this perfect plastic world, I started when I heard an adult's voice call my name.

"Frankie, what are you doing? Get out of there. Those are Patty's old toys. You're not supposed to play with them."

Something in their tone caught my attention and connected with a new place inside me, a sensation I'd never known before. It was the first time I remember feeling shame. From that point forward, I internalized every disapproving message I received from my parents, my teachers, my psychiatrist, and even kids at school. Whether explicit or unspoken, their disapproval highlighted that unbearable yet inescapable feeling: *There is something seriously wrong with you. You are not normal, and if you ever hope to be loved and accepted, you need to change.*

Fortunately, I was a quick study.

CHAPTER TWO

MOM AND DAD

"Blown Away" | **Carrie Underwood**

Oh, how I wished I too could shatter every window, destroy every brick, eliminate every slamming door, and wipe away every tear-soaked, whiskey-stained memory that existed in my childhood home growing up. I felt trapped and alone but held on to the hope that someday, it would all be blown away.

* * *

My father, Louis Dominic Guastella, was born in Chicago in 1929. He developed a heart murmur after contracting rheumatic fever as a little boy and was enrolled in a school for sick children who needed special attention. Coddled by his mother because of his condition, he wasn't allowed to run around and play like other boys. Nevertheless, he grew up to be a quintessential Chicagoan, with a strong build that loomed large and powerful to me as a child and classic Italian features: black hair parted to the side, dark eyes, a Roman nose, olive skin.

Louis had a brother, Frank Anthony; I was named after him in accordance with Italian tradition, but everyone called him Tony. Healthy, smart, funny, and above all successful, Uncle Tony was the oldest of three siblings. They had a younger sister, Mia, who was quiet and more reserved unless her temper flared up. Their mother, Katie, was stern, while their father, Ross, was a kind and gentle soul. Grandma Katie seemed like a mean old lady to me when I was a kid. I liked my grandpa Ross much better, and he liked me too. He would often slip me a five-dollar bill after Sunday dinner, with a whispered warning and a wink: "Don't tell Grandma."

Despite being born in the US, Grandpa Ross had an immigrant's spirited work ethic. At age 12, he'd been forced to quit school and start working to support his family after his father died unexpectedly. Ross built furnaces for a living and took pride in honest labor, but he wanted his sons to live the American Dream in a way that he never could have. His firstborn son achieved that dream by becoming a doctor.

Louis, on the other hand, tried to follow in Tony's footsteps but flunked out of a pre-medicine program in college. He then worked as an airline ticket agent for a short period of time before deciding to enroll in pharmacy school. He set out to achieve his parents' aspirations of success by building a drugstore empire. During that time, my mom, a licensed practical nurse, worked the overnight shift at the hospital to cover the rent and help pay the bills. This meant my dad was often left alone at night with a crying baby in the crib while trying to study for his pharmacy exams.

Maybe it was because his illness had deprived him of a normal childhood. Maybe it was because his brother, the doctor, was more widely respected and admired. Maybe it was just how he was wired. Regardless of the reason, my father could easily become angry, volatile, and out of control. One too many martinis only aggravated his precarious mood.

Some boys might have been content with simply avoiding the rage and dodging the blows. But I was determined to figure out how to win my dad's love and attention. Just being myself wasn't working—my dad took little notice of my natural talent for drawing or my knack for telling stories. He showed far more interest in my brother and his hobbies— baseball, fishing, shooting guns.

It was my grandpa Ross who finally helped me find my opportunity. His stories of bootstrapping his way up from poverty ended with a maxim I heard over and over again: "Education is the most important thing."

My dad had a maxim of his own that expanded this idea: "The smarter you are, the luckier you become."

Once I caught onto the importance of education and success to this side of the family, I set to work getting my father to love me by being a straight-A student. Each academic quarter, my parents rewarded me and my siblings with a dollar for every A on our report card. But I wasn't after money—I wanted the kind of recognition that proved I was headed for success. In my grade school, that meant getting a gold star, the shining symbol of making the honor roll.

At Oak Lawn Elementary, report cards were passed out by the principal, Mr. Kernwyne. Most kids were terrified when he entered the room. But not me. When he called out my name, I leaped out of my desk and rushed to the head of the class. He placed his arm on my shoulder and, with a warm smile, handed me my card. "Another great quarter, Frank. Congratulations!"

I thrilled to the sight of the star on top and the words *Honor Roll* written in the teacher comments section. I couldn't wait to show my dad. But later, as I watched him open the envelope and inspect my report card, the proud excitement began to curdle in my stomach. As his eyes scanned the grade point column, he remained impassive. He merely reached into his pocket and, true to his word, fished out the dollar.

Dejected, I went upstairs to the bathroom and looked at myself in the mirror. *What is wrong with you?* My grandfather cheered me on for studying, my teachers rewarded me with praise and wide smiles, Mr. Kernwyne had congratulated me with a warm hand on my shoulder. *You must be a worthless piece of crap if your own father doesn't love you.*

I looked down at the dollar in my hand, smoothing its crumpled surface with my thumb.

Something is better than nothing.

* * *

I continued getting A's and gold stars, quarter after quarter, needing to believe that someday I'd achieve something lofty enough to earn my father's love and recognition. My determination was fueled by my mom's unflagging encouragement that I could accomplish anything in life. Her affirmations of my potential protected me from the self-hatred that I had already begun to internalize from my father's antagonism. Throughout my life, I've heard her voice in my head during pivotal moments: "Frankie, you can do whatever you want to in this world."

Like my father, Margaret Rose Florenza was born and raised in Chicago, the baby in a family of three girls. An attractive woman with a girl-next-door look, she had chestnut hair, brown eyes, a big, pearly white smile, and a prominent nose that she passed down to me. Her father, Sam, died of a brain tumor when she was six months old, leaving her mom, Grace, to raise three daughters alone.

Over the course of her long life, my grandma Grace spent time with at least two men after her husband died: one named Joe, whom she briefly married and who cheated on her, the other a drinker whose very name elicited a look of horror from my mother whenever it was mentioned. With no one to support her, Grandma Grace got a job at the post office working the night shift, which meant the two older girls, Edith and Dorothy—eight and ten years old at the time—had the responsibility of looking after baby Margaret all night long. With two sisters who were considerably older and a mother who worked constantly to support the family, Margaret was often left alone as she grew up; she described herself as a "widowed child." Having lost her father when she was an infant, as well as his two less-than-ideal replacements, I believe she grew up yearning for love from a strong father figure.

My mom often told the story of seeing a new kid enter her eighth-grade classroom and saying to herself, "I'm going to marry that boy someday." True childhood sweethearts, my parents have spent the majority of their life together. Though just a year older than my mom, my dad represented both the caring father Margaret never had and the dysfunctional fathers she often feared. He was dominant and controlling, and she was dependent on him. Despite her quiet intelligence, outgoing personality, and attractive features, she was deeply insecure and had a terrible time making decisions. For example, she loved playing sports and always wished she had become a gym teacher, but my grandmother discouraged her from pursuing it as a career. In Grandma Grace's eyes, my mom would be better off enrolling in secretarial school, which promised far more valuable opportunities for an eligible young lady. They finally compromised on nursing school.

My mother and I were similar in temperament, boasting big personalities and an irrepressible *joie de vivre*. We had a lot of fun together, often sharing inside jokes with only a glance. Our close relationship seemed to further enrage my father. Whenever I caught a glimpse of his hateful look out of the corner of my eye, I instantly shut up and shut down, tempering the laughter with my mother in the hopes of averting another explosive attack.

Still, while my relationship with my father was marked by physical, verbal, and emotional abuse, it was at least straightforward: He was the father in control, I the obedient son. I understood the expectations attached to our roles, even if I hated them. My relationship with my mother was much more complicated. From a young age, I saw us as emotional allies under the weight of my father's unpredictable temper. As a result, I did too much with her and for her. When she got in a fight with my father, I listened. When she was overserved at one of our family's wild parties, I served as her "morning after" nurse. In addition to being her son, I became her friend, her confidant, and, starting in grade school, her personal stylist. I have vivid memories of sitting on the floor of the women's dressing room at Marshall Fields department store, looking up at the framed reproductions of classic Chicago scenes that decorated the white walls, trying to avoid being pricked by the fallen pins stuck in the carpeting, while my mother turned back and forth, examining her reflection in the full-length mirror.

"What do you think of this one, Frankie?"

Just nine years old, caught between boredom and the tension of trying not to look at her naked body, I nevertheless felt obligated to help my mother make her decision. "The rhinestone straps are really cool," I said, "and I like the red color. It's fancy."

"Hmm . . . I wonder, is it too dressy for the party?"

"I don't think so, Mom," I said. "Remember the last party you went to with Uncle Tony, Auntie Anna, and a bunch of their friends? You thought you were underdressed. Those people have a lot of money and they wear expensive clothes. This one is perfect."

"I guess you're right, honey, but I'm just not sure about the color." Mom lifted yet another dress from the hook on the wall. "Here, let me just quickly try on this strapless one. Can you unzip me?"

Another vivid memory from around the same time starts with Mom coming home from an appointment at an expensive salon in downtown Chicago, right off Michigan Avenue. She only went to this hairdresser once in a while for a "special occasion" cut and style. This time, however, she didn't stop to show off her new coiffure but instead went straight into the upstairs bathroom. Shortly afterward, she called out for me to join her. This wasn't unusual—the bathroom was where she and I spent a lot of time together talking. I found her looking at herself in the mirror, lamenting.

"Oh Frankie, I just hate it. It's way too short. What am I going to do?"

"I don't think it looks bad," I reassured her. "I like the wave in the front."

She picked up the handheld mirror and turned around to see the back. "Oh, would you look at this? It's much too short. I look like a boy."

"I think it looks modern."

"Your father is going to kill me. You know how he likes me in longer hair, and he's going to be mad at me for spending this much money on a haircut he won't even like."

"You deserve a nice haircut. You shouldn't worry about what he thinks about your hair. And you don't have to tell him how much it costs. Besides, it's only hair. It'll grow back."

"Are you sure?"

"Yes, I promise."

I loved my mother dearly; I also needed her desperately. Sensing how much she needed me too, I tried my best to build her up. While she has always been my greatest supporter and we are very close to this day, I've come to realize that our relationship was overwhelming for me as a child. Even while she instilled in me the confidence to be successful, she revealed too much of herself in the service of love and self-survival. Of course, I had no awareness of this at the time. By then, I was proficient at pushing uncomfortable feelings away. All I knew was that I felt responsible for protecting my mother from the control my father imposed on her, even if it meant greater violence inflicted on me.

* * *

At seven years old, I woke up in the middle of the night to booming voices. My parents had gone out to dinner earlier that evening, and the babysitter had put us to bed well before they got home. Disoriented, I rubbed my eyes, trying to wake myself up. I heard swear words and violent language, followed by sounds like someone was in pain.

Is Dad hurting Mom?

I got out of bed and walked toward my parents' bedroom. The room was dark, but the door was slightly ajar. I saw shadows moving. Rather, one shadow, a big mound, covered by a blanket, moving in a strange and rhythmic fashion.

Oh my God. Is that what sex is?

I was frozen in terror, not just by what I was seeing but what I heard him saying—words almost just like the ones I'd heard him shout at me. I was afraid for my mother's safety. *I've got to get out of here, but I need to protect my mom.* Suddenly, my blood began to boil with anger. *I won't let you hurt her the way you hurt me, you monster.* That impulse, too, fell prey to the overriding threat of my father's wrath. *If Dad finds out I'm here, he's going to kill me.*

I ran back to my bed, my heart pounding. *What just happened? Was that even real?* I squeezed my eyes shut, willing myself to go back to sleep, to forget what I'd just seen and heard. *Please make it go away. Make it go away.*

I fell asleep.

By this point, it was almost second nature for me to shut down or disconnect when confronted with something scary or overwhelming. It was life-saving, but it also set me up to constantly second-guess reality as well as my sense of right and wrong. The few actual memories I have of my early childhood, good as well as bad, are the ones that I later managed to find proof of.

A year or so later, I was again catapulted out of a deep sleep, this time by several loud voices, not violent but screaming with laughter and talking loudly over each other to be heard. It came from the basement, so I left my bedroom and went into the upstairs bathroom, where the laundry chute reached all the way down to the washer and dryer, right next to the basement bar.

The sound carried up from the basement to the bathroom with remarkable clarity: the woozy strings of Burt Bacharach's "What the World Needs Now," the hiss and pop of beer cans being opened, women's voices that I recognized as my mom, our neighbor Mrs. O'Connor and, I thought, my Auntie Anna too.

"You guys are crazy! We're not going to burn our bras. That's ridiculous."

I heard a cacophony of men's voices cheering at them. "Come on, let's have a little fun! Take them off."

"Oh, all right, why not? Let's do it, girls!" More laughter, and some scuffling. My body tensed in alarm as images of women's breasts popped into my mind. *I'm not supposed to be hearing this.* The combination of emotional closeness and physical overexposure to my mother, not to mention witnessing my parents having what seemed to be violent sex, resulted in an overwhelm and disgust with all things sexual. I ran back into my bedroom, pulled the covers over my head, and tried my best to push it all away and go back to sleep.

In the quiet of the next morning, I sneaked down to the basement and found the night's festivities in full evidence: half-empty glasses and beer bottles, full ashtrays, plates of picked-over food, the familiar smell of moldy cigarettes and spilled beer mixed with soured liquor and the pungent remains of French onion dip. Venturing over to the fireplace, I combed through the ashes to find, sure enough, charred hooks and fasteners, fragments of fabric and elastic straps, scattered throughout the firebox. *I wasn't dreaming; that really did happen.* Again, my mind was flooded with unwanted images of nipples and breasts: my mom's, my aunt's, Mrs. O'Connor's.

The 1960s were an era of political turmoil, racial injustice, women's liberation, antiwar protests, and passionate fights for freedom and equality, and my parents were young adults doing their best to balance being responsible and taking good care of their children with finding a way to still have some fun. Dad was overwhelmed at work, Mom was trying to raise four small children, and when the opportunity arose to let off steam, a big drunken party wasn't atypical. However, it led to me seeing myself as the responsible one in the family system, the one who looked after everyone's needs while my parents acted wild and free.

This role was reinforced one night when my parents brought us along for a pinochle game at Auntie Edith and Uncle Leo's house across town. It was getting late and my two sisters, about two and three at the time, were practically falling asleep in their chairs.

"Louis, we have to get these girls to bed," my mom admonished.

"Oh, come on, Maggie, don't be a party pooper. Let's finish this game. It's really close, and I want to whip Leo's ass." My dad gave his brother-in-law a wink and a grin. "Why don't we drop the kids back home? Frankie can watch the girls, and we can come back here and finish our hand."

"But he's not old enough to babysit—he just turned nine," my mom protested, trying to be the voice of reason. "And you know how fussy the girls can be when they're tired."

"I have an idea," my dad said. "Let's bring the kids home, then come back here. We can call Frankie on the phone and have him leave it off the hook. That way we can hear what's going on and rush home if anything happens. Come on, it will be fine. It's not that far away, and he's such a responsible kid. Don't worry about it. Trust me."

As usual, my mom caved in.

This plan may have worked for them, but it didn't work for me. The whole way home, my mind raced with the thought of being alone in the house, the only one in charge of keeping two toddlers safe. *This is too much for me to handle.* At the same time, I desperately wanted to show that I was the child they could count on. *They like me when I'm responsible.* I double-locked all the doors, closed the curtains in every room, then took my post beside the kitchen telephone. Once it rang, I sat there, my ear glued to the receiver, listening to my parents finishing their game across town.

"Fifteen and pass. Hearts are trump. Who threw down that ace?"

It occurred to me later that my parents had effectively invented the first baby monitor. If they had only acquired a patent for their idea at the time, our family would be living the high life. As it was, the situation was another triumph of the will for my dad, and another confirmation of the parentified role I'd more or less accepted by that time. From picking up the slack for my father to picking out dresses for my mother, I'd do anything it took to prove there was nothing wrong with me. I was determined to be loved.

. . .

It was Uncle Tony who originally suggested to my parents that I go to therapy. My mom and dad trusted his opinion because he was a doctor, and it was clear to them something had to be done. I was highly emotional, anxious, and fearful. I bit my fingernails until they bled, had frequent stomachaches, and was preoccupied with being physically hurt. My interests and hobbies were artistic rather than athletic. In short, I wasn't like other boys.

Today, I can appreciate that my parents sent me to therapy out of love and genuine concern. They wanted to make me fit into mainstream society, to make me safe and successful. With that goal in mind, the therapist told my parents that it would be good for me to get involved in sports. They signed me up for tennis lessons, which I liked, and had me join the town's baseball team, which I didn't. But I complied because I was determined to fit in and do the right thing.

On the first day of baseball practice, the coach asked, "Who wants to be the catcher?"

I raised my hand immediately. I was terrified of getting hit by the ball, and the catcher had all this protective gear. Face mask, a chest plate, chin guards, even a bigger mitt. Little did I know that, as the only catcher on the team, I had to play every inning in every game for the entire season. At least I'd be protected when that ball came flying at me.

Preseason practices had taught me that I wasn't a good hitter. Before the pitcher even threw the ball, I had already decided if I would swing at it or not. I always bent my knees and crouched down while at bat, deliberately making my strike zone smaller, hoping for a walk. I got only two hits the whole season, and they were both at the one and only game my father came to see.

By this time, Dad's dreams of success were starting to show signs of coming true. With the help of loans from our entire family—his parents, his aunts and uncles, all his siblings, even relatives on my mom's side— he'd just purchased his first pharmacy. It was a big pharmacy, complete with greeting cards, jewelry, children's toys, and a sizable liquor section.

He worked twelve-hour days from Monday through Saturday, barely making it home before we went to bed, and was rarely present for family events, school assemblies, and extracurricular activities. While life at home was calmer and more peaceful without him around, effectively growing up without a father stoked my desperation for his interest.

It was one of the first games of the season and, as it happened, my tenth birthday, when I came up to bat and caught sight of my dad in the stands. He was on his feet, grinning with pride and anticipation. A wave of confidence surged through me—I felt unstoppable, even willing to take a risk. When the pitcher released the ball, I stepped into the pitch and swung.

It was a day like no other. Not only did I connect with the ball, but I hit a single *and* a double, and for the first time, I saw my dad look thrilled at my performance. In celebration of my unprecedented success, he bought Fudgsicles and ice cream sandwiches for the whole team. For the first time I could remember, we both got what we wanted from each other.

I hoped that after this, things would change at home. They didn't. My dad never attended another game and I didn't get another hit. He still flew off the handle and I still went to therapy every Tuesday evening. I didn't fully understand what my problem was or why I needed to be fixed in this way. I only knew that, compared to other people, kids and adults alike, I was different . . . and not in a good way.

CHAPTER THREE

THE KIDS

"Bohemian Rhapsody" | Queen

The confusion, the contradictions, the mixed messages created a Bohemian Rhapsody in my mind. What was reality? What is fantasy? Did I want to live or die? Mama, I needed to kill off that little boy inside in order to survive.

* * *

For obvious reasons, my baseball "career" didn't last. Tennis was a much better fit. In terms of sports, it felt safer than baseball. Not only was there less to fear from being hit by the ball, but it allowed me to rely only on myself rather than try to fit into a team. To my surprise, I found that I genuinely liked playing tennis. To my parents' surprise, I proved very good at it, and they encouraged my new interest by paying for private lessons. As a freshman in high school, I made the varsity tennis team, won my share of tournaments, and even got a job as a ball boy at the tennis club in Oak Lawn. It was a revelation: an activity I genuinely enjoyed that also helped me earn a sense of confidence and self-esteem.

My parents' counselor, knowing that they were supporting me emotionally and financially in pursuing this hobby, suggested that tennis might be a "good family activity" for all of us. Mom and Dad started playing tennis too, and before long, my brother joined in. It would be nice to say that tennis brought us together. But inevitably, it turned out to be much more complicated.

We always played doubles: Mom and me against Dad and Ross. To call our matches competitive would be a massive understatement. We fought ferociously and shamelessly during our tennis outings, no matter the venue: indoors at the racquet club, outdoors at local parks and playgrounds, even on our family vacations.

The fighting on the courts only fueled the naturally occurring divide within our family—that is, "Team Mom" versus "Team Dad." It wasn't unusual for my father to call on one of us kids at family dinner and ask, "If Mom and I got divorced, who would you choose to live with?" The answers were always the same: Luna and Frank would choose Mom, Ross and Sophia would choose Dad. This was because, in addition to being divided into "the boys and the girls," we were also split down the middle according to our looks and temperaments. Luna and I were more like our mom—outgoing, talkative, intellectually curious, and okay, a little dramatic. We looked more like her, too, with our fair skin and lighter hair. Ross and Sophia were dark-skinned Italians who looked more like my father and, like him, were more reserved and practical rather than intellectual and, supposedly, more reasonable. (Though it could be argued that regularly asking your kids which parent they would choose in a divorce is anything but reasonable.) In Louis's eyes, this made his "side" the winners and, by definition, the rest of us "losers."

While my father prided himself on being ethical in business, he wasn't above cheating on the tennis court. When I hit the ball in and it was a close call, my dad would call it out, not only to get an advantage in the game but mainly to get a rise out of me.

"Watch," he'd say to Ross, "Frankie's going to lose it when I call this ball out." And he was right. I went nuts every time.

One such occasion happened on Thanksgiving Day, after we watched Björn Borg and Jimmy Connors play an incredible tennis match on TV. Jimmy was such a hothead and exciting to watch, while Björn was calm, collected, and consistent. With all of us still lively from the thrilling match, my dad suggested that we get dressed and play some tennis before we went to Auntie Edith and Uncle Leo's house for dinner.

Playing tennis in November in Chicago was an audacious venture. The courts were predictably empty. Of people, anyway. The asphalt was littered with puddles of water and piles of fallen leaves that we had to sweep up before we could play. Lucky for us, it was one of those rare warm days that seemed to come out of nowhere, the air crisp and clean, the sun radiant. I was stoked, still on a high from watching the TV match, and I loved when our family was fun and spontaneous.

It started out so well. Then it all turned to shit.

"40–15," I said, as I got ready to serve.

"No, it's not. It's 30–30," retorted Dad.

"No, 40–15," I insisted. "You hit a backhand into the net, I served an ace, and Ross just missed the last shot."

"No, I didn't. That was last game."

Are you kidding me? Rage started to build within me. "Mom, you tell him," I pleaded.

"I don't remember," Mom said, trying to keep the peace. "Let's just say it's 30–30 and move on."

I sighed but gave in and sent another serve. Ross returned it and we had a great rally. Then he lobbed the ball, and I hit an overhead smash.

"Out," my dad called.

What? Not again. Are you serious? When I started to protest, my dad cut me off.

"It's on our side; it's our call," he said firmly. "The score is 30 for you, and 40 for us. Let's keep playing."

This time, even Mom chimed in. "Louis, are you sure? It looked in from here."

"Yep, I'm sure. Frank's ball was out." A smirk played on his face.

I couldn't take it anymore. I smashed my racquet on the ground, screaming. "I hate you! You're such a cheater!"

My father started yelling. My sisters ran over from the playground to see what was going on. The neighbors across the street from the courts came outside to stare. But the embarrassment did nothing to temper my rage. Chafing under his constant authority and control, I had a fire in me to stand up for what was right.

"That's it! Game over. We're going home," said Dad.

"That's fine with me," I muttered under my breath, as we all packed up and went home. So much for family fun.

After high school, my brother gave up tennis and refuses to play to this day. Luna and Sophia, unsurprisingly, never picked up the sport. I can't blame any of them. In the end, family tennis proved to be fertile ground for us to physically act out the angst we were unable to express verbally. For whatever reason, the tennis court was the one public place where we could be the fucked-up family we were in private.

• • •

My siblings and I were all affected by our mother's passive nature and our father's controlling behavior and unpredictable rages. But while I know Luna and Sophia witnessed a lot of dysfunctional behavior and were directly impacted by it at times, being much younger gave them a different experience from mine growing up. Along with things being less explosive at home as they grew older, thanks to what my parents had learned in counseling, being female meant they were held to a different standard than the boys, with fewer demands placed on them but also fewer opportunities to excel.

Starting when Ross and I were nine and eleven years old, my dad had taken us to work with him at his pharmacy every Saturday, where we worked alongside him from nine in the morning to nine at night. My sisters, meanwhile, were rewarded for cooking, baking, and helping Mom around the house. It was understood that Ross and I *had* to go to college and make something of ourselves; for Luna and Sophia, though, college was purely optional. The inequity was nothing unusual for that time and place, especially within the old-world culture of our Italian family circle, but something about it felt unnerving in a way I couldn't articulate. Today, the word that comes to mind is *misogyny*.

Luna was vivacious, precocious, and intelligent. She excelled in school and often did Ross's homework assignments for him, even though she was five years his junior. With her long brown hair, fair skin, and eyes that were big as buttons, she always lit up the room when she entered. She had boundless energy and a heartwarming smile. But for some reason, she became the family punching bag for a period of time. While Ross and I physically fought out our feelings against each other, Luna became the verbal target of our frustrations whenever the four of us kids played together. She became the brunt of our inside jokes and got teased for saying stupid things or for being spacey, messy, and disorganized.

Most of this happened when Dad was at work. Mom was no disciplinarian—she would chase us around the dining room table with a wooden spoon in her hand, yelling at the top of her lungs, "I'm going to tell your father about this when he gets home tonight and then you'll all be in trouble." But her threats rarely came to fruition. However, we all knew Mom held a special place in her heart for Luna, and she did her ineffectual best to protect Luna from our bullying.

Kids can be cruel, and even I was no exception. I still hold guilt about being an active participant in taunting Luna. On some unconscious level, I must have been relieved that it was happening to someone else instead of me. Sophia, on the other hand, despite her participation in Luna's taunting, simultaneously became her fiercest protector, much like Ross was for me. The classic youngest sibling, Sophia was a quiet peacemaker who avoided conflict at all costs and did everything in her power to keep the family together. Despite having strangers routinely comment on her movie-star beauty, Sophia grew up largely under the radar, an observer who rarely spoke up. On the surface, she was the easy child, the one who seemingly didn't need much to get by. No one ever thought to ask her how she was doing or if she was affected by what was going on at home. As she recalls it now, our parents weren't there for her during the milestone moments in her life; her primary memories include rarely having a birthday cake, driving herself to college, and moving into her first dorm room all alone. Unfortunately, I wasn't there for her either. I was off at college, driven to succeed, doing what I could to manage my own inner turmoil.

. . .

Growing up, my brother and I were starved for our father's attention. He never did the typical things dads did with their sons back then: play catch in the yard, teach us to cut the grass, show us how to use tools. Since he worked long hours at the pharmacy, we were in bed more often than not when he finally got home from work. Beyond willing ourselves to stay awake to see him, we often resorted to provoking him into seeing us with a game we'd invented. After we were sent to bed, we would wrap ourselves in blankets—six or seven at a time, layer after layer, all tucked up under the mattress—and proceed to yell and scream.

"Shut up, Ross, you're a big fat idiot."

"You shut up, Frankie. Your farts smell like moldy cheese."

"Oh yeah? You smell like rotten diarrhea."

Before long, Dad would yell up the stairs, "Shut up, you sons of bitches. If I hear your mouths one more time, I'll give you something to scream about."

A few moments later, Ross and I would start up again.

"You're the stupidest kid in your class."

"Well, you're the biggest teacher's pet in the whole school."

"At least I'm smart, not stupid like you."

"You're a loser. Your only friends are teachers."

"That's it!"—At Dad's scream, I would look over at Ross and he would signal two thumbs up from across the room. As my dad's footsteps *thump, thump, thumped* up the stairs, I stared at the door, the same door I'd watched hundreds of times before while hiding from one of his rages. This time, I felt excitement combined with the fear. After all, it was a game that Ross and I initiated, so we were the ones in control. Sort of.

The door burst open.

"I work all goddamn day long, and all I want to do is come home, relax, and have one fucking moment of peace and quiet! But you sons of bitches think it's funny to scream and yell up here, is that right?"

With one fell swoop, he ripped all the covers off my bed, the one closest to the door, then moved to my brother's bed and did the same thing. He gave us each a swift smack on the ass and walked out the door.

Grinning with our success, we turned over and fell asleep. Negative attention was better than none at all. In our chaotic and, at times, violent home, we did whatever we could to get contact and connection.

When we were very young, maybe three or four years old, my brother and I had another game we played, one that only he and I knew about. A few times per week, my mom filled up the tub with Mr. Bubble, then left us alone together in the bathtub. Naked, unsupervised, and curious, Ross and I touched ourselves, counting to 10 or 15 before switching to touch each other. Was it sexual? Not really. We were just little kids. Was it shameful? Definitely. To this day, we don't talk about it. Was it soothing? Undeniably. It was a way for us to comfort ourselves as well as each other in the midst of all the chaos.

Our traumatic bond as young kids shifted to resentment of each other once we reached grade school and high school. This was partly the result of my father's inexplicable preference for me as the target of his physical and verbal abuse. Ross got hit occasionally for acting up at home or getting in trouble at school, but my father seemed to like him more, perhaps because he took after my dad's side, from his athletic and aggressive nature to his mischievous smile and a bowlegged walk just like our grandfather's. The difference in our treatment was exacerbated by typical big brother-little brother tension. All through my teen years, just as I was awakening to the thrill of having friends, I was forced by my parents to take Ross along when I got invited to a party.

"Come on, Frankie," Mom cajoled. "Your brother is younger than you, and he doesn't have as many friends as you do. Bring him to the party and introduce him to your group."

"But Mom, that is so lame," I protested. "No one brings their little brother along with them to a party. My friends will think I'm a total loser."

"I don't care what your friends think," said my dad. "We said bring your brother. If you want to go, then he goes with you. End of story."

The tables were turned when Ross was a sophomore in high school and got a car. From the time Ross was about twelve or thirteen, our neighbor and family friend Albert O'Connor had told him, "As soon as you turn sixteen, you're getting my car." He was a man of his word. On Ross's sixteenth birthday, a classic 1969 Chevy Impala showed up in our driveway. My blood boiled at the injustice of it. My younger brother, a sophomore, had a new car while I, a senior, had nothing but a free ride to school.

Of course, it was Mr. O'Connor's choice to give his car to whomever he pleased, and it had always been clear that Mr. O'Connor favored Ross over me. In fact, he never showed any particular interest in me. He was another man who had more in common with my brother—hunting, fishing, boating, baseball. What I found confusing was why my parents allowed it.

"Oh, Frankie, you don't need a car. You'll be going off to college soon," my mom said.

Dad backed her up. "Rossie will be here for two more years. He needs a car more than you do."

"It's totally unfair," I protested. "I'm being driven to school by my little brother! C'mon, Mom, do you know how embarrassing that is? Can't we at least share the car?"

Neither of my parents uttered a word in response. Furious, I went upstairs into my bedroom and put "Bohemian Rhapsody" on my stereo. By then, music had become the companion I needed to put words to what I was feeling, or sometimes to tap into feelings when there were no words.

As I lost myself in the layering melodies, I thought back to the time when I was nine or ten years old and Ross and I were in Mr. O'Connor's basement, playing with his old army gear: duffle bag, mess kit, ammunition holder, an empty hand grenade, and some stray bullets.

Through the window we could hear our dad, our uncle Ted, and several other men from the neighborhood in Mr. O'Connor's backyard having a beer and listening to music on the radio. The men were all laughing—someone must be telling a joke. Then Mr. O'Connor's voice bellowed through the laughter, his words loud and distinct: "They were all a bunch of fudge packers."

My mind puzzled over the words until I put two and two together. I said to Ross, "I think he's talking about a gay person."

Ross looked at me blankly. "I don't get it."

"Don't worry about it," I said, feeling confusion and disgust rise up inside me.

With Queen's harmonies swelling in the background, I felt that same disgust and confusion again. Why was it okay for the men on my dad's side of the family to kiss each other in greeting? Why could Freddie Mercury preen on the stage in full makeup and rhinestones? Why was it okay for Mr. O'Connor to put down "fudge packers" when he was the one who dressed up for Halloween as the Miller Babe with a blond wig, white skirt, even big balloons for breasts under his T-shirt?

I reached out and whacked the needle off the record with an ear-splitting scratch.

* * *

Outside of my siblings, the kid who had the biggest impact on me was Mr. O'Connor's son, our neighbor Mateo. Adopted at birth, his backstory was shrouded in mystery—yet another secret we knew better than to ask about. With his glossy curls and darker skin, he fit in better with our family than with his fair-skinned Irish parents. Perhaps that's one reason why he was constantly at our house. Most days I'd come home from school to find him playing with my younger sisters; he regularly stayed for dinner with us and often slept overnight on the weekends during the summer. Knowing that Mateo loved to go fishing, we even took him on our family vacations to a lakeside cabin in Tomahawk, Wisconsin. He felt like part of our family.

I will never forget the day when the course of Mateo's life permanently changed. It was a Sunday evening, the one night of the week when my dad was home for family dinner. Mateo was there and I noticed a bizarre look on his face, as if he were present but, at the same time, somewhere else. He had a strange smile on his face, too. It looked like he was stoned, but I knew that was unlikely, because he was only eleven years old.

Without warning, the unsettling look turned into a terrifying rant.

"Spiders! The spiders! Get them off me. Help! Somebody, do something—they're crawling all over my face! They're everywhere! Aaaaaargh I can't stand it!"

We all stared at Mateo, stunned. *What is he talking about?* None of us saw any spiders on his face or anywhere in our kitchen. But his panic was undeniably real.

"Mateo, what do you mean?" Mom said, trying to keep her voice calm. "There aren't any spiders, sweetheart. Everything's okay."

"Yes, there are!" Mateo swiped frantically at his face and shoulders. "There are spiders everywhere! I can see them and feel them. Make them go away!"

"We don't see anything, Mateo," Dad chimed in.

Then Mateo burst out laughing, loudly and inappropriately, as if reacting to a joke that only he could hear.

"Honey, you're scaring me," Mom said. "What is going on? I'm going to call your mother."

Mateo's strange behavior went on for days. He would be his usual self, then suddenly slip into one of these episodes. Sometimes it lasted several hours, sometimes it went on for the whole day. Mr. and Mrs. O'Connor were beyond baffled; they seemed in shock, utterly helpless. Desperate for advice, they turned to my dad, the pharmacist, and my mom, the nurse, for recommendations. Mateo was shuttled to one doctor after another, undergoing blood tests and filling out questionnaires, as they looked for obscure medical conditions that might be causing his hallucinations. He was put on high doses of antipsychotic medication. He was hospitalized once, briefly, and then again, and then again. All summer long, he went in and out of psychiatric hospitals. Between these visits, poor Mateo would walk around our house like a zombie, a vacant stare in his eyes.

"Hey Mateo, how's it going?" I said to him one afternoon.

"How's it going. That's a good question. A very interesting question indeed." He spoke in a puzzled tone, with a faraway look in his eyes. "Frank is asking me how it's going."

It was devastating to see little Mateo like that. I remember going to bed one night and thinking, *We are all having a bad dream. When I wake up in the morning, this will all be over.* But it didn't stop. In fact, it got worse—much worse—before it got better.

When fall came, Mateo struggled so much to function normally that he could barely go back to school. My parents kept helping his parents search for answers. At one point, Mom and Dad suggested that Mateo go to the prestigious Mayo Clinic in Rochester, Minnesota, for an evaluation. Mateo remained there for several weeks, undergoing various tests and treatments. During Thanksgiving vacation, our family went up to visit him.

The hospital building was new and modern looking, with fancy carpeting and furniture, big paintings on the walls, and windows everywhere. But when we arrived at the psychiatric ward, it was a different story. We walked up to two white, windowless doors with a button to the right under a sign that read "Private—Ring to Enter." A lady dressed all in white opened the door and welcomed us in a whisper: "Whom are you here to visit?"

"Mateo O'Connor," my parents said in a matching soft tone.

"Oh, yes, we've been expecting you," she intoned. "Mateo is very excited to see you. He's told us all about you and what a nice family you are. Come in—I'll escort you to the family conference room and I'll have Mateo join you there."

The contrast from the rest of the hospital was remarkable. The walls were painted beige, hung with a few scattered pictures of nondescript landscapes. The floor was linoleum. All the windows had bars across them. An eerie silence and a sterile smell pervaded the unit. Bleak, vapid, reeking of secrecy and shame, it felt more like a prison ward than a hospital. I felt lonesome just walking down the hall, with every patient diverting their gaze as we walked past them. My siblings and I kept looking at each other. No one said a word, but we were all thinking the same things: *Poor Mateo!* and *Get me out of here!*

Mateo told us that he'd been diagnosed with bipolar disorder and put on Lithium and Haldol, that he would soon be discharged home, that he'd try his best to get back to school and resume a normal life. We had a nice visit with Mateo, but it was dreadful to see him in a place like that. During the long drive home, I couldn't get the image of those kids out of my mind. I saw the sorrow in their eyes and felt their heartache as keenly as my own. The helplessness of the doctors, the O'Connors, and my own parents was intolerable to me. I knew too well what it was like to be not only in pain but utterly alone. I left the psych ward with a conviction that I had to do something to stop the suffering I had witnessed. I might be the perfect person for the job.

Mateo gradually became more stable, returned to school, and successfully reengaged in his studies. With his parents' help, he managed his symptoms, and despite intermittent relapses, entered high school, graduated, and was accepted into college at DePaul University in downtown Chicago.

Meanwhile, in light of what we'd all gone through over the last few years, my parents decided to plan a trip to Florida and invited the O'Connors to join us. We didn't go on many big vacations, but when we did, family life was at its best—spontaneous, fun, and full of adventure. Dad wasn't stressed out from overworking, Mom got a well-deserved break from all her household duties, and we siblings got to spend quality time together. Moreover, having Mateo and his family join us helped everyone be on their best behavior—at least, once we arrived at our destination. Getting there was the hard part.

"I hate sitting in this car," said Ross, voicing a sentiment we all shared. Even a big Cadillac like the one Dad always drove was a cramped cross-country ride for six people. There was just enough room for three of us in the front seat and three of us in the back. Whoever was in the back stared enviously out the rear window at the O'Connors, trailing behind us in their own vehicle, quiet and with all the room they needed.

My dad kept his focus on the road, singing under his breath as the soundtrack from *The Godfather* played over and over again on the car's eight-track player. To help us pass the time, my mom would intermittently suggest we all play a game together. "Name an animal that starts with an A, next a B . . ." When we wearied of the game, my sisters would color or play word puzzles together while Ross occupied himself with contradicting what anyone else said or breaking up quiet moments with controversial statements.

"All lions are male, and all tigers are female," he'd announce.

"No, Ross," everyone retorted.

To keep myself busy, I'd brought along plenty of books, only to remember that reading was nearly impossible because I was prone to carsickness. Instead, I sharpened my dissociation skills with a little game of my own invention. I'd stare out the window, let my eyes go blurry, and see how long I could successfully block out everyone's voices before some new controversy broke the spell.

We arrived in Sarasota around six o'clock in the evening and began unpacking our cars into our respective condos. As soon as we walked in the door, we kids started fighting over which bedroom we would take for the week. Dad pulled me from the fray and asked me to make the martinis. We always traveled with a cooler full of alcohol so my parents could save money by having a cocktail or two before heading to a restaurant for dinner. And as a teen, I had proved a natural with the shaker, earning rare praise for my signature recipe: four shots of Stolichnaya vodka, a cap full of dry vermouth, served on the rocks with a twist of lemon rind and two anchovy olives.

After a few sips, my mom surprised us all by saying, "I hate this place. It's not at all what they described when I made the reservation. Let's get out of here and go somewhere else. I wonder how the O'Connors like their place?"

Is this the martini talking? None of us knew what to make of this suggestion, especially coming from Mom. Drinks had been made; we'd already started to unpack. But as we watched, Mom picked up the phone, dialed a number from her purse, and talked to someone for about twenty minutes. When she hung up, she announced, "Everyone pack up your stuff. They're giving us a new condo in a different location."

Despite her usual acquiescent attitude, Maggie could be powerful when she made up her mind about something. Her insistence that night paid off—our next place was huge and beautiful, way up on the eighth floor, overlooking the beach. The next day, when we entered the Magic Kingdom, the crowds were overwhelming, but my sisters and Mateo were thrilled to be there. Whether still high on her own display of agency or simply overtaken by the joy of the moment, my mom called out, "Hey kids, do you want one of those big balloons over there?"

They shouted, "Yes!"

"Well, too bad. You can't have one—they're too expensive." Mom looked over her shoulder for support from Mateo's mom. "Don't you agree, Molly?"

We all burst out laughing—Mom and Molly included—at how her frugal mindset quickly reined in her offer. To this day, it remains a beloved family memory, referenced hundreds of times: "Do you want a balloon? Too bad."

After the dark period we'd all gone through together, the light-hearted absurdity of that moment set the tone for the rest of the trip. We visited each other at our posh vacation digs. We ate at fancy restaurants. We each got to pick a special activity—going to Disney World had been the girls' choice, Ross and Mateo picked deep-sea fishing, and I took a private tennis lesson.

On the long car ride home, I remember thinking, *It's important to have these happy moments to balance out the bad ones.* Dad seemed to agree, proclaiming, as the theme song from *The Godfather* played yet again, "You only live once. *Alla famiglia*—to the family!"

CHAPTER FOUR

ALLA FAMIGLIA

"Speak Softly Love" (Love Theme from *The Godfather*) | **Andy Williams**

The love and the hate, the traditions and the tragedy, the fun and the fear. The gentle beauty of a love that never dies was always in the air in my big Italian family, until it wasn't. In the blink of an eye, the love died and you feared for your life.

* * *

Growing up as a purebred Italian certainly had its benefits but also its downsides. At times, it felt bipolar. There are many things about the culture that are wonderful and other things that aren't so great. Our love of family, our pride in our culture, and our passionate emotional expression could make everyday life brilliant and beautiful, but at the drop of a hat, it could become ugly, overbearing, or downright cruel.

Growing up, we spent most of our weekends at Uncle Tony's house. He was a family physician at the time, who frequently made house calls and even accepted forms of barter for his services if his patients couldn't pay. I remember seeing all kinds of weird and fun stuff he'd received as payment, including a memorable jar of homemade maraschino cherries well over a gallon in size. The adults used them when Manhattans replaced martinis as the drink of the evening, and the kids used them to make Shirley Temple mocktails. Once the drinks got flowing—and they always did—the adults got hangovers, and the kids got stomachaches.

When we got together, we typically had a big pasta dinner complete with noodles, sauce, salad, zucchini or eggplant, bread, and meatballs, all made from scratch. Preparing the meal was an all-day event for the women in our family. I vividly remember what it was like to walk into the house when they were cooking, the mixture of sights and smells that instantly hijacked my senses: scarlet tomatoes blistered and bubbling in the sauce pot, beef broiling in the oven, freshly baked bread filling the room with its soothing aroma. Food created home, and sharing a meal was what life was all about for our family.

Many of these gatherings ended in slumber parties with my cousins—Louie (the oldest, named after my father just as I was named after my uncle) and his three younger sisters, Isabella, Nancy, and Gianna. Our cousins were our best friends, and most of my happiest childhood memories are from times spent with them. I remember sitting on the couch in their basement at night, covered in blankets, as we watched the latest *Creature Features* on TV. When Frankenstein or the werewolf showed up, we notoriously threw the blankets over our heads to avoid the jump scare.

With festive weekends like these being the norm, it was only natural for our holiday parties to be larger than life. Christmas, New Year's Eve, Memorial Day, Fourth of July, Labor Day, birthdays, graduations— if there was a reason to celebrate, my big extended Italian family threw a party for it. Each family took their turn hosting, and let me tell you, planning these parties was stressful. Typically, both sides of the family were invited, which meant there were usually thirty to forty of us at each celebration. Needless to say, it was challenging to get everything ready— preparing the food, the drinks, and the decorations, cleaning the house, setting up the tables and chairs, and, of course, ensuring that everyone looked their best. For us, that meant Mom taking us shopping at JC Penney to buy a new outfit whenever it was our turn to host. Even with immediate family, we knew appearances mattered.

My dad had an unusual (and baffling) nickname for my mom: Butch. In the days and hours leading up to our party, we'd hear him screaming it, again and again.

"Butch, how many bags of ice did you buy?"

"Butch, I don't think we have enough Smirnoffs. Goddammit, we're going to have to switch over to gin martinis when the vodka runs out."

"Butch, where in the hell are the bags of Fritos and French onion dip you bought the other day?"

My mom shouted out the answers to my dad's requests amid managing her own level of stress. "If you boys don't get into that shower immediately, you're going to be grounded for a week. Do you hear me? I have to finish putting together the lasagna and get it into the oven before everyone gets here. And I haven't even started the artichoke and spinach casserole. Frank and Ross, why don't you just take a shower together? At this point, we're running out of time, and there won't be enough hot water for your father and me."

My dad would add his signature brand of support: "If you boys don't do what your mother says *immediately,* I'm going to come upstairs and put you in the shower myself, and I promise you, it won't be pretty. *Capisci?*"

My mom chimes in again. "Boys, don't forget to put on the new leisure suits I bought you. Frankie, just put safety pins in your new pants if they're too long—I don't have time to hem them right now. And when you're done with your shower, I need you to wake up the girls from their nap and put on their new dresses, the matching purple ones hanging in the closet with the tags still on them."

Utter mayhem abounded throughout our house in preparation for the party. But as soon as the first person knocked at the door, we pulled it together, ran downstairs, and welcomed our guests with smiles and open arms. No matter what happened behind closed doors, we looked, sounded, and acted like the perfect family when others were watching.

Uncle Steve's family was the first to arrive. I greeted him with a kiss on the cheek, and immediately regretted it when I saw the look on his face.

"Men don't kiss each other, Frankie."

Oh, crap! I remembered too late. *The men on my dad's side of the family kiss on the cheek, not the men on Mom's side of the family—they shake hands.* With a shrug and a muttered apology, I gripped his hand, then made myself scarce.

Along with holidays and special occasions, our family gathered annually around our passion for two ethnic traditions: canning tomatoes and making wine. These were more than seasonal hobbies—they were a rite of passage, a beloved part of our heritage preserved from the old country and incorporated into our Italian American life in Chicago.

When the weather began to turn toward fall, Grandpa Ross ordered boxes of Zinfandel grapes from a distributor in California and spent the entire week before the delivery pulling the equipment out of his garage, making sure it was clean and ready to use. The arrival of the wooden crates brought Uncle Tony, Uncle Steve, Uncle Leo, Uncle Ted, my dad, my brother, and my cousin Louie out to help. Winemaking was a man's job in our family.

There are many steps involved in making wine, and it was all done by hand. First, we opened the crates and rinsed the grapes off with a hose, raising a sweet smell and making their purple color even more vibrant. We then put the grapes in barrels and smashed them with a special mallet. This part was the most fun. The squishing noise was wildly entertaining, and by the end, we were covered from head to toe with grape juice. Seeing us, my grandpa would spread his arms expansively and proclaim, "We're making nectar of the gods."

However, it was nectar of the bees, too. The grown-ups would tell us not to worry about them—they were there for the grapes, not us—but for city kids like us, it was terrifying to see these hordes of bees swarming around or feel one buzzing close to our ear. In this instance, though, their brushoff was valid—the bees mostly left us alone.

Next, we put big rubber gloves on to pick out the stems from the mash we'd created. Being perfect wasn't necessary; Grandpa used to say,

"Don't worry about it—you'd need to eat a bushel of dirt before you ended up in the hospital."

The juice was then siphoned off and put into clean barrels while the residual skin and pulp was placed into the wine press to extract the remaining liquid. This was the hardest step, requiring us to crank it by hand. Everyone took turns, even the kids. The men would cheer us on: "Come on boys, it's good for you. It builds muscle and character."

Amid all this activity, winemaking required a lot of standing around and waiting. That was when the stories started flowing. The men reminisced about "the old country." My grandpa told us crazy things he did with his buddies, as well as with the ladies, when he was a young adult. My uncles told stories that we were explicitly warned not to repeat in the company of women. I loved listening to all these tales. Beyond just the history of our family, they taught me what it meant to be an Italian, and what it meant to be a man.

When the grape juice was completely drained and filtered, we carefully poured it into fifty-gallon oak barrels and my grandfather added a special mix of ingredients, including sugar and sodium metabisulfite to help start the fermenting process. The recipe, he told us, came from "Ut" (short for uncle) Angelo, a long-lost relative on my grandma Katie's side who, according to family lore, was the reigning champion of the winemaking competitions in the old neighborhood. Ut Angelo gifted my grandpa all the winemaking equipment, along with his secret recipe, before he died. Stories about him were the stuff of legend. One evening, when my sister Sophia didn't want to eat her peas at dinner, Grandpa Ross launched into a familiar classic.

"Did I ever tell you the story about Ut Angelo's dog? That dog was picky, and he only liked a certain brand of dog food. So, you know what Angelo did?"

Despite having heard this story a hundred times before, we all said in unison, "No, Grandpa, what did he do?"

"He took that dog and put him in the coal shed. He put him in there for thirty days and thirty nights. That dog began eating and shitting coal, he was so hungry. He ate and shat coal for thirty days straight. And you know what happened when Angelo let the dog out of the coal shed?"

Yes, we did.

"That dog ate everything that was put in front of him from that day forward. He was never picky again."

Ross, Luna, and I looked at each other, grinning. We were used to our relatives' way of teaching us life lessons through telling stories. None of us were totally sure if this particular fable was completely made up or not. But Sophia picked up her spoon and started eating her peas.

Once the barrels were filled and the chemicals were added, the bulk of the winemaking process was done. Now it was time to wait. It took months for the wine to fully ferment. We typically had our first glass of wine during one of our family Christmas celebrations. Again, this included the kids—another Italian family tradition.

Canning tomatoes was similar to making wine, except the women were included, which meant that the stories were mostly G-rated. It started with ordering large quantities of tomatoes—twenty to thirty bushels' worth. Italians go through a lot of tomatoes when everyone eats pasta at least every Sunday; we typically put up 250 or 300 quarts of tomatoes to get us through the winter. We all gathered for most of the weekend and rotated between the various jobs so it didn't become too monotonous.

Just as the kind of grapes chosen was important to winemaking, so was the variety of tomatoes used for canning. "This year we were lucky enough to get beefsteak, Roma, and Tom-Tom tomatoes," my grandmother would boast.

The work started with cleaning and blanching the tomatoes; this made them easier to skin. Next, someone diced them, and someone else put them through the hand grinder, which was as tiring as the grape press; no one stayed at this station for very long. We first cranked with the left hand, then switched to the right hand, and eventually used both hands before taking a break.

Meanwhile, another person sat and picked basil leaves off hundreds of plants. The mound of emerald-green leaves spread across the kitchen table, filling the room with their pungent sweetness. Another person put salt into the tomato mixture and watched over the huge pots simmering. When that step was done, we all worked together to ladle the tomatoes into mason jars, and it was my dad's job to seal them properly. We had to make sure each lid popped—otherwise, the tomatoes would spoil and have to be thrown away.

The weekend was always rewarded with a big pasta dinner, which naturally included homemade fettuccini and fresh sauce. Those meals were special, signifying not only the end of our hard work but also the importance of our heritage as a culture and a family. My dad always began the meal by holding up a glass of homemade wine while offering his favorite toast: "*Alla famiglia!*"

• • •

I grew up on the South Side of Chicago, an area that was predominantly Irish Catholic at the time. Kids who grew up there identified themselves not by the town they lived in but rather by the church they attended.

"I'm from St. Gerald's. Where are you from?"

"I come from St. Linus, but we used to live in St. Germain."

This made another place in my life where I didn't quite fit in, a full-blooded Italian in a sea of O'Malleys and O'Briens. Our family dinner conversations didn't include getting a South Side Irish jacket for Christmas or figuring out how to get accepted into Notre Dame College someday. Instead, our family banter revolved around our Mafia ties.

The story goes that the notorious Genna brothers, a mob family that controlled Chicago's West Side (also known as "Little Italy" or "Little Sicily"), sold alcohol during the Prohibition era. One of them wanted to marry my grandmother, Katie, and when a leader of the mob wants to marry you, you don't have much to say about it. But he and two of his brothers were gunned down within two months of each other, just before the marriage was to take place. Apparently, the Italians had infiltrated the Irish neighborhood to sell moonshine, and the Irish mob retaliated with a massacre.

This bloody event let my grandmother off the hook, leaving her free to marry her true love, my grandpa Ross. However, it turned out that Grandpa Ross's history wasn't as squeaky clean as he led us to believe. His sister Jenny, also a kind and gentle soul, married a man named Tommy, who was connected. Tommy served as a pallbearer for the Genna brothers' funerals and later was instructed to move to Los Angeles for a new "business venture." Apparently, the two guys who accompanied him out west got shot and killed within a month of arriving. At that point, Tommy was directed to leave his family and "go into hiding." This lasted a total of three years, leaving Jenny alone to raise three kids by her-self—with financial support from the mob of course. The nature of the business venture, as well as where he went to hide, remained a mystery.

We never got the full story when it came to these kinds of memories. Catching us listening, the grown-ups would say, "You kids don't need to hear this," then switch from English to Italian. This tactic only escalated our fear and curiosity. The Italian swear words we learned—*puttana* for whore, *vaffanculo* for fuck—were as fascinating as the stories themselves.

To make some extra cash for his upcoming nuptials, Grandpa Ross briefly worked for Tommy. I learned more about the nature of that work when my grandpa came down to Champaign, Illinois, to pick me up from college before Christmas vacation.

"I remember this town, Frankie," Grandpa said to me. "This is where I did some time before your grandma and I got married."

"What do you mean?" I asked, surprised.

"I got caught delivering moonshine to some of the saloons down here and was thrown in jail a week before our wedding. Boy, was your grandma furious with me! She had to borrow money to help get me out of jail. I guess she wanted to have someone to kiss and say 'I do' to at the end of the ceremony after she walked down the aisle in her new wedding dress."

Sure, I thought to myself, *why not add in a little jail time to the family saga?*

Kids at school thought it was cool to have Mafia connections, but I held a constant level of fear in the background of my mind, especially when my dad shared from his own arsenal of stories about relatives and the Mafia.

"I've never taken any money from the mob," he told us with pride. "They've offered it to me several times, but I've always said no. Once you owe them, they own you for life. And I don't want to owe anyone anything. Uncle Nino took a loan once for his gas station. He had trouble paying them back, and you know what? They blew up his gas station."

Each time I heard one of these stories, a pang jolted through my body, not panic or excitement but something in between. *I wonder if Tommy or Uncle Nino or Ut Angelo ever knew Al Capone personally. Wouldn't that be cool?* Some kids grew up fearing the boogeyman; I grew up fearing mobsters. They were out there and could come for you at any moment if you missed a payment or made them mad—a threat I was all too familiar with. *What if they know where I live? What if our house gets blown up some day?* It was hard to differentiate fact from fiction in these stories, and given that secrets were a part of the fabric of our family, I never knew what or whom I could trust. I pictured dead bodies on the street, pools of blood spreading below them, or imagined the gas station down the street erupting in a huge explosion and raging flames. Not only was being inside my home unpredictable and often scary, but the world outside our house could be scary, too.

• • •

Mafia connections weren't the only family scandal. One came to light when I did a genealogy report in my sophomore year of high school. We weren't allowed to put anything in the report unless it was backed by an official document. When I was working on my mom's side of the family, I noticed something odd in the papers belonging to my grandma Florida (so called because she frequently traveled there when we were young): her birth certificate and her marriage license had the same last name. To gain some clarity, I called her up.

"Hey, Grandma Florida, it's Frankie. I'm confused about something. It seems that you and Grandpa Sam had the same last name before you got married?"

"Oh, Frankie, isn't that funny? It only looks that way," she assured me. "His name was pronounced 'Florenza' and my name was pronounced 'Fiorenza,' even though they were spelled the same on some of the papers."

"Oh, okay. That *is* strange." We said goodbye and hung up the phone.

It turned out that my grandmother in fact married her cousin, Sam Florenza, a secret she carried with her until the day she died. She had so much shame around her marriage to my grandfather that she made up a story about pronunciation differences to use whenever she was confronted with it.

After my mom confirmed my suspicions, I was reminded of how everyone commented about my resemblance to Grandpa Sam: "You look just like him." In the way that a child's mind works, I grew up believing that I, too, would die early of a brain tumor. At the same time, hearing about his kind nature and his uncommon intelligence made me feel a special connection to him—to this day, I often feel him as a presence in my life. I never held any judgment toward my grandmother or my grandfather for their secret, and it seemed no one else in the family did either, though they never shared any details about their courtship or relationship. It simply disappeared into the vault of family stories, a rare instance of our secrecy protecting something out of love rather than shame.

There were also scandals that seemed to belong in neither category—the ones that were talked about as funny or trifling but felt in memory as though they crossed a line. One such scandal took place during Christmastime in 1979, the year the song "Grandma Got Run Over by a Reindeer" was released by Elmo & Patsy. We sang it constantly that holiday season but changed the lyrics—we sang "Daddy" instead of "Grandpa," poking fun at how my father had almost succeeded in killing off his mother-in-law.

It started with a holiday celebration at Uncle Tony and Auntie Anna's house. Theirs were the best parties: fancy catered appetizers, platters of meat and seafood—including filet mignon, king crab legs, shrimp cocktail, clams, oysters, and octopus—and a variety of side dishes, including the latest and greatest Jell-O mold. That year's model featured orange Jell-O with carrots, walnuts, cranberries, and Cool Whip. There were always two punch bowls, one spiked and one alcohol-free, and a whole room dedicated to desserts. After dinner, the most inebriated uncle would dress up as Santa Claus and pass out the presents. The younger kids would cry when Santa arrived, and the adults made naughty comments when the women sat on his lap.

At the end of the evening, after a lavish meal, a brand-new sweater, a few new toys, and lots and lots of drinking, we packed our Christmas haul in the trunk of the car and headed home. Grandma Florida, who was going to spend the night at our house, was crammed next to me in the back seat of Dad's latest Cadillac, which was fire-engine red with a white top.

Uncle Tony and his family lived in a wealthy, secluded suburb of Chicago surrounded by woods, about a forty-five-minute drive from our house. That winter evening, as my dad steered over fallen snow through the impending darkness, his driving was clearly impaired by alcohol.

"Louis, slow down," Mom pleaded. "The roads seem icy."

"Yeah, Dad, I keep bumping into Grandma back here," I chimed in.

"Would you and your mother be quiet and let me do the driving, for Christ's sake?" he snapped back.

Without warning, we started bouncing up and down and side to side. Our bodies were flailing out of control. Grandma and I were literally lifted out of our seats, our heads hitting the ceiling of the car. *What the hell is happening?* Abruptly, the car came to a stop. No one said a word. A combination of shock, terror, and relief had us speechless.

"Well, that was strange," said Dad. "Why didn't they put a road sign back there telling me I was supposed to turn left?" It took him a good ten minutes to back out of the snowbank and get back on a paved road.

Are you serious? You've driven home from Uncle Tony's house hundreds of times. We all know that curve in the road. You just drove off the road into the forest preserves. You almost killed us. That's what I was thinking, but I knew better than to open my mouth.

"Louis, maybe I should drive the rest of the way home," Mom suggested.

"No, Butch. Shut up and stop worrying. I'm fine. I have no trouble driving home. Everyone needs to relax, and no one will mention a word of this to anyone. Got it?"

We drove the rest of the way home in total silence.

My mind festered with a mixture of anger and fright. *Shouldn't you be saying, "Hey, is everyone okay? I'm so sorry. I think I had too much to drink. Butch, why don't you drive home from here?"* I was enraged by his denial and tired of living through yet another scary experience. *I wish our family was normal.*

Once again, my dad had created a story that matched the reality he desired, while attempting to save face in front of my grandmother. But my reality was different. A delightful Christmas Eve party had been followed by one of the scariest moments of my life and ended with the usual anticlimax of distorted truth. No big deal, nothing really happened. It felt like an episode from a sitcom: *The Crazy Italians*, starring alcohol, mood swings, and too much pride.

It all boiled down to the fact that families are incredibly confusing. Ours had moments of greatness, even if it didn't always seem that way on the inside. It was also full of heartbreak and rage and tension and misunderstanding that lasted for years. Sometimes it felt worth it, other times, not at all. In the end, it was all that we had, because it was all that we knew.

• • •

My dad's mother, Katie Sabalone, came to America from Sicily as a young child. She grew up to be a striking beauty, but she was one tough cookie. Short in stature, with well-defined facial features and medium-length wavy black hair, Grandma Katie was a self-taught seamstress who wore gorgeous clothes, expensive jewelry, pointy glasses studded with rhinestones, and frequently, a harsh look that revealed her legendary mean streak. When her husband did something that was, according to her, out of line, she would often scream, "For Christ's sake, Ross, shut your goddamn mouth!" at which he would bow his head and look away in shame.

After fate saved her from marrying into the Mafia, Grandma Katie ended up marrying Ross Guastella, who shared her Sicilian roots. He was strong and handsome, a man of integrity with a kind soul. Grandpa had a round face with a boyish smile, brown hair thinning at the crown, and a body like a boxer or a professional weightlifter. As kids, we often said, "Grandpa, show us your muscles." He flexed his bicep and let us squeeze it, giving us a wink when we reacted with amazement and delight.

Grandpa Ross loved connecting with the earth and growing his own vegetables, particularly tomatoes, basil, zucchini, and eggplant. To this day, I have a love of nature and gardening because of him. In my grandfather's eyes, there was not one thing wrong with me; I was perfect. Besides slipping me money, he constantly praised me for my academic achievements and was there for every graduation and awards ceremony. He took me to fancy clothing stores and bought me real tailored suits so I would look professional when I interviewed for college and medical school. He treated me special and, feeling his love, I believed that my grandfather deserved to be treated special too, not constantly berated by his domineering wife.

I hope Grandma Katie dies before Grandpa Ross does. He's so nice, but she is so mean to him. She's constantly yelling at him. She's not even that nice to me or my brother and sisters. I wish he never married her. My other grandma is so much nicer. She takes us to fun places and is always buying us things.

Sadly, many years later when Grandma Katie did pass, my grandfather became a shell of his former self. He was totally lost without his wife. Even with her cantankerous disposition, she offered him something he needed and couldn't uphold on his own: perspective and self-restraint. Without her, his racial and ethnic tribalism went unchecked. Despite his kind heart, my grandfather was notorious for judging others—you were either "good people" or "bad people." Outsiders were quickly sized up and fell on one side of the fence or the other: "We like them, they're our kind of people" or else "He's no good. We don't associate with his kind."

This attitude could go to hurtful extremes, such as the time when my grandfather took his firstborn son, the doctor, out of his will because Uncle Tony had betrayed the family by getting divorced and remarrying an Irish woman. While not technically a sin, divorce is taboo in the traditional Italian culture, and as I later learned, so was marrying someone of Irish descent, especially in light of the Prohibition massacre inflicted by the Irish bootleggers on the Italians.

I was puzzled by the contrast between my grandfather's gentle soul and his harsh, irrational treatment of his son. It felt as though I'd lost one of the few safe people in my family circle. The only sense I could make was that asserting our own superiority by putting down other people seemed to be another family tradition. At times, it even applied to our own extended family.

"See, we don't fight like they do," Dad would remark to us kids after we got back home from visiting one of our relatives. "Their smoking is awful. I'm telling you, they're gonna end up getting lung cancer someday, mark my words. I told you, having money causes problems. See how unhappy they are."

I vowed to never participate in this behavior when I grew up, knowing how bad it felt to be judged myself. At the same time, the general judgment offered some relief for being at the bottom of my family's pecking order. Seeing ourselves as manifestly superior to everyone else we knew, especially in knowing how to have a good time, helped us overlook our obvious dysfunction.

"Look at Albert next door," Dad would say. "Every Saturday morning at eight o'clock, without fail, he's out there washing his car. I bet he gets up at the same time every day, takes a shit, wipes with the same hand, gets dressed, and drives the same route to work, week after week. Not us. We're a family who knows how to have fun!"

It was a beautiful summer afternoon, Dad was home from work, and we were all outside waiting for the barbeque to heat up. Suddenly, my dad picked up the hose and sprayed my mom with it.

"Louis, stop that," she said, annoyed.

"Oh, come on, Butchie, what's wrong with a little water? What's wrong with having a little fun? You're not going to melt!" He sprayed her again.

Ross and I saw the look in his eyes—one of fun, not fight—so we ran into the garage and grabbed two big buckets. Once filled, we started dumping water on each other. Then we headed straight for Luna and Sophia. But my sisters were fast—they ran into the house, and my mom quickly followed. Dad was right behind her, hose in hand. Suddenly, there was water everywhere. I took my bucket, ran into the bathroom, filled it up, and waited for someone to come by. *Sploosh!* I dumped the whole bucket full of water on Sophia as she ran from the hallway into the kitchen. Before I could get back to the bathroom for a refill, my dad caught up to me and sprayed me with the hose.

Finally, my mom couldn't take it anymore. "Everyone stop!" she screamed. "I'm going to have a nervous breakdown."

Game over, Dad ordered us all to help clean up the mess we'd made. For Ross and me, spending the afternoon soaking up water from the rugs and furniture was a perfectly fair tradeoff for the fun we'd had. We couldn't deny it had been damn crazy, too. *Do other families do this?*

That fall, someone gave my mom a basket of freshly picked apples, and she decided to make them into pies. Mom was not a baker, so this was a big deal. Her full day in the kitchen resulted in three pies, crust and all baked from scratch, sitting on the dining room table to cool. We were all excited to eat them.

Then I heard a thud and crash, followed by a scream from Mom that gave way to crying. I ran into the dining room to find pie crust and baked apple filling plastered all over the wall and strewn on the carpeting. It didn't seem like they'd had a fight; instead, out of nowhere, my dad had simply picked up the pies, one by one, and thrown them against the wall.

I stood there looking at what had just happened, not quite sure how to feel. *Stay vigilant; things can turn on a dime in this house.*

As usual, Dad tried to normalize it. "It's not the end of the world. It's only food and carpeting, for Pete's sake. Everything can be cleaned up. Worry about the big problems in life; don't sweat the small stuff. I was just having a little fun. They're just pies."

A knot swelled up in my stomach. It was all so confusing. On some level, it *was* fun—exciting, anyway. Out of the norm, certainly, but we were unique, not like other families. On another level, it felt out of control, unsafe. *Is it better to know how to have fun, if fun looks like this?*

Then there was our menagerie. My dad loved animals; every day, as soon as he came home from work, he'd kiss our dog, Puggie, followed by a hello kiss for my mother. It was always a waggish bone of contention between them.

"Louis," my mom often remonstrated, "you like animals more than you like people."

Animals were indeed a better fit for him—they were always happy to see him, and they never talked back or challenged his authority. In addition to Puggie, we kept angel fish (we often had twenty fish tanks going at any one time), a parrot named Taco, and a pet monkey named Sunshine.

One day, with the monkey's cage smelling up the house, Mom asked us to clean it. Ross unhooked the latch and Sunshine promptly escaped, running all over the kitchen with the squealing noise that said he was enjoying himself. He crawled across the curtain rod, then jumped onto the kitchen table and grabbed a stick of butter, thinking it was a banana. Butter in hand, he scampered off, continuing his spree throughout the house.

"Boys, get that damn monkey back into his cage immediately," Mom pleaded. "He's making a total mess!"

I stood next to the cage with several pieces of banana at the ready. I put one piece on my shoulder, one piece on my extended hand, and two more pieces in the cage. Eventually, Sunshine spotted the treats and climbed up my body, onto my arm, and back into the cage. Ross quickly closed the door. Another day in the life of having a monkey. Another Guastella family crisis narrowly averted.

Yeah, we're definitely not like other families.

• • •

Why is family so complicated? How can so much love be accompanied by so much pain? I love my ethnic identity and the sense of belonging and heritage that comes with it. I love the fun, the laughter, the joy my family has brought me; I appreciate that they've seen me at my worst and still showed up the next day. On the other hand, I cannot believe how much stress, sadness, and heartache they've also caused me. Many of the best moments of my life have been with my family; so have many of the worst.

Distortion and dichotomy were two of the things that bound our family together. This was a puzzling way to live as a child. Contradictory thoughts constantly went through my mind, leaving me to wonder if something I remembered was true or fabricated, fun or terrifying. I struggled to trust my own judgment, my own thoughts and feelings about what went on in my family. *That didn't really happen. I didn't feel that way. That wasn't true.* It was hard for me to stand up for what I believed in, partly because it was too dangerous, partly because I really wasn't sure what my own beliefs were. To cope, I always looked at the positive side of everything. To a fault, I would not see the downside in people. I was always pushing for hope, looking for the positives, seeing the good in everything and everyone. The idea of focusing on the negative was too overwhelming.

It's true that having a positive outlook often cultivates a resilience that supports mental health, but not when it blinds you to what's real and prevents you from listening to your inner voice. From a young age, I had to choose between my dad's reality and mine. To survive, I chose his.

CHAPTER FIVE

MADE IT TO "NORMAL"

"Roll with the Changes" | REO Speedwagon

Being a smart, resourceful kid, I knew it was time to be done with the same old story; I knew I had to turn some pages. I learned to ignore, suppress, deny, succeed, and move on. I learned how to roll with the changes. I learned how to be normal.

* * *

During the last year of my therapy with Dr. Dwight, when I was in sixth grade, a woman in the waiting room offered to do a needlepoint for me. Her teenage son had the session right before mine, and each week she sat in the same chair, working on her craft. To pass the time, we'd talk over whatever project she was working on as it progressed from one week to the next. Her kind interest made the tedious wait more bearable. For a few minutes, I felt like I was special, rather than a problem to be solved.

"I hear you're ending therapy soon," she said. "I've been wanting to try a new project. Why don't you bring me in a picture of your favorite animal? Anything you want."

"Really?" I said with excitement. I loved watching her projects over the years—and now I'd have one made just for me?

The next week, I brought her a page from my sisters' coloring book featuring the mouse from *Tom and Jerry*. Looking back, it was an uncannily accurate reflection of how I felt at the time—small, meek, and powerless. However, her gift meant the world to me then, and still does to this day. It was a sign of accomplishment, like a diploma. My parents must have thought so, too, because they made a big deal of the finished piece and had it professionally framed. That embroidered mouse was a symbol that I was done with my "special meetings"—the therapy had done its work, and that chapter of my life was finally over. For my parents, it meant that the family could be normal now. For me, it meant that I'd endured and, apparently, succeeded. I was "fixed," and my parents were happy.

It was true that by that time, I'd gained a pretty good idea of what I needed to do to act "normal." I've always been a quick learner and keen observer, and from an early age, I took in all the unspoken lessons from my Midwestern life about what toys I was supposed to play with (army men and battleships: good, my cousin's dollhouse: bad) and what activities I was supposed to participate in (baseball: yes, arts and crafts: no). I took in cues from the kids on the playground, from television, from the men in my family. Reading my father's moods led to learning how to read people's faces, their subtle reactions, and what they wanted from me. For a while, these skills served me well, especially throughout my teenage years and well into young adulthood. It felt good to fit in and be like everyone else, and it definitely eased the conflicts and chaos at home. Somewhere between his counseling sessions, his thriving pharmacy business, and my convincing imitation of "normal," my dad had become much less explosive; the screaming, vile language, and violent outbursts had quieted down. Occasionally, Louis Guastella even seemed proud of his firstborn son.

"Nice job last night at the matchbox derby, Frank. Even though your car didn't win, you gave it your best shot. That's all I can ask for."

"Wow, thanks, Dad," I said, trying not to show how keenly I felt his approval.

Middle school, however, brought a new set of hurdles to overcome. I remained an extremely dedicated and disciplined student, getting up at five every morning to study while the house was quiet. Most semesters, I made the honor roll and enjoyed glowing accolades from my teachers.

But while being the teacher's pet certainly had its perks, like being picked first for fun projects and field trips, it also had its disadvantages, especially when it came to recess.

Back when I was a kid, schools didn't acknowledge bullies. If they had, Bernard certainly would have qualified as one. He was a big kid in the grade above me, athletic but not very smart, and for some reason, he had it out for me. Whenever he passed me in the hall, he poked or pushed or punched me, depending on whether a teacher was nearby. During recess, he chased me. But thanks to my father, I'd had a lot of practice escaping from bullies. My constant vigilance tipped me off even before I saw his large frame bounding toward me. As soon as my heart started pumping, I took off for my daily mini-marathon around the recess yard. I ran from one end to the other, dodging in and out of the play structures at lightning speed, keeping Bernard at a safe distance until he got tired out or frustrated and gave up. We kept playing this exhausting game throughout our middle school years until, thank goodness, we ended up in different high schools.

Worse than Bernard's persecution was my father's persistent lack of enthusiasm about my academic success. While he wasn't yelling as much or calling me names, I still wasn't earning his love or even his attention. Nevertheless, I kept pushing myself to achieve. If the honor roll wasn't enough, maybe something even greater would be. At my eighth-grade graduation ceremony, I was called to the podium to receive the coveted AMVETS scholarship. This was the first award I ever received, and while it still didn't win my father over, it drove my ambition to new heights. I became obsessed with going to a private high school.

As hardworking, middle-class Americans, Louis and Maggie Guastella had no experience with private school. Paying for a high school education? To my parents, this was not simply unheard of; it was absurd. But I was determined. Back then, the South Side's public high school, Richards, was known as an "end-of-the-road" school—kids who went there typically didn't go to college. I set my sights on attending Marist, an all-boys Catholic high school known for its academics. Kids who went to a private high school like Marist were smart and motivated. They went places. That was where I wanted to be.

Growing up, I didn't ask my parents for much. I saw how hard my dad was working to strike it rich with his pharmacy empire. By this time, he'd paid back everyone who had lent him money for the first store, down to the penny, and had purchased two additional smaller pharmacies. He had a vision of himself as the next Charles Walgreen, the Chicago-born pharmacy mogul, and aspired to own a chain of pharmacies—in that spirit, he'd return from work proclaiming, "The king is home!"

But even with his business thriving, the late 1970s brought tough times for everyone: high inflation, 20 percent interest rates, horse meat at the supermarket, grain alcohol at the gas stations. This kept my dad working harder than ever before; we were effectively growing up without a father. Behind his comments about how other people cared too much about money, or his disparaging remarks about Uncle Tony's lavish life-style—"Oh my God, a new Mercedes? What's next, a Rolls Royce like his friend Angelo's?"—I saw how much he envied the prosperity and opportunities his brother could afford. I wanted those things, too. Education was my ticket to freedom, to success, to getting out of the house. I knew that pleading my case wouldn't be enough; I had to show my parents that their hard-earned money would be well spent. First, however, I had to get accepted to Marist. I took the initiative and signed myself up for the entrance exams.

On the morning of the exam, I again got up while it was still dark out and crept down the stairs to prepare. I reviewed the requirements for acceptance. I looked over some math and science material, my favorite subjects, to make sure I performed at my best. A few hours later, my mom came down the stairs, groggy and rubbing her eyes.

"Frankie, honey, hold on," she said. "Before you go, let me make you some breakfast. Can I get you a cup of Linco?"

What? I looked up from my books, startled. *Is she trying to trick me into drinking bleach?* I watched her for a moment as she stumbled around the kitchen. *Oh, she's just tired.* Whether from a lack of sleep or, perhaps, too much to drink the night before, she wasn't thinking clearly.

I got up out of my chair and patted her on the shoulder. "Thanks, Mom, I'm good. Why don't you go back to bed? I'll grab a Pop-Tart before I go."

After a blank pause, my mom started laughing. "Did I really just offer you a cup of Linco for breakfast?"

"Yep, you sure did," I responded. It crossed my mind, as I looked at her guilty smile, that it was just the sort of thing my dad might have done—"C'mon, Frankie, what's wrong with a little fun?"—a practical joke that would have thrown off my focus. But feeling my mom's love for me made the whole situation land differently. Indeed, the "Linco incident" has become another fond family memory. Whenever my siblings and I get together, someone inevitably brings it up sooner or later: "Frankie, can I get you a cup of Linco?"

Mom leaned over and kissed me on the forehead. "Good luck today, honey. I know you'll do great. You always do."

The Linco story was certainly told later that night, but the headline was that I was accepted into Marist. I did so well on the entrance exam that I got placed in a mixture of advanced and honors classes. This was enough to win my parents over, even with the tuition price tag of $3,000 a year. That was a lot of money at the time, and a considerable hardship for my parents. Still, as second-generation Italian immigrants, my parents believed in the promise of the American Dream, and I was determined to prove that the investment in a private high school was an opportunity worth the sacrifice. In the end, I was a successful test case. After me, all my siblings went to private high schools.

* * *

High school marked the start of my "normal" phase. At Marist, being a good student was reinforced and expected—for the first time ever, I fit in. I made friends who weren't family members. I started feeling like a typical teenage boy. After all the turmoil of feeling different, compounded by the trauma at home, I was finally happy. *Maybe my therapy was successful,* I thought.

Since Marist didn't provide a school bus service for its students, my resourceful mom found a carpool, consisting of four students, that was looking for an additional member. Each mom rotated shifts as the week's designated driver. I was the only freshman in the carpool—the others were sophomores and juniors—but regardless of my age, they all liked me. Furthermore, since these older boys had been going to Marist for a year or more already, they had become acquainted with a group of students at the Catholic girls' school, Mother McAuley. As a result, most of my weekends were spent with my friends from Marist and the cohort from our "sister school." We'd be on the phone all week, making plans: Whose house was available for a party? Could anyone get hold of any alcohol? Did anyone hear about a party that another group was having?

It felt awesome to fit in and be included in something bigger than me. It felt even better to have something to contribute to the group. After all, since my family had a lot of parties, I knew what it took to successfully pull one off. One Saturday night, my parents had plans to go out to dinner with their group of friends to Phil Smidts, a favorite special occasion restaurant for our family that was fortuitously located in Indiana. With my parents scheduled to spend the evening nearly an hour's drive from our house, I seized the opportunity to host a party of my own.

The minute my parents pulled out of the driveway, I called my friend Rob. "Okay, the coast is clear. You can tell everyone to head over to my house."

Ross was home and supposed to babysit Luna and Sophia, so I invited him to the party. The only question remaining was how to buy my sisters' silence. *I know—I'll bribe them.*

"Luna and Sophia, come here for a second. I'm having some friends over, and I don't want you to say anything to Mom and Dad."

"But I thought you were going out tonight," said Luna.

"I know, but plans have changed. Hey, what if I pay you five dollars each?"

Seeing their faces light up, I repeated, "But you have to promise not to say anything to Mom and Dad. Not one word. Do you promise?" They looked at each other, hesitant, then nodded their heads yes. *Phew!*

Word of my party spread like wildfire. Before I knew it, there were forty to fifty people crammed in my basement. In addition to the beer some of the kids brought to the party, I tapped each and every bottle of hard liquor in my parents' huge bar. As we drank, I replaced the alcohol with water, confident that my parents wouldn't notice. I also played DJ, queuing up the eight-track player with Journey, Foreigner, REO Speedwagon, Aerosmith. I paid my sisters another five dollars each to put some frozen pizzas in the oven for the hungry guests; they eagerly helped out, excited by the responsibility and overwhelmed by the generous wages I was offering. Looking around the room, I was on cloud nine. *I'm having my first party, and everyone's having a blast!*

But then there was trouble.

"Frank, get over here," my friend Theo called out. "Suzie just puked all over the rug in the kitchen. She's wasted, and her clothes are a mess."

Shit! Think fast!

"Have Carol and Karen throw her in the shower," I commanded, "then have someone drive her home."

"Seriously?" Theo responded.

"Yeah, why not?" *I can handle this.* I knew we had enough time, because my mom would call Ross to let him know they were on their way home. Besides, life in my family had made me adept at running interference for a gang of rowdy drinkers. This time, it felt great to be the one in charge.

When Mom eventually called, we moved into high gear.

"Okay, listen up, everyone. My parents just left the restaurant. Everyone has to help clean up and be out of here in thirty minutes."

Big, loud, and drunken, my first official party was a huge success (with the exception of Suzie, of course). The whole house, puke and all, was wiped clean of evidence. When my parents returned, happily full and buzzed after their swanky dinner, they had no clue what had just gone down under their roof. In fact, they never found out until about five years ago, when my siblings and I were visiting during the holidays and the subject of the party came up.

Parties weren't the only "new normal" in my high school experience. Girlfriends were, too. My dating adventures began with the homecoming dance my freshman year. All the guys in my group of friends spent the weeks leading up to the dance planning the best moves and maneuvers for getting to the proverbial bases with their dates. I sat back, listened, and learned.

I will never forget going "parking" after the dance. I double-dated with Dan, one of my carpool friends, because he was old enough to drive. Dan and his date were making out in the front seat of his car while in the back seat, my date Joanne and I were doing the same. Kissing was okay—it was a bit sloppy and awkward, being my first attempt, but I guess I liked it. After getting up enough courage, I made the big move to put my hands on her breasts. This was terrifying but exciting. So exciting, in fact, that I instantly came, right there in my pants.

"What's wrong?" Joanne asked when I pulled away from her.

"Nothing, I'm fine." It was all I could do to keep cool.

"Are you sure? All of a sudden you got so quiet."

"Yeah, I'm fine. I'm just tired," I lied. "Hey Dan, we're ready to go whenever you are."

I went to many more dances in high school and dated many more girls. But Carol Montgomery was my first real girlfriend, and the saying is true: You never forget your first. Carol was the prettiest girl in our group, and she picked me over older, more popular guys, which boosted my popularity along with my confidence. Throughout my dating adventures in high school, I learned important skills, like how to French kiss, unhook bras, put my hands down girls' shirts and, eventually, their pants. Despite getting to all the bases, I never hit a home run. Luckily, though, I never had another unwanted orgasm, either.

* * *

During my junior year, I got my first taste of college, and it proved just as exciting as throwing my first party. After hours of pleading with my parents, they agreed to let me go away for the weekend to visit Dan at Bradley University in Peoria, three hours from Chicago. I told them the purpose of the trip was to check out the college, but I had other plans in mind, too. Other than sleepovers with my cousins, this was my first real trip away from home. Dan and I smoked cigarettes, got stoned, and hooked up with girls all weekend long. I felt pretty damn good about myself: I was having a lot of fun, experiencing my first taste of freedom, behaving like a normal teenager.

Chicago has several great schools—Northwestern, Loyola, and the University of Chicago, for starters. But I wanted to go to the University of Illinois; in addition to being a great school, it was more than two hours' distance from our house. I had to work hard to convince my parents. While they were impressed by the notion of their son attending a Big Ten school, they didn't grow up in an environment in which going away for school was commonplace. "There's no need to go far away for college. There are plenty of good schools right here in Chicago. Paying room and board is a waste of money. Why don't you just pick a local school?"

Once again, with a lot of hard work—filling out the application, paying the application fee, visiting the college, and taking the placement exams—I won them over.

However, their agreement had a condition: I had to pay for my own college education. My father was scrupulous about passing down the strong work ethic he'd developed as a second-generation immigrant.

From the time I was twelve through eighteen, I'd work alongside him two weekday evenings and all day Saturday during the school year, and during summer vacations, I'd work twelve hours a day, six days a week. When it came time for college, I'd saved a lot of money, and since U of I was a state school, I was able to cover the cost of room, board, and tuition all four years between my savings and the help of student loans.

As soon as I was accepted to U of I, I started looking forward to being on campus. I wanted to get there as soon as the dorms were open. But my father had a different plan. He refused to take the day off from work to drive me to school. We had a huge fight about it.

"But Dad, New Student Week starts on Monday. Why can't I be there on the first day?" I pleaded with him. "They have a bunch of activities planned for all the new freshmen."

"Because life doesn't only revolve around you. Missing a day of work costs the family a lot of money. And besides, your mom has to take care of your brother and sisters. It's not all about you, Frank," he proclaimed, the anger growing in his voice.

"Why don't they stay home and you drive me, then?" I suggested.

"Absolutely not! We do things as a family—how many times do I need to remind you? If one goes, we all go. And let me be clear: Everything you bring to school must fit in the trunk of the car. That's all the space you get, so you better think twice about what you want to bring."

"Are you kidding me?" I slammed my fist on the kitchen table and stormed out of the house.

My father eventually relented, taking a day off work so I could arrive on Wednesday of Freshman Orientation Week. My excitement renewed—midway through was better than nothing—I got to work streamlining the stash of dorm room essentials I had been assembling for months: sheets, toiletries, a hot pot, clothing, a typewriter, a boombox to play music, and, of course, cool decorations for my room, including a big neon Budweiser sign from the front window of my dad's store. *This will be a huge hit at school,* I remember thinking. *Everyone will see how cool I am.*

The trunk of the car looked like a jigsaw puzzle when I finished packing everything in. With the six of us piled into Dad's latest Cadillac, and the Budweiser sign in my lap, we were off on the family's latest adventure: taking Frankie to college. Everyone helped unload the trunk, my mom made sure my bed was properly made, and I got busy scouting a small refrigerator for my room. After dinner at a local restaurant, we all went back to my dorm, said our goodbyes, and with that, I watched my family drive away.

Holy shit, is this really happening?

It felt fantastic to be out of that house. *For the first time in my life, I'm free.* At the same time, I was surprised to feel a lump in my throat. It was one of the most exciting times of my life, yet here I was, scared to be living on my own. I also found myself feeling angry at my dad for all the conditions and restrictions he'd placed on me while moving in. Was his reluctance to take a day off work purely a financial issue, or was it his way of expressing how much he would miss me when I was gone?

I was just as surprised to find that whenever I came home for a weekend visit during that first semester, my dad would slip me a fifty-dollar bill, just like my grandfather did when I was younger, to help with spending money. *Is he rewarding me for good behavior? Did I become the son he always wanted? Is he proud of me?*

* * *

My father, who flunked out of pre-med before becoming a pharmacist, had repeatedly warned us, "College is hard. If you don't do your work, you're going to flunk out. And it doesn't get any easier—some make it, and some don't."

With that fear drilled into my head, it's no wonder I studied like crazy. I was determined to maintain my record of being an all-A's student. Good thing I loved learning! I got so excited each semester to see my new class schedule. I loved looking through my textbooks and thinking, *I can't believe I'll know all this information by the end of December.* I allowed myself one B every semester, and I chose which class it would be before the semester started. Everything else had to be an A.

Fueled by my drive to succeed, I stuck to a strict schedule, even tracking the hours I put into studying. It was common for kids to start partying on Thursday to get a jump on the weekend. I, on the other hand, never allowed myself a break before Friday night, and when I did go out, it was only for one night each weekend. I would often say to myself, *Good job, Frank, another Friday afternoon of studying while everyone else was at happy hour. You're three hours ahead of most of your class right now.* In the evenings, well after dinner service, the cafeteria would stay open to allow students to study there. Since it was much quieter than the dorms, I went there to study most evenings, often staying up until four in the morning. It reminded me of getting up early in the morning to study when I was living at home.

My commitment to my studies was supported by having almost no way of leaving campus. At that time, U of I was essentially an island in the middle of southern Illinois' vast farmland. Apart from the quaint fringe of shops and cafés surrounding the campus, there wasn't much to do in town. If you wanted real fun, you had to drive to find it.

For a brief time, I did have a car . . . sort of. The year Ross entered college, our dad bought a secondhand station wagon for my brother and me to share. (Unsurprisingly, Albert O'Connor's ancient Chevy Impala hadn't lasted very long.) However, Dad's car-sharing plan had one major problem: Ross went to school in Indiana, and I was in Illinois. It turns out that it's really hard to share a car when you're in different states. The "sharing" system quickly turned into a custody dispute, determined by whoever was in our father's favor. If Ross did something to piss him off, Louis commanded him to return the car to me. I got to enjoy the privilege of having a car for two or three months until, inevitably, I did something wrong; then back to Ross the car went.

Neither of us was terribly surprised by the outcome of this arrangement. What was surprising was that, rather than making us rivals, it brought us closer together. Trying to figure out who got the car from one week to the next gave us an opportunity to talk more often. Griping about my dad's arbitrary temper led to reminiscing and even laughing over the crazy childhood we'd undergone together. Against all odds, our old trauma bond turned into a true brotherly closeness.

In all four years of college, I remember just one evening when I decided to do something other than study. One of the fraternities hosted free movie screenings on Wednesday nights. With my homework done early, I decided to treat myself to a relaxing midweek evening out. Instead, I spent two hours riveted by a story that looked in many ways just like mine: a boy growing up in the Chicago suburbs, a terrible experience of trauma, a series of visits to a psychiatrist. The movie was *Ordinary People*, a true story based on a book that I immediately bought and read. While I related deeply to the young patient, I found myself more drawn to the psychiatrist character. Ever since I'd visited Mateo in the psych ward, I had wished there was a way to rescue people from the pain that lived inside their minds. This was my first inkling that it was, in fact, possible. I wondered what it must feel like to be such a person—someone who could be there for someone else's suffering, to listen, to understand, to offer them the help they couldn't get on their own. I read the book until the cover was tattered; I watched the movie so many times that I memorized every line.

* * *

I chose chemistry as my major, with a minor in math. Ironically, my first semester class in chemistry would prove to be the one C I'd get in my four years as an undergrad. I loved chemistry, but I was adjusting to the rigors of college-level courses. I was devastated by this blight on my straight-A record, but in hindsight, this class taught me something even more valuable than basic chemistry: how to learn on my own.

When I was a sophomore in college, I met my second—and last— serious girlfriend, Elizabeth. She had brown eyes, long brown hair, and an ethnic look about her, though not of the olive-skinned variety I was used to. She was German, with fair skin, prominent cheekbones, bushy eyebrows, and a sculpted chin. She had a bohemian fashion sense, with a penchant for oversized clothing that looked like it came from a trendy thrift store. Her favorite jacket was a men's full-length tweed overcoat, which she wore as a badge of individuality. She was smart, unique, extremely kind; I was intrigued.

We met in organic chemistry class and quickly became lab partners. While it made for a good "meet-cute" story, our personal chemistry was less sexual magnetism, more intellectual passion. I started taking Beth out on study dates to my favorite spot, David Kinley Hall (DKH), an old-fashioned red brick collegiate building with light that poured in through floor-to-ceiling windows. Nearly every night after dinner, we walked to DKH and found a quiet room where we could stay late into the evening, studying or, more often, talking endlessly about homework, life, each other's interests and hopes.

One night during junior year, Beth and I were in DKH reviewing the Krebs cycle for a biochemistry exam. Before we tackled the last section, I told Beth that I needed a bathroom break. She decided to take a quick break, too, and called her sister. In those few minutes that we were apart, something unsettling happened.

It was late by that time, the halls dark, not many people around. Surprisingly, the light was on when I entered the bathroom, dimly reflecting off the dark wooden walls and raising a glow from the polished white mosaic tiles on the floor. There were three stalls, and I went into the first one on the right. Suddenly, a man—older than me but clearly not a professor—knelt down in the stall next to me and exposed himself. He then dropped a magazine with pictures of naked men on it and started masturbating.

"What are you doing?" I blurted out.

He responded to my question with another question.

"Do you like it?"

I couldn't seem to look away. "Why are you doing this?" I responded with a frozen stare, taken over by a wave of undefinable emotion.

He came all over the floor. Snapping back to reality, I quickly left the bathroom, my heart pounding a mile a minute. *What in the fuck just happened?*

I returned to our study room as Beth wrapped up her call with her sister. We proceeded to study the last section of the Krebs cycle, but I couldn't concentrate. My mind was flooded with images of the previous five minutes. Without warning, I had a spontaneous orgasm—the second one in my life.

Flummoxed, I made an excuse to Beth. "It's getting late, and I'm tired. Let's go home and finish this tomorrow, okay?"

She agreed, we packed up, and I walked her back to her dorm.

I didn't realize at the time that I had caught a man cruising in a public bathroom. All I knew was that this was the first time in my life anyone gay had crossed my path. Confused and ashamed by the way my body reacted, I pushed the entire incident out of my mind, just as I'd done hundreds of times in my childhood. Thanks to my well-honed powers of willfully forgetting and moving on, I aced my biochemistry exam, ranking 11 out of 550 students, putting me on track for another A in what happened to be a "weeding out" course for pre-med.

• • •

I loved college life: studying like crazy, dating Beth, hanging out with friends. Our group studied together, ate together, played racquetball at the rec center, and occasionally went out to the bars. I felt so connected. I was living my best life. Unfortunately, as hard as I tried to bury my past, my deep-seated insecurities started surfacing. If one of my organic chemistry labs went beyond 5 p.m. (as they often did) and the rest of the group went down to dinner without me, I panicked. My heart pumped faster as negative thoughts raced through my mind: *They left without me. They really don't like me. If they did, they would have waited for me. I'm not worth it. I'm irrelevant.* Most young people have occasional bouts of insecurity; today, we call it FOMO (fear of missing out). But my reaction was too intense. I got hurt so easily, and I felt rejected and betrayed. Having a group of friends was amazing, but it was also hard when my fear of abandonment was activated.

After sophomore year, students were no longer allowed to live in the dorms. Instead, our friend group divided up and looked for apartments off campus. I decided to get an apartment together with my best college friend, Jim Nichols, a cattle farmer from southern Illinois. His girlfriend, Ronda, who was his high school sweetheart, lived across campus. Jim was also serious about his studies, and we got along well. We often ate meals together, especially when he brought back amazing cuts of meat from his family farm. We watched movies together and even wrestled in our apartment during study breaks. Wrestling with Jim made me feel uncomfortable, yet I once again ignored my gut and told myself, *This is normal. This is what guys do.* It was harder to persuade myself of this, however, when Jim left to spend the weekend with Ronda. Even though I had a girlfriend of my own, I felt abandoned and alone. *What is wrong with me?* I thought. *This is not normal.*

Instead of sorting out what was getting stirred up inside of me, I shifted my focus to a different problem: the terrifying task of telling my father I wanted to go to medical school. Back home, everyone, including my dad, assumed I would follow in his footsteps by becoming a pharmacist and taking over the family business. I'd already spent my freshman and sophomore years in the pre-pharmacy program, completing the requisite courses for entering U of I's pharmacy school the following year. But seeing how I was outperforming most of the pre-med students in those classes had sparked my ambition. Biology had activated a new and unexpected interest in how the human body worked. Most of all, I adamantly did not want to go back to Chicago.

Back at home for Christmas that year, I struggled with how to break the news to my dad. As usual, we were having a big holiday party, our house filled with relatives, everyone drinking heavily. Because I was now considered one of the adults, I played Santa Claus that year—a rite of passage that proved surprisingly fun. After disrobing and taking off my makeup, I sat at the corner of our famous basement bar, a real seventies relic with its Naugahyde-wrapped bumper, yellow Formica top, and burnt-orange shag carpeting up the sides. I found a sympathetic ear in Johnny, a cousin by marriage. Eight years older than me, he grew up in the "hippie" generation. He was tall and thin, had a head full of frizzy blond hair, and smoked like a chimney. Though we hadn't talked much before, we sat up together for the rest of the night while the other party-goers continued their revelry upstairs.

"Nice job up there, Frank. You're a natural Santa," Johnny said. "You better be careful, or you'll have that job for the next decade. It was mine for a few years, but I was happy to pass on the torch. It gets old fast."

I thanked him for the heads-up. Then he asked me the question I'd been dreading.

"So, how's school going?"

"Really well," I told him. "Almost too good, honestly. I'm doing better than most of the kids around me." I hesitated, then dove in. "I'm actually thinking about becoming a doctor instead of a pharmacist. I love my classes and being away at school, and if I get into pharmacy school, it means coming back here to Chicago. But if I tell my dad about it, he'll kill me."

"What do you mean by that?" Johnny inquired, taken aback.

I tried to explain. "My dad flunked out of pre-med in college. If I do what he failed at when he was younger, he's going to hate me even more than he already does. It's like shoving his failure right in his face."

Johnny blew out a cloud of strange-smelling smoke. "Frank, your dad might surprise you. I think he would support you going to medical school if that's what you really want to do." He grinned encouragingly. "Have a little faith. You'll never know unless you give it a try."

Maybe it was the aroma from Johnny's hand-rolled cigarettes. Maybe it was his outsider perspective. Maybe it was just the right time in my life to consider my situation from a different perspective. Though Johnny was unaware of what went on behind closed doors between my father and me, his reasoning reassured me. At the end of the night, when the party was nearly over and everybody was leaving, I walked upstairs to the kitchen, where relatives were packing up leftovers, sneaking extra nibbles of dessert, waiting for their buzz to wear off. Seeing my dad sitting at the kitchen table, I took a deep breath, and dove in.

"Dad, I need to talk to you about something. I've been doing really well in school . . ." I swallowed hard, my heart beating faster. "And I don't want to go to pharmacy school. I think I want to stay at U of I and transfer into the pre-med program. I want to become a doctor."

My body tensed up, waiting for his response. There was a long pause before he replied.

"Well, it's the ultimate in the healthcare profession. And if you want to go for the ultimate, then go ahead. It'll be a lot of work, but if that's what you want, do it."

And that was that. Once again, Louis's reaction had taken me by surprise. It was kind of a strange comment—"the ultimate in the healthcare profession"—but that was the way he viewed it. The shock and relief made way for a sense of freedom within, as I conquered the next hurdle on my journey. I was confident that I could get into medical school. But would it make him proud of his son, the doctor? That remained to be seen.

• • •

When I returned to college from winter break, I transferred into pre-med. Beth and I continued dating, looking forward to a future together. Hoping to continue our education alongside each other as well, we took the MCATs (the standardized exam to enter medical school) and applied to the same medical schools. While Beth wasn't sure what branch of medicine she wanted to pursue, a couple of months before graduation she had already been accepted at three medical schools: University of Illinois, Loyola, and Rush Presbyterian. Meanwhile, I got waitlisted at U of I, rejected by Loyola, and hadn't yet heard from Rush. Working hard in school didn't make everything come easily to me. Despite my stellar grades, it turned out I wasn't a great standardized test taker. I started to panic. *What if I can't get into medical school? What in the world will I do?*

As graduation approached, Beth had to choose which of the three medical schools she would attend. She picked Rush Presbyterian in the hopes that I would get in there. Knowing I couldn't face another summer of going home to work at my father's pharmacy, I reassessed my strengths and began searching for PhD programs in biochemistry. I loved biochemistry and was highly ranked in the class; on a whim, I reached out to Purdue University, filled out their application, and received not only an acceptance letter but a full scholarship of $25,000 per year to earn my doctorate in biochemistry. There was only one problem: I didn't want to be a biochemist. I didn't even know what type of job one ended up with. I wanted to be a doctor.

Graduation weekend arrived. Despite not knowing what my next step would be, it was wonderful. Both our families were there to celebrate our graduation, so we decided to take them to an upscale restaurant together. It was the first time Beth and her parents met my parents. Everything went smoothly, everyone got along, but it felt strange to me, a bit too grown-up for my liking. I was inducted into the Phi Beta Kappa honor society during our graduation ceremony, which helped counteract some of the fear I carried about my future. Then I packed up all my belongings, said goodbye to my roommate, Jim, and moved back home to Oak Lawn for the summer. *At least I have Purdue—just two more months of working at the pharmacy,* I thought as I drove away, looking at U of I in my rearview mirror.

The very next morning, my mom called up to my bedroom.

"Frank, you got some mail."

When I walked downstairs, she was holding a letter up to the overhead light in our kitchen. I grabbed the envelope from her, opened it, and read: "It is with great pleasure that we offer you a position in the 1985–86 entering class of Rush Medical College."

CHAPTER SIX

FOR THE LOVE OF DOCTOR

"Lose Yourself" | **Eminem**

I lost myself, not in the moment but in a lifetime of studying and working to achieve my goal. It paid off and I got my shot. I owned it, I captured it, I took full advantage of it. I was a wounded healer; I was exactly where I belonged.

✴ ✴ ✴

"I got in! I got accepted to medical school!"

I will never forget that moment, standing in my childhood kitchen opening that letter. All the years, months, days, and hours of hard work and dedication were represented in the words on that page. I had accomplished something I was truly proud of. I breathed a gigantic sigh of relief and thought, *Everything is finally falling into place.*

Amid the flood of thrill and relief, my mom's response intruded like a record scratch: "Oh, Frankie, congratulations! How wonderful! I'm so proud of you! That's the same hospital you went to for psych testing when you were young."

What? I was speechless.

My memory flickered with faint images as Mom shared the details: the pictures I'd drawn, the questions I'd filled out, the inkblot images I'd stared at. Who could have predicted that my therapy experience as a child would bring me right back to the institution where the whole journey started? The belief that I was broken and abnormal had propelled me to excel in school, and now here I was, with my highest achievement to date coming from the same place where that belief was born. It had an eerie feeling of being beyond coincidence. I'd come so completely full circle that it made my head spin.

· · ·

In college, I'd fully devoted myself to studying—seven days a week, often six to eight hours a day—with Beth by my side. During our first semester at Rush, we repeated the pattern. My devotion to working nonstop, sacrificing sleep and a social life, was rewarded with high honors on my first exams. But our breathless pace was interrupted when the news broke that one of our fellow classmates, a woman I'd briefly dated at U of I, had been brutally murdered. The news shook us all to the core. *You could be dead tomorrow,* I reflected. For the first time, I wondered if I should look for more meaning in my life than simply achieving the next success. I'd come so far already—even if I hadn't earned my father's love yet, hadn't I at least earned the right to take my foot off the gas pedal and enjoy life? I decided it was time for a radical change.

Here's a secret most people don't know about medical school: Getting in is the hardest part. Things change once you're accepted. Most schools invest a lot of time, energy, and financial resources in educating you to become a doctor—for that reason, they're committed to keeping you enrolled and helping you finish. Since we've already proven ourselves as exceptional students, with good study habits and the ability to digest large amounts of information in short periods of time, medical students don't have to worry so much about getting straight A's. Instead, most medical schools are based on a system of pass, fail, or honors. It's true that getting honors does give you an advantage in terms of your residency placement, especially if you're planning on going into the competitive programs such as cardiac surgery or orthopedics. In general, however, as long as you continue to work hard, retain the vast amount of requisite material, and pass your exams, you will move on to become a resident and, ultimately, earn your MD.

Finding this out after my first semester of pushing and sacrificing for honors, I made a pact with myself: *I'm going to try for once to have balance in my life.*

* * *

At Rush, Beth and I had an amazing group of friends. There were six of us who studied together, hung out during down-time, and shared the same philosophy of getting good grades while maintaining balanced lives. At some point, we began a monthly ritual of wowing each other with our cooking skills, which led to dubbing ourselves "The Supper Club." Every month, one of us would host a dinner party, a five-course meal complete with cocktails. One month, I called my grandmother to get her recipes—I wanted everyone to experience authentic, made-from-scratch Italian food the way I had it growing up. It was a huge production, but it was worth it. I made oysters Rockefeller and eggplant caponata for appetizers. The main course was angel hair pasta Fra Diavolo with clams, shrimp, cuttlefish, and octopus from the fish market, accompanied by breaded zucchini, a Caesar salad, homemade bread, and tiramisu with limoncello shots for dessert. It was a recreation of the big Italian parties of my youth, minus the yelling, the puking, and the driving off the road into a snowbank. The meal lasted for hours as we ate, drank, laughed, and gossiped.

"What about that histology exam last week? It kicked my ass," said Saul.

"Agreed," said Aleesha. "But I was surprised at how easy the pathology exam was."

"That's because Dr. Hoffman thinks you're a babe," Saul said, as he shot her a devilish wink.

"Shut up. He's a creepy old man, and you're disgusting," Aleesha retorted. "Finish your dessert, and let's help Frank with the dishes. We have a psychopharmacology lecture at eight o'clock tomorrow morning."

Being a part of The Supper Club turned out to be a brilliant distraction, providing sweet relief from the stress of studying. Together, we developed a camaraderie that was essential for surviving the rigors of medical school. It was a novel feeling to be a part of the "fun" group by just being myself.

Of course, medical school wasn't all fun and dinner parties. Medical students spend the first two years studying—anatomy, physiology, histology, microbiology, pathology, pharmacology—with the goal of not simply passing exams, but applying all that book knowledge over the next two years, under intense pressure, often in life-or-death scenarios, with real-life patients in the hospital. That's when you discover a fact none of your professors tell you: The medical system has its own secret world. It's extremely hierarchical and even, at times, abusive.

The third and fourth years of medical school are dedicated to clinical rotations, what insiders call "working on the floors." You learn on the job as you rotate among different specialties—internal medicine, pediatrics, obstetrics and gynecology, surgery, neurology, cardiology, and more. But to get into the clinicals, you first must pass a comprehensive national board exam. Passing the exam means earning the right to wear a short white coat and work with real live patients. Long white coats were reserved for residents and attending physicians. The length of the coat is a sign of status, power, and privilege in the hospital. To achieve that power and privilege, you first had to be thrown into the fire.

Our first task in working on the floors was to "round" on the patients. This involved standing by the patient's bedside, or outside their room, as the long coats drill the short coats with question after question after question.

"What's the differential diagnosis for this?"

"What lab test would you run to confirm that?"

"What's the standard treatment for this condition?"

We had to know the correct answers and answer quickly. If we blurted out something wrong or took too long to respond, we'd be humiliated in front of our peers, a fate worse than death for this group of the best and the brightest.

"Dr. Guastella, what are the risk factors for developing gallbladder disease?"

I know this. I just read about it last week. Just relax, Frank, you've got this.

"The risk factors for gallbladder disease are females, over forty years old, who are still fertile, with fair skin, have increased flatulence, and are obese," I recited.

"Good job," said Dr. Evans. "Dr. Guastella just stated the six F risk factors for gallbladder disease; however, he didn't say them correctly, did you, Dr. Guastella?" He grinned. "As the mnemonic goes, *fat*, not obese; *forty*; *female*; *fair*; *fucking*, not fertile; and *farting*, not flatulence." He made a mark on his clipboard. "Okay, next patient."

I breathed a sigh of relief. Reluctant to use the crude version, I'd knowingly flubbed my answer a bit, but it could have been a lot worse—I'd been spared the public shaming that other residents had suffered when they failed to answer perfectly. I had hoped to get away from nasty authority figures when I decided to go into medicine, but it seemed that dictatorial smart-asses weren't limited to the pharmacy profession.

Some might call this harsh practice "education." Medical students have another name for it: "pimping." So widespread and recognized is this practice in the medical industry that it's been the subject of an article published in the journal *BMC Medical Education*:* "The *pimp* (attending, fellow, or resident) is a supervisor who evaluates the student. The *pimped* (medical student) must appease the attending, a performance necessary for career advancement."

Pimping was a thinly disguised form of hazing and a daily reality for myself and my classmates throughout our medical training. We didn't question it any more than we questioned getting paid next to nothing for

---

* Chen, D. R., & Priest, K. C. "Pimping: A tradition of gendered disempowerment." *BMC Medical Education 19*, no. 345 (2019). https://doi.org/10.1186/s12909-019-1761-1

the staggering responsibilities we undertook. During my residency, just for fun, we periodically calculated our hourly wage; some weeks it came out to fifty cents an hour.

Medical education was designed to train future doctors to handle whatever emergencies or challenges come their way. In theory, it results in resilient physicians with top-notch skills, but in practice, the training can be brutal and harmful. Marked by lack of sleep, poor eating habits, and relentless stress, medical students develop a lifestyle that's incredibly unhealthy, all in the service of helping sick people become healthy. In turn, the workload, pressure, and sheer exhaustion often led students to slowly stop caring about their patients, the reason they went into the profession in the first place. It's a huge paradox.

• • •

For a medical student, clinicals are stressful and grueling, not to mention unpredictable. Eventually, that unpredictability became its own thrill, like flying without a net. As I took ownership of my position as a doctor, the feeling went from *This is terrifying; what do I do now?* to *This is fucking awesome—I can save someone's life.*

The very first person I treated was an AIDS patient. This was in the mid-eighties, when AIDS was relatively new and widely feared due to stigma, ignorance about how it spread, and uncertainty in how best to treat it. I had to put on a hazmat suit to interact with my HIV-positive patient, a woman who was a heroin addict. Why was I, a third-year medical student, given one of the sickest and potentially most contagious patients as my introduction to clinical medicine? Talk about trial by fire!

I remember the attending physician saying to me, "Whatever you do, don't stick yourself with one of her needles." I was clueless and terrified, but she was so kind and gentle to me, I will always remember her fondly.

I also remember responding to my first Code Blue. I was leaving the cafeteria with my team—consisting of an attending physician, a few residents, and several fellow medical students—when I heard it crackle over the intercom.

"Code Blue, Room 357 West. Code Blue, Room 357 West."

If you're a fan of medical dramas, you're familiar with how hospital color codes refer to a specific emergency situation—for example, Code Red typically indicates fire or smoke in the hospital, and Code Gray is usually a call for security. Calling a Code Blue means that the patient is in respiratory or cardiac arrest. My team all started running and I followed them. When we arrived, the room was noisy and full of activity, with three or four people already hovering over the patient, a gentleman suffering a heart attack.

The senior resident on my team, who was in charge of the code, started shouting out orders. I took a step back and watched it all for a few moments. Then I heard her say, "Frank, you take over chest compressions."

People made space for me as I stepped up to the patient's bedside. I tentatively put two fingers at the base of his sternum, looking for the proper position, clasped my hands together, and began pumping on his chest.

Holy cow! Is this really happening? This guy is having a heart attack right before my eyes and I'm doing chest compressions on him.

I felt a rush of adrenaline pulse throughout my body in a way that was oddly familiar. As my arms worked up and down, I remembered the sound of footsteps pounding up the stairs, the frantic reach for the crawl-space door, the musty scent of old clothes and suitcases. The feeling of life-or-death urgency was the same one I had when my father chased me through the house. *But now,* I realized, *that feeling is helping me save this man's life.* In a flash, I was hooked. The commotion and chaos faded into white noise around me. *I'm no longer at the mercy of someone else; it's not my life or death this time. It's someone else's life or death, and I'm going to help save him.*

"Okay, Frank, let Aleesha take over now. You can run this blood gas down to the lab. Tell them you need the results stat."

I ran down the hall, exhilarated. *This is exactly where I want to be. This is exactly what I want to be doing with my life. I am where I belong.*

Along with the intense stress and life-or-death urgency, medical school mirrored my childhood by requiring students to develop effective coping mechanisms to survive the pressure and fulfill what is expected of them. I learned to work smarter and faster, to multitask with precision and focus.

To this day, more than thirty years later, people often say to me, "How do you manage to do so much? You're taking on multiple creative projects along with your demanding work schedule, yet you seem to manage it all so well?" I tell them that as a medical student and resident, if you weren't resourceful and efficient, you'd quickly become overwhelmed and end up far behind. Thanks to the quick reflexes I developed as a kid avoiding my father's rage, I became a fast swimmer in this sink-or-swim environment.

• • •

During the fourth and final year of medical school, every student must decide which specialty they're going to pursue as a career. The point of clinical rotations at this stage—which includes stints in more specialized fields like radiology, pulmonology, the emergency department, child psychiatry, neurosurgery, and pediatric intensive care—is to narrow down your choices to the specific branch of medicine you want to focus on during your residency. Two key events helped to shape my choice, and the first happened in the hospital during my clinicals.

I always thought pediatrics would be my specialty until I worked in the pediatric intensive care unit. It was a heart-wrenching experience to see so many kids suffering and dying with terminal illnesses like leukemia or brain tumors, or suffering from tragic accidents, like the little boy who swallowed a balloon at a birthday party and asphyxiated; he was barely alive, hooked up to tubes to keep him breathing. Because I truly loved kids, it broke my heart to see them suffer; on some level, I suspect that it activated suppressed memories of my own childhood misery. Thanks to my clinical rotation in pediatrics, I came to a realization that I couldn't be a pediatrician. I wasn't objective enough.

The other event that transformed my career in medicine involved my neighbor, Mateo. In the middle of his first semester in college, Mateo had a second psychotic break and went missing. He was eighteen years old, extremely fragile, and lost (or worse) in downtown Chicago. After my parents called to share the news, I rushed home to see what I could do to help.

My parents and I immediately went next door to visit Albert and Molly. We found them sitting at their kitchen table, looking shattered.

"We have to do something," insisted my father. "Mateo's been missing for almost twenty-four hours. Shouldn't you call the police or something?"

"I don't know what to do," mumbled Albert.

"Well, I think you should at least file a missing person's report," I urged.

"Okay, Frankie, if you think that will help," whispered Molly.

If I think that will help? I felt an adrenaline surge bubble up inside. *Don't just sit there—your son is missing. Do something!* I looked over at my parents, and they nodded their heads in approval. They knew I could get shit done.

Clicking into high gear, I called the police, found the precinct associated with Mateo's college, and drove downtown. The police chief helped me fill out the appropriate paperwork and instructed me to bring some pictures of Mateo to the station, as well as a few articles of his clothing to be used by the search-and-rescue dogs for picking up his scent. He asked me to find out what he was last wearing and to notify administration at his school, DePaul University. He also advised that I make a hundred or more copies of a missing persons sign with a recent picture of Mateo, and round up a group of people to help post them all over campus and the surrounding area.

Before I left, the police chief pulled me aside. "The longer he's missing, the worse the outcome." His voice was gentle but somber. "Tell his parents we'll do whatever we can to find him." He gave me his number and told me he would be in touch soon.

I felt a sense of unreality, like I'd been dropped into an episode of *Law and Order*. The familiar beats of a cop show were very different when they happened in real life, and when the victim was someone I knew and cared about. Images of Mateo in the hospital as a teen flashed before my mind, overtaken by images of him lying in a pool of blood in a dark alley. I steadied my growing dread with the direction the police chief had given me. Armed with a plan, my family and I got to work while the O'Connors sat helpless, fearing the worst about their son.

Four days after he went missing, Mateo was found in the back of an abandoned van on a residential street in Chicago. He was incoherent and traumatized, unable to say how he'd come to be there and what had happened to him. Using my medical school connections, I got Mateo admitted to Rush under the care of a highly qualified and compassionate doctor. This unit was nicer than the one he was at as a teen, but the doors were still locked, the ambience still sterile and bleak. Knowing I was one of the few people who could connect with Mateo, I visited him as often as I could after my classes were over for the day. When I looked into his eyes, he looked utterly lost, beyond anyone's reach. We later learned he had been assaulted during the time he was missing.

My heart ached for him, even more than it did the first time I saw him in the hospital. We'd both endured a childhood of pain and loneliness—why did I manage to get free when he didn't?

I was gripped by that same conviction I'd had back then; no longer just a sense, it was stronger, more defined. When Mateo was found, I found my purpose: to help him, and others like him who suffered with mental illness and trauma, find safety and healing. In my fourth year of medical school, I shifted my focus to becoming a psychiatrist.

* * *

Initially, I thought child psychiatry would be the perfect blend of my two interests, children and mental health. Accordingly, I signed up for the child psych ward as my next rotation. What I would learn, yet again, was that working with kids hit too close to home.

Like all kids, patients in the child psych ward need to go out and play. For this, Rush provided a playground, complete with a slide and swings, located just outside the hospital in a little fenced-in area. During my time there, I was asked to help supervise the young patients during their play time. One afternoon, a little girl ran over to me and asked, "Hey, can you help me? I want to get on that swing. Could you pick me up?"

"Of course," I said, and I picked her up and placed her on the swing. I wasn't alone with this little girl—there were other staff members and other kids on the playground as well—so I thought nothing of it. That is, until I got a call from the dean of the medical school.

"Dr. Guastella, we have to pull you out of your child psych rotation, effective immediately."

"I don't understand," I replied, perplexed. "It's supposed to be a four-week rotation and I'm only halfway through it. Why?"

"All I can tell you at this point is that you've been accused of inappropriate behavior with one of the patients."

What? Now I was really baffled, not to mention agitated. *I didn't do anything wrong.* An all-too-familiar feeling welled up. . . . *Or did I? I'll fix it—just tell me what it is!*

"There will be an investigation," the dean continued. "We'll contact you when it's completed. I suggest you go home and spend some time with your family while you wait."

"Okay . . . Thank you." I didn't know what else to say.

With no other option, I went back to my parents' house, reeling from disbelief and unmitigated shame. For three weeks, I sat and wondered what in the world had just happened to me. *Is my career in medicine already finished before it even started?* It was surreal to sit and wait, day after day, with absolutely no idea about what I did or to whom.

My mom and dad seemed as confused as I was, but they were both supportive of me, seeming to understand that I didn't need to be questioned or judged. To my admitted surprise, they offered me the love and unconditional acceptance I needed at that time. It was relieving to know that in a true emergency, my parents were on my side.

When you're pulled out of a clinical rotation, people start to wonder. My friends started calling to inquire about me; however, I'd been explicitly instructed not to say a word about the situation. Besides my parents, the only person I told was Beth. I didn't have much to tell, anyway—I was completely in the dark. I just knew that it must be bad. Or that *I* must be bad.

Several weeks later, I got a call from an investigator with the Department of Social Services. He wanted to set up a meeting to discuss my case. We met at Rush and took a walk around the grounds.

"Nice to meet you, Frank," said the investigator.

It's not nice to meet you, but I have to be polite. "Nice to meet you, too."

"So, first I want to say that you did nothing wrong."

Oh, thank God . . . But wait, I already knew that!

He continued, "One of the patients on the child psych unit claimed that you inappropriately touched her on the playground. She fabricated the story to get her mother's attention. Apparently, her mother is a child therapist who specializes in trauma and works some pretty long days. The little girl thought this would be a good way for her mom to focus more on her and less on her work."

Are you kidding me? I instantly felt a wave of relief, followed by anger toward this little girl. *How dare she?*

"Anyway, your record is totally clear, and I was told by the medical school that they're giving you credit and a grade of high honors for the rotation. You can start your next clinical tomorrow."

Taken aback, I felt a mixture of relief and rage toward the medical school, too. *Honors and move on—that's it?*

"That's great news," I told the investigator, because, despite everything, it *was* great news. "Thanks so much for letting me know. I hope you have a good day."

As I walked away, the fear and tension I had carried in my body for the last three weeks slowly dissipated. I couldn't ignore the way this whole experience activated feelings of shame from my childhood. As a kid, I believed that I was bad and must have done something wrong, though I never knew what. Being pulled from clinicals for some unknown offense brought that feeling right back. It had even concluded in a way that was familiar from my childhood: I was expected to simply put the experience behind me and move on. *Oh, I know how to do that!* Bitterness filled the back of my throat. No amount of success, it seemed, could help me outrun this mysterious "abnormal" quality that seemed to hover around me. *What will it take to prove I'm not broken?*

Surprisingly, this thought helped me discover a connection to the kid who almost destroyed my career. This little girl and I had something in common: We were both searching for love and attention from our parents. I focused on success and achievement to get my father to notice and be proud of me, while this little girl had tried to become the type of child her mother cared about and focused on the most: a victim of abuse.

• • •

On the whole, doctors are exceptionally smart and driven people. As I know all too well, driven people are driven for a reason—to chase away their demons, to get attention, to feel successful, to counteract low self-worth, or (as in my case, and even the case of the little girl who accused me) to be loved. That drive can take a toll on your physical, emotional, and mental health. Doctors are not gods or angels. They are human beings just like their patients—often unhealthy and sometimes impaired. The medical profession, even the entire healthcare system, would be more effective and salubrious if we all were able to acknowledge that. As it is, many doctors cope by adopting unhealthy behaviors—from lack of sleep and poor nutrition, to substance abuse and letting off steam by impulsively having sex with members of the hospital staff, or even their patients. Whether it's a doctor helping others heal to address their own wounds, or a little girl telling lies to make her mother notice her, or a fourth-year medical student whose desperation to be loved leads him to accept an unfair accusation without protest, we all are driven to make up for what we've missed in our childhoods. Ultimately, it was this human frailty that sealed my decision to become a psychiatrist. I wanted nothing more than to help people who are in pain find love.

CHAPTER SEVEN

HAPPILY EVER AFTER?

"Never Die Young" | James Taylor

On the surface, we were the golden ones—a little too sweet, a little too tight. But just below the surface, under all the red flags, we were desperate for help. We needed to be held up, not lay prey to the rust and the ruin. It was a silent cry for help.

* * *

After a long period of uncertainty, Beth finally decided on internal medicine as her specialty. Meanwhile, I focused on a different life decision. I still loved children and wanted to become a father someday. Why not marry Beth? We complemented and challenged each other intellectually and supported each other's professional goals and ambitions. Most importantly, we were best friends. Dr. and Dr. Guastella—it had a nice ring to it.

That was what I kept telling myself, anyway. It all made logical sense, and I was good at creating the narrative I needed myself to believe. But in reality, my heart was not involved in this thought process, and I ignored the red flags that both of us brought to our relationship. From the beginning, the more serious our relationship became, the harder my insecurities and need for validation kicked in. Now, with life seeming to point us in the direction of marriage, I took on a quality I had witnessed in my father in his behavior with my mother: I became controlling, the man in charge. And Beth, whose own insecurities complemented mine, became compliant and accommodating, much as my mother had been.

Beth was (and still is) a woman of superior intelligence, a STEM whiz before "STEM" was even a thing. She was also easy to talk to and fun to be around, with a sweet disposition and a kind heart. But before long, I learned that under her oversized coat, baggy pants, and untucked shirts was a woman who felt uncomfortable with her body and lacked confidence about the way she looked. Since I loved and cared about her, I said to myself, *I can help her with that.*

While in college, I'd shared Beth's struggle with my roommate Jim. His advice: "You know, her personality is what matters, and that's what you care about—it won't vary over time. It's easy to change a body." Remembering that suggestion, I took Jim's words to heart and made them part of my personal mission to create the perfect life, complete with the perfect wife. The next time Beth expressed dissatisfaction with her looks, I stepped in with an offer to become her personal health coach. How hard could it be? After all, I was a doctor, one with a lifetime of experience taking responsibility for other people's problems.

"I know you can do this, Beth, and I'm happy to help. It's really just about choosing healthy foods. Salads are super healthy. During the week, you can make a salad at home and bring it to the hospital to eat for lunch. On the weekends, we can go to the new restaurant in the hospital and eat at their buffet. They have a ton of interesting options to choose from, and it will feel like a treat. I'll do it with you. Come on, it'll be fun. And you'll feel better about yourself."

"I would love your help, Frank," Beth said. "Thank you."

Over the next several months, upon my suggestion, we started grocery shopping together, reading labels and only buying healthy ingredients. We meal prepped together, brought our lunches to work, and ate our dinners together. The more I took charge, the more Beth settled into the role of the good student. Encouraged by the results we were seeing, I proposed we next focus her efforts on exercise.

"But I've never been much of an athlete," Beth hesitated.

"You don't have to be an athlete to exercise," I assured her. "The medical school offers an aerobics class for students. Why don't you and I go this week and see what you think?"

With her reluctant agreement, I took her out to buy some new exercise clothing and went with her to aerobics three days a week. Despite her initial apprehension, Beth gradually began to enjoy exercising; she even became the instructor for the aerobics class. The more confident she became, the better we both felt about ourselves. It was a win-win, until it wasn't anymore.

Over time, it became clear that my brilliant plan came at a cost to both of us. My drive to succeed, or at least to appear successful, became the dominant force in the relationship. I became more controlling around our food choices, more insistent about our exercise schedule. In response, Beth became more and more preoccupied with pleasing me. No matter how much she did, she never felt successful at living up to the standard I set for her.

This dynamic played itself out around sex, too. Up to that point, I'd been reluctant to "go all the way." Despite dating for five years, we'd never had proper sex. It wasn't out of a desire to be a good Catholic boy saving himself for marriage. Rather, it was because I thought there was too much at stake.

"We can do a lot of things that are fun and feel good," I assured Beth. "Foreplay and oral sex are great. But actual sex is too risky for me. For us. God forbid, you get pregnant—it will ruin everything. Our careers would be over. Are you willing to throw it all away?" I repeated it with extra intensity. "*Are* you? I'm not. We've both worked too hard to get here. That's the bottom line for me."

"Okay, I get it," replied Beth, though we both knew she was frustrated. "I'm fine waiting."

The "no sex" rule continued until our fourth year of medical school, when Beth and I moved into an off-campus apartment together. My brother, Ross, and his new girlfriend, Marla (who's now his wife) came to visit us once for the weekend and ended up "christening" our apartment with actual sex before we did. At the time, we all couldn't help but laugh at how ridiculous it was. But soon after, the situation, and the dynamic beneath it, started taking a toll on both of us. I couldn't ignore the signs Beth was showing of being depressed, nor the way I was sounding more and more like my father every day. I felt trapped, yet I didn't know how to change anything without putting all our plans in jeopardy.

That's when the thought popped into my head for the first time: *If—God forbid—Beth were to die in some tragic accident or because of some horrible sickness, I would be off the hook.* As soon as I thought it, I was horrified by my own imagination, and even more so by how seductive the idea remained. *I'd be out of this relationship, and everyone would have sympathy for me.* Despite repressing the thought, my self-loathing only continued to grow. As we neared our graduation date, in an act of desperation, I proposed the only solution I could think of.

"I think it's time, Beth."

"Time for what?"

"I think it's time we went all the way. Had proper sex. I think we're ready. What do you think?"

"Sure, I'm ready."

We jumped in the car and drove to a local grocery store with a pharmacy attached, where I bought a pack of condoms, then came back to our apartment and had intercourse. Neither of us quite knew what we were doing. I remember thinking, as we went through the motions, *This is what all the hype's about?* Not to say it wasn't physically pleasurable. I had an orgasm; I think Beth did too. But it felt more mechanical than romantic—hardly the relationship fix I'd hoped it would be.

The next day, I felt perplexed. *Maybe it's like this for everyone the first time.* Unable to focus on my patients, I kept flashing back to a moment at the kitchen table in my childhood home when, out of the blue, my mom said, "Louis, you need to talk to the boys about sex. It's your job, not mine. Now is as good a time as any."

Ross and I rolled our eyes—we were way past that point.

Dad, for his part, appeared nonplussed, even annoyed. "What's to talk about?" he demanded. "I'm sure they already know what to do, and what *not* to do. The bottom line is, boys, don't get the girl pregnant."

The memory brought a sudden revelation, striking in its obviousness: *Oh, that's where I learned to be afraid of pregnancy.* But it didn't explain why sex had been so lackluster. As if on cue, another flashback followed: that dreadful night when, as a young kid, I heard my parents having sex. I winced in disgust. Despite growing up in such a passionate Italian family, I never saw sexual intimacy demonstrated with romance or tenderness. No wonder it hadn't seemed to bring Beth and me closer.

I did what I always did with introspections like these: pushed it aside and pushed forward with my plans for a successful "normal" life. With sex checked off the list, it was time for us to focus on the next step in our life path: telling our parents that we wanted to get married.

I'd always been good at winning over the parents of friends and girlfriends: I was polite, well-mannered, top of my class, and now about to become a doctor. Plus, to all appearances, their daughter was thriving in our relationship, happy and healthy like she'd never been before. One evening, when Beth was on call, I went over to their house and asked her father for her hand in marriage. As I'd expected, both her parents were thrilled.

My parents, however, were a different story.

* * *

I had a month off between clinical rotations to prepare for my future. It wasn't a month of leisure—I was doing something valuable that I loved, working part time in the hospital, entering patient data for the liver transplant department. But my father had other plans for my time off. He wanted me to come back to Oak Lawn—he had a project for me, one that he thought would be more profitable for me than working in the lab. His main pharmacy had an extensive liquor department, and all the whiskey and wine bottles on the shelves needed a serious dusting, one by one.

Hearing him recite this plan as if it were already decided filled me with resentment. I was about to graduate from a prestigious medical program and become an actual working doctor, but my father wanted me to come home and devote twelve hours a day, six days a week, to a job he could have hired a high school kid to do. *You don't see me at all; you don't care about what's important to me. All you see is what I can do for you.*

I have stood up to my father three times in my life. This marked the first, and it was a major milestone. Gathering my strength, I picked up the phone and dialed his number back.

"Dad, I need to talk to you. I'm not going to come home to work in the pharmacy this summer. I'm going to stay here and work at the lab."

"But that's just a part-time job, Frank," he scoffed. "You can make more money working at the pharmacy."

"I don't want to work at the pharmacy anymore." Even while saying it, I couldn't believe I found the courage to speak so clearly. My body trembled as I spoke. "Dusting off the liquor bottles for a month will drive me crazy. I'm in medical school now and heading off to residency soon. I'm done working at the pharmacy."

"You little shit." I heard the anger rising in his voice. "So, you think you're too good for the pharmacy now, do you?"

"Yes, Dad, I do. I hate it there." Despite my fear, it felt as though every cell in my body was saying, *No, I'm done.* Finally I was saying what I'd been feeling for years. "And there's another thing you need to know: I'm going to ask Beth to marry me. We want to get married before we start our residencies."

"Who do you think you are?" he roared. "You entitled little bastard! You're refusing to work at the pharmacy, and you think you can afford a wedding ring on top of it all? You're out of your goddamn mind!"

Our voices got louder by the second, quickly becoming a screaming match that felt like it lasted for hours.

"You can't tell me what I can and can't do anymore," I told him, excitement surging through my body. "I'm an adult now, and I'm making my own decisions."

"Well, good luck with that. You're not getting a cent from me."

"I don't need your money. Goodbye."

When I finally hung up, I felt elated and terrified at the same time. I had finally stood up to my father! It felt amazing, but would this act of defiance come back to bite me? *Thank God I did this over the phone,* I thought, trying to convince myself that it would keep me physically safe from his rage. A tiny part of me feared that he would drive downtown to come after me. Even if he didn't, I knew from experience that my father wasn't one to forget things. One day, when I least expected it, would he try to show me that he was still the king?

• • •

I took Beth to dinner on the ninety-fifth floor of the John Hancock building, produced a diamond ring bought with my savings from summers and vacations, and asked her to be my wife. She instantly said yes. However, just like our first time having sex, I remember thinking to myself, *Shouldn't I feel different?*

Still, despite the lack of fireworks, I was happy, and Beth was thrilled. To be getting married, yes, but even more to plan a wedding. Between studying and working at the hospital, she spent hours combing through stacks of bride magazines. However, when it came time for a final decision, I jumped in. I picked out the color theme (black and white—a bold choice, I thought, a real style statement), the menu (spinach salad with poppyseed dressing, Cornish game hen, wild rice with mushrooms, roasted root vegetables), and even had final say on the bridesmaid dresses (black skirts with a white V-neck top). As usual, Beth fell in line with all my decisions. The one thing she chose for herself was her wedding dress. She really wanted to wear her mother's dress, and it wasn't my place to say otherwise. I wanted her to be happy, too.

Despite my dad's rant about my inability to afford a wedding ring, he embraced my choice in a fiancée. He was as charming to Beth as my mother was awkward. Mom kept repeating a phrase that I thought was strange: "I'm not losing a son; I'm gaining a daughter." It was only later that I considered how much she'd always depended on me, even once I was out of the house. The last thing she wanted was to be replaced as the woman in my life. Perhaps it was easier for her to think of Beth as a daughter than a daughter-in-law.

With our wedding plans gathering momentum, Beth's parents offered to cover the costs of the wedding reception, except for the alcohol. Since my family couldn't fathom the idea of any celebration without drinking, my father graciously agreed to foot the bill for the booze. Everything was going smoothly, according to plan.

Then, two weeks before our wedding, I caught Beth in a huge lie. The topic is too personal to share; suffice it to say that we got into a huge fight over it. The realization came like a kick from a steel-toed boot. *Can I ever trust her again?* was the thought that kept running through my mind.

Beth was terrified that I would call off the wedding. But after several days of not talking to each other, I approached Beth to reconcile.

"Don't worry about it; everything will be fine. Of course we should go ahead with the wedding. But you need to promise me one thing. Promise me that you will always be honest with me moving forward, no matter what."

"Oh yes, Frank, I promise, with all my heart," she said with tears in her eyes.

At that moment, I wasn't strong enough to express the misgivings I'd been hiding for weeks: that I thought I should be feeling differently about her, that I loved her more like a best friend than the love of my life. I wasn't aware that the lie had triggered something powerful within me: the betrayal I had repeatedly experienced with my mother growing up—"I won't say anything to your father, Frankie, I promise."

I wasn't brave enough to say what I should have said: "Let's postpone the wedding. I have things I need to work out before I fully embrace this commitment to you or to anyone, for that matter. I'm acting like my father, and you're reminding me of my mother. I don't want to enter a marriage with all this baggage." Instead, I did what I was used to: suppressed my feelings, glossed over the problem, and did what "normal" people do.

• • •

On June 21, 1988, Beth and I tied the knot. I felt a rush of freedom unlike any I'd ever felt before. I was finally on my own, no longer tethered to my father. After the ceremony, during the reception, I felt elated, carefree, so overtaken by joy that I danced on the tables, waving my hands in the air and flashing my black-and-white polka-dot socks for all the guests to see.

Beth, however, wasn't fully present that day. My sisters Luna and Sophia, who were bridesmaids at the wedding, remarked that she looked dissociated in many of the wedding photos, almost like a Stepford Wife. She kept saying to them, "I can't believe he's marrying me. I just can't believe we're getting married." I do know that Beth adored me unquestioningly, but her devotion to me nearly destroyed her. Suppressing our true feelings has a way of doing that.

We went on a honeymoon trip to Fort Myers Beach, Florida, where a friend of the family had offered us the use of their condo for a wedding present—a wonderful gift, since we didn't have much money to spend. We did everything newlyweds were supposed to do: We ate, we drank, we had lots of sex. After our well-deserved vacation, we returned to Chicago and focused our attention on getting into our specialty of choice: psychiatry for me, internal medicine for my wife.

We narrowed our focus on residency programs that were away from Chicago, primarily in the Northeast. Since we were married, we entered what was called the "couples match," which meant we were a package deal in terms of our applications. The National Resident Matching

Program had to place us in programs that were at the same institution or at least in the same city.

Match Day, the day that all fourth-year medical students find out what residency program they've been accepted to, is typically the third Friday in March. With everyone throughout the United States finding out where they've been accepted on the same day, it's a watershed moment for thousands of hopeful students, one usually followed by a big celebration, especially if you get your top-ranked choices.

On the big day, our whole medical school class gathered in Rush's main lecture hall, the place where we spent thousands of hours together over the last four years. I had spent most of my life—grade school, high school, college, medical school—preparing for this day. Now, for the first time, the direction my life would take was out of my control. All the faculty were present as the dean called out our names and handed us envelopes. We were told to wait until everyone received their letters before being instructed to open them. As I looked down, I knew my fate, my future, rested in the envelope I held in my hands. I was nervous but mostly eager to find out where Beth and I had matched.

The dean then proclaimed, "Rush Medical Class of 1989, you may open your letters!"

I glanced over at Beth, smiled, and slowly opened the cream-colored envelope that had my name, *Frank Louis Guastella*, printed on the front and the Rush University logo on the back.

"It is with great pleasure that we welcome you to the Department of Psychiatry at Harvard University . . ."

I couldn't believe my eyes. Time stood still. It was surreal. *Is it really true? Did I really do this? Is this really happening?*

Beth had been accepted to Tufts University, less than three miles away from the Longwood Medical area where all the Harvard hospitals were located. It was one of the best moments of my life: I was in the "ultimate medical profession" at one of the most prestigious teaching hospitals in the country, and I had a good woman by my side for the journey ahead. What could possibly go wrong?

CHAPTER EIGHT

HARVARD, REVEALED

"Losing My Religion" | R.E.M.

My life became bigger than the façade I built up over the years. I was used to hiding in the corner and it was time for me to be in the spotlight. I said too much, but I hadn't even begun to speak. It was just the beginning.

* * *

My big Italian family threw us a big Italian graduation/going-away party in classic Guastella style, rowdy and fun, with lots of food and lots of booze. I surprised everyone, including myself, by bursting into tears at the end of the night. With everyone gone, it finally hit me that I was leaving behind the place I'd known my whole life. Even with all the pain I'd endured, all the struggles I'd gone through, this was my home, and I would miss it.

The next day, Beth and I packed everything we owned into a U-Haul. With our car in tow, our cat in a carrier, and the greatest hits of James Taylor on cassette, we left Chicago behind and headed to Boston, singing the lyrics of our favorite songs in unison. We'd leased a lovely apartment in Beacon Hill, right in the heart of the city, and were looking forward to starting our residencies and our new life together.

After two full days of driving, it was thrilling to arrive in Boston. It felt prodigious to be starting a new life in a new city, with my new wife, in a new apartment. Admittedly, it was just a one-bedroom in a four-story walkup—the best we could afford in that expensive city on our new two-resident salary—but it had at least the virtue of authenticity, being located directly across the street from the Public Gardens and just one block away from the original *Cheers* bar. I loved when tourists asked me to take their photo in front of the bar, as I walked home from the corner grocery store. Our new home felt like a new start at life. I could fit in here being whoever I wanted to be.

Because we didn't yet know anyone in town, Beth and I had the daunting task of unloading the entire truck by ourselves. Up and down those four stories we went with our bed, dressers, couch, kitchen table, and countless boxes. It was as grueling as it was exciting. *This is a whole new level of being on your own now, Frank—no one to tell you what to do, but no one to help you out either.*

After just a week of settling in, it was time to start work. Harvard required that all psychiatric residents spend the first year of their residency in a medical internship to gain a solid basis in traditional medicine before focusing on patients with mental health issues. Accordingly, I applied to work at Framingham Union, a community hospital where I offered general medical care to patients. Unlike the rotations in medical school, I wore the "long" coat this time. This meant I was now teaching the students who wore the short coats. In addition, I was assigned a list of patients to take care of and I wrote orders in the charts. I rotated through every department at the hospital: geriatrics, cardiology, pediatrics. I delivered babies, took care of infants in the NICU, assisted in surgeries, dressed wounds in the ICU, and, within the first month of work, had to "pronounce" someone. That is, pronounce them dead.

It was a particularly busy night on call, and I had just finished my last admission for the night. It was about four o'clock in the morning when I headed up to my room to finally get some shut-eye. I fell asleep as soon as my head hit the pillow. But forty minutes later, I was awakened by the sound of my beeper.

"Excuse me, Dr. Guastella. I'm sorry to bother you, but Mr. Jones in Room 223 just expired. Would you come down and pronounce him?"

For real? I'm so friggin' tired right now. My exhausted annoyance was overtaken by an alarming realization: *Wait, I don't even know what it means to pronounce someone.*

"Thanks, Viola," I replied, trying to sound lucid and professional. "I'll be right down."

I splashed some water on my face and walked through the darkened halls of the hospital to arrive at the nurse's station on the second floor. The head nurse that night was Viola, an experienced professional in her late forties, who told me that Mr. Jones had been diagnosed with pancreatic cancer. One of the nurses discovered that he had died when she went in to check his vitals.

I thanked her for filling me in and went over to Mr. Jones's room. When I first stepped inside, he looked like he was peacefully sleeping. But then I saw that his chest wasn't moving up and down. I placed my stethoscope on his heart to make sure—no heartbeat. *What else should I do?* I looked at the clock in his room; it read 4:52 a.m. *I guess that should be the official time of death?* I stood there for a moment. *I'm actually standing next to a dead person. Okay, now what? Is that all? What else am I supposed to do?*

I headed back to the nurse's station. "I'm sorry," I confided to Viola, "but I've never actually done this before. What am I supposed to do to pronounce Mr. Jones?"

As I quickly learned, being kind to nurses could make all the difference in your experience as a resident or medical student. Nurses essentially ran the hospital—they knew what needed to be done and how to do it. As a result, they could make your life a living hell or they could guide you through the many challenges you would inevitably face when you were on call. Relative to nurses, there were two types of doctors: those who were cocky and arrogant, and those who were considerate and kind. Because of my history, I was afraid of authority figures; far from challenging them, I did whatever I could to please them. In this setting, my history benefited me. I naturally fell into the "kind and considerate" category, which made me a favorite with the nurses. (I suspect that the arrogant doctors' behavior was also tied to their upbringing. They don't call us "wounded healers" for nothing.)

Viola started asking questions. "Did you check his vitals? Pulse, heartbeat, and respirations?"

"Only his heartbeat," I answered.

"Did you notice the time when you examined him?"

"Yes," I told her. "4:52 a.m."

"Good," Viola assured me. "You now need to write an order saying 'Deceased: please prepare body,' fill out the death certificate, and call the family. You need to tell them that their loved one has expired and ask if they want to come and see him before his body is sent to the morgue."

Yikes, that's going to be one helluva call.

"Then write an order for the morgue to come and get the body," Viola added. "That's basically it."

"Thanks so much. I really appreciate your help."

"You're a good kid, Frank," Viola said with a warm smile on her face. "I'm happy to help."

It was surreal and slightly creepy, but nonetheless it was a profound experience to pronounce Mr. Jones. I will never forget it, and I will remain eternally grateful to Viola and the many other nurses along the way who helped me survive my nights on call.

The first year of residency didn't offer much time off and only paid a basic living wage, which didn't go far in an expensive city like Boston. As a result, Beth and I couldn't afford to go back to Chicago for Thanksgiving. Up to this point in my life, I'd only known holiday celebrations as big, rowdy parties full of family, food, music, and noise. The thought of spending the holiday alone with Beth, strangely enough, elicited some mild panic. What in the world would we do? Was it even a holiday without a party?

With no plans and no local friends we could count on for an invitation, Beth and I decided, on a whim, to take a quick trip up to New

Hampshire and rent a small cabin for the night. I was nervous about it, not knowing this part of the country or what to expect from this unfamiliar way of celebrating the holiday, but it turned out to be a great time. We spent a beautiful fall day in New England, starting with a hike in the mountains and ending with Thanksgiving dinner at a local restaurant. To my surprise, it was refreshing to celebrate as just the two of us, quietly and intentionally. Instead of a family brawl on the tennis court, we reveled in the silence and the spectacular colors of the forest. Instead of cramming ourselves around a table with inebriated adults and sugar-buzzed kids, we enjoyed a civil meal in the prim and proper company of fellow travelers. Instead of piling on top of cousins for a monster movie afterward, we cuddled under a blanket beside the wood stove. Being on my own, having experiences that were different from what I knew growing up, felt expansive.

During the last rotation of my medical internship, I was responsible for monitoring the patients in the psychiatric ward. To my surprise, the facilities at Framingham Union proved to be a far cry from the bleak despair of the psych wards where I'd visited Mateo. What stood out most was "community meeting." Each day, everyone in the psych wing—doctors, nurses, aides, even patients—took time out of their day to gather together in a room, sit down in a circle, and check in with each other.

"Rodney, how are you feeling this morning? What are your plans for the day?"

"Joy, how did the psychological testing go yesterday? Was it as scary as you thought?"

As the charge nurse went around the room, I sat back and observed with my pad and pen in hand, taking notes on each patient's progress. After a few minutes, the nurse looked directly at me.

"Frank, what do you have on your schedule for today? Are there any patients you want to see? We can make sure they're available when you need them. Is there anything else you'd like to share with us?"

After all the rushing and stress of the other rotations, this community meeting time was beyond refreshing; it was a revelation. *You mean we can stop for a moment and listen to each other in psychiatry?* It was compassionate. It was humane. It was about genuine connection. My entire body relaxed, my mind stopped racing, and my heart opened. At that moment, I thought to myself, *Psychiatry is where I belong. I picked the right profession.*

* * *

I will never forget the first day I walked into Massachusetts Mental Health Center, an enormous old red brick building on the edge of the Longwood Medical area, where I would spend the next three years of my life in residency. All the patients were homeless, had no medical insurance, and suffered from major mental illnesses. Several of them were hanging out at the front entrance of the building, smoking cigarettes and sizing up the new crop of doctors who would be caring for them. Once again, I was thrilled and terrified. *What in the world have I gotten myself into?*

All the new residents were instructed to sign in and proceed to the main auditorium, where grand rounds and all our lectures would be held. A group of attending doctors entered the room and took seats on the stage.

"Welcome to Harvard, everyone. You have earned a seat here because you've demonstrated exceptional academic and clinical skills during your medical school training. You will be taught by some of the best and brightest minds in the field and exposed to cutting-edge research. When you open any top-tier psychiatric journal, you'll probably recognize the author of the publication because they've likely trained or worked at Harvard at some point during their career. It is our mission to help you become a leader in the field of psychiatry. You are now a part of the Harvard family. Welcome aboard."

I looked around the room at my fellow residents, and thought to myself, *How in the world did I get here? Will I ever measure up?* It was undeniably intimidating.

We were then escorted upstairs to the third floor, the locked unit. No white coats were worn here; that would intimidate the patients. Instead, we were instructed to present a more familiar professional look: shirts, ties, and dress pants for the men, skirts or slacks with blouses or a sensible dress for the women. We were then given a set of keys—those who held the keys had the power in psych units—and directed into a conference room, where we met the staff. The charge nurse Seanne gave us a list, along with brief descriptions, of the patients we would be following during our first rotation.

"Frank, you'll be working with Newman S. He was a former neurosurgeon here at Harvard and had a psychotic break over twenty-five years ago. He never fully recovered from that episode and has been inpatient here ever since.

"Next is Josephine W. She experienced postpartum depression after the birth of her fourth child. She's been inpatient here for the last four years and recently lost custody of her children. She is currently receiving her third round of ECT treatments, which will be the maximum allowed for the year.

"You'll also be working with Larry R., who has been homeless and struggled with addiction for most of his adult life. He just got back into the hospital after he left his group home and relapsed with cocaine and alcohol. He was found unconscious in the streets and is here for detox and long-term day treatment.

"And then there's Brenda B. She was admitted from the Framingham State Penitentiary. She's here for a psychiatric evaluation to determine whether she's competent to stand trial for murdering her grandfather six months ago. She just turned twenty-one years old."

No doubt about it—this was the big leagues. Devoutly grateful that I'd be supervised by Harvard-trained psychiatrists, I felt scared but also excited to be working with such an extreme caseload. The intensity of this program had called to me from the moment I began interviewing for residencies. Still, being on call at this place was nothing like I'd ever experienced. Anyone picked up by the police or found homeless on the streets of Boston was brought to us; our job was to evaluate whether they should be admitted to our unit or go first to a medical hospital to be stabilized. The admittance office, located just off the main lobby, was equipped with a panic button under the desk in case we needed assistance. For extra protection, a security guard was stationed outside the door.

We were called constantly throughout the night to assess people who seemed unstable, unsafe, or unable to care for themselves. One particular night—more like early morning—my beeper had already gone off three times by three o'clock, and I had just settled down when it went off yet again.

"Dr. Guastella, we have another man coming in to be evaluated in about ten minutes. The police found him combative and disoriented in the Public Gardens downtown."

"Okay, I'll be right down," I responded with a sigh, not at all in the mood to do another evaluation.

The security guard and I met the patient, Duane, at the hospital entrance. The police officer who brought him in removed his handcuffs and handed me some paperwork. "Good luck with this one," the officer muttered as he headed out the door.

"Hi, Duane, nice to meet you," I said as cheerfully as possible, hoping to create rapport. "Why don't you come with me and we can sit and have a talk about what's been going on for you lately?"

Duane nodded, followed me into the office, and took a seat across from my desk. I had just started asking him the standard questions when, out of the blue, he pulled out a knife and pointed it right at me.

Maybe it was the exhaustion I felt at that point in the night. Maybe it was a lifetime of being confronted with violence. Whatever it was, it saved me from feeling any fear at the sight of this man pointing a weapon at me. All I felt was pissed.

"Put that knife down right now," I demanded, my voice strong and stern.

Duane immediately put the knife down on the desk. I quickly moved it out of his reach and pressed the panic button.

The "knife incident," as it became known, made me a celebrity of sorts among my fellow residents and attending physicians. My reflexive actions that night defied all that we'd been taught about how to deescalate potentially dangerous situations, how to restrain patents that were violent and out of control, and how to keep patients, staff, and ourselves safe. In other words, everything I did was totally wrong . . . but it totally worked. I took the accolades in stride, but all I felt was lucky. That night, someone was looking out for me.

* * *

The training I received at Massachusetts Mental Health Center and Harvard Medical School was truly outstanding. I learned how to handle the most extreme and severe cases of mental illness under the field's best practitioners, and even some pioneers. It was here that I met my first mentor, Dr. Bessel van der Kolk, one of the world's preeminent experts on trauma, who would later author the *New York Times* bestselling book *The Body Keeps the Score.*

At that time, trauma was barely acknowledged as a general factor in mental illness. The conventional wisdom was that posttraumatic stress disorder was something experienced only by war veterans; all other mental illness, the thinking went, resulted from genetic or chemical imbalances in the brain. Bessel was taking trauma out of the war context into the general population, showing how PTSD can also result from relationship violations such as physical, verbal, and sexual assault, even non-physical causes like betrayal, neglect, and shame.

While the establishment regarded his work with skepticism, it was a lightning rod for me. This, I realized, was the reason for the deep connection I felt to my patients. I understood their suffering at not only a clinical but also a personal level. In fact, because of my childhood experiences with abuse, betrayal, and shame, I might be uniquely equipped to help them heal.

With this in mind, I dove headfirst into the emerging field of trauma therapy. I went to every conference, attended every workshop, read every book. This naturally brought me into closer proximity to Bessel himself. Being taken under his wing revived the hero worship I'd felt for my principal, Mr. Kernwyne, and all the teachers that affirmed my intelligence. My eager dedication to the work quickly established me as a rising star in the field, as well as Bessel's personal protégé. He made me staff psychiatrist for the Trauma Center; I served as psychiatrist for the first EMDR versus Prozac study; he even proposed that I should marry his daughter (jokingly—he knew I was in a committed relationship).

Working with Bessel, I came to understand that all the patients I treated were genuinely good, sometimes great, people who had gone through some of the most horrific life events imaginable, leaving them locked in a torturous cycle neither they nor their loved ones could understand.

What took me by surprise was that working with that level of psychic trauma stirred up my own history. I was consumed by the intensity of my patients' lives. It was all I thought or talked about when I got home from work. The stories they told me during our therapy sessions swirled through my head at night, keeping me from sleep. My usual efforts at disconnection and suppression were no match for the personal revelations that my work kept bringing to light. Eventually, I went to my supervisor and asked him for the name of someone I could see for my own personal therapy.

It was standard for psychiatric residents to go into therapy at some point during their training, but it typically happened during the third year, when we focused more on outpatient care. However, I couldn't wait. I felt as though a volcano had erupted inside me. Overwhelmed by feelings I couldn't control and didn't understand, I needed help to figure things out.

My supervisor gave me the names of two male therapists. The first guy was nice enough and friendly—I had a pleasant session with him. The second guy didn't say much during our session, but when I left, I felt extremely anxious and didn't know why. I had never chosen a therapist on my own before, so I didn't know what to look for. When I asked my supervisor for his expert opinion, he advised me, "If you can tolerate the intensity, you might get to a deeper place with the second therapist."

So I picked the quiet guy, Mike Frost, a short, balding man with a beard and a gentle smile.

Boston was known as a hub for psychoanalysis at that time, and technically, that is what I was doing with Mike. But I refused to lie down on the couch and have him sit behind me, taking notes. I needed to see my therapist, to sit up in a chair and talk face-to-face. Thankfully, Mike was willing to accommodate my request. I had found a safe man who cared about me and was willing to help me work through my trauma history. He explained to me that sitting with people in pain often activates the hidden pain within ourselves. During my sessions with Mike, I started connecting to my childhood experiences of abuse—first a little, then a lot. After a few months of seeing Mike weekly, I started increasing the frequency of my visits. I went from going once per week to twice, then three times a week, and within six months or so, I was going to therapy five times per week. This was both intense and expensive. Luckily, I was able to moonlight at some local hospitals in town to be able to pay for my sessions.

This experience of therapy was vastly different from my initial experience as a child. This time, it was my choice, not a mandate from my parents. I felt how much I needed to go, and I looked forward to my sessions with Mike. He was kind, grounded, reflective, and nonjudgmental.

For better or worse, I transferred my attachment issues onto him—
which, I was told, was where they belonged—so he could help me work
through the dysfunctional dynamics that were established with both
parents. He provided a supportive environment for me to slowly sort
through what happened to me as a kid and see how it affected my decisions and behavior as an adult.

As we started unpacking my childhood, it became clearer to me
that what I experienced growing up wasn't normal. Memories began
resurfacing of the violence inflicted upon me by my father, the blurry
boundaries with my mother. Images and recollections from my past
intruded on my daily life, and I developed symptoms of PTSD. I started
having nightmares again, just like in my childhood. (At least this time
I wasn't wetting the bed, which would have definitely been problematic
for my marriage.) I startled easily, became guarded and mistrusting of
people, and at one point, developed symptoms of depression.

Late one night, Beth and I were in our apartment watching a movie
together in bed—I don't remember the title, but do remember the violence—when, out of nowhere, I was catapulted back into my childhood
bedroom and began frantically screaming, "Make him stop. Please make
him stop. Make it go away!"

"What's happening, Frank? You're scaring me," Beth said, a panicked
tone in her voice.

"Just make it stop. Please, make him go away." I curled into a fetal
position on our bed, crying and hyperventilating.

"I'm the only one here," Beth insisted piteously. "Who are you
talking about?"

"My father. I need to get away from him . . . he's going to kill me."

"Frank, no one is here right now except you and me. Your dad's in
Chicago, we're in Boston. You're safe."

Beth gently stroked my back, arm, and forehead. At her touch, I was
almost instantly soothed, just as I had been by my mother's comforting
presence more than twenty years earlier.

Later, I called Mike, desperate for some support. "Why did that happen out of the blue?" I asked Mike. "What can I do to prevent it from recurring?"

"Flashbacks are a common occurrence when working through trauma," he told me. "Try your best to stay present and know that it won't last forever."

This was less than reassuring. Thanks to both my childhood and medical training, I was well versed in pushing through almost anything. While I often felt anxious and overwhelmed during my time in therapy, I had never experienced anything that had affected my ability to see reality or to function. After that experience, I got apprehensive about ever reliving the past again, and a wall went up inside me. It didn't feel safe to go to those places, with Mike or with anyone else.

* * *

Every medical student self-diagnoses and makes adjustments to their lifestyle based on what they're learning. When you're studying cardiology, for example, you stop eating salt and fat. When you're studying neurology, you're convinced you have memory loss. But this type of self-experimentation is a whole different thing when it concerns mental health. I knew about PTSD from my studies, but now I was consciously experiencing it.

As overwhelming as it was to have these feelings that had been buried for years, I was grateful for the way it helped me better understand what my patients were going through. Moreover, I was determined not to let PTSD get the best of me. For a time, I white-knuckled my way through processing the feelings that therapy had brought up. Then I took an antidepressant, which improved my mood and my ability to function. Eventually, though, I decided that what I really needed was to process some of these memories with someone who could validate them firsthand.

Ever since college, I'd continued my habit of calling my parents weekly to check in. Since Dad was usually at work, I mostly talked with my mom. She would ask me about Beth, about my work, and finally, inquire whether I was still in therapy. But when I attempted to discuss with her what I was discovering in my sessions, it was consistently met with denial, dismissal, or a firm repudiation.

"I don't understand why you need to see a therapist, anyway," Mom said. "I thought things were better for you now. Is he really helping you? You seem to be doing worse since you started seeing him."

"I'm realizing that Dad was abusive to me as a kid," I stated, "and that he treated Ross differently than he treated me."

"Oh, that's not true, at all," she protested indignantly. "Your father's a good man and he loves all his children the same. You're making him out to be a monster. Why don't you stop dwelling on your past and move forward with your life?"

"That's what I'm trying to do, Mom. I'm doing my best to have a good life, and it's important for me to figure out what happened. I buried a lot of my past. And besides, Dad and I have never had a good relationship."

"That's nonsense," she pushed back. "Stop blaming him, Frank."

A week later, I received a card from my mom that included an article from Ann Landers, the famous *Chicago Sun-Times* columnist, about how false memories are created in therapy and how they can destroy families. Yet again, I felt that I was being blamed for what happened to me. After so many years of repressing so much, all I wanted was to get it all out on the table and have my experience validated. Instead, month after month, my perspective was disregarded or refuted as untrue. Not by just anyone, but by my mother.

At that point in my life, I wasn't strong enough to withstand the pushback or stand up for myself with confidence. Instead, I decided to temporarily cut off communication with my parents. I needed some distance to hold on to my truth and maintain a sense of independence from my mom's views. This ultimately became a period of no face-to-face contact that lasted for seven years. I had no idea—or intention, for that matter—that it would go on for that long, but apparently I needed that much time and space from her reactions and his rejection. I learned in the process that silence can be a powerful change agent. I know the break was difficult for my parents—they said as much to my brother whenever he talked to them—but it showed them (and myself) that they no longer controlled me or dictated what I said, did, or believed. I was becoming my own person.

* * *

As intense and overwhelming as it was to process all this for the first time, it was making me stronger. I was feeling better about myself. The therapy was working.

Still, the way I reenacted my father's behavior with my wife continued to be a concern. I shared with Mike how Beth could be submissive to a fault, like my mother, while I could be domineering like my father. Why did I act like him when I hated the way he treated me? Even though I had tried everything in my power to break away from him, there were times when I felt as if I was possessed, unable to resist repeating his worst behaviors.

One particular incident still haunts me. Beth and I were "post call" and exhausted after working thirty-six hours at our respective hospitals. She was in the bedroom changing clothes while I stood in the doorway, the two of us dissecting our experiences that week: difficult cases, hospital drama, rewarding moments. Something she said caught my attention; when I asked her about it, I immediately noticed her hesitation. Her answer, when it came, was inconsistent. I realized that I had caught her in another lie.

"How many times do I have to tell you?" I was livid. "It's the only thing I asked for, Beth. The only thing that's important to me. I told you that I need you to be honest with me, no matter what. Why can't you get that through your head?"

"I'm sorry, Frank," Beth said, her voice trembling. "I didn't mean to lie. I know how important it is to you."

Half-blinded by rage, I couldn't see her vulnerability. All I could see was another woman trying to deny reality right to my face.

"How in the fuck am I supposed to trust you? How many times do I have to ask you for this? Why should I believe that it will ever be different?" I went from ranting to shouting. "Honesty. Honesty. Honesty. That's all I want. That's all I've ever wanted!"

Beth put her hands over her face and started crying. As I looked at her, half-clothed and huddled on the floor, sobbing, my reason finally returned.

What in the world is wrong with you, Frank? You're totally out of control. Look what you're doing to her. She doesn't deserve to be treated like this. No one deserves to be treated this way.

In a sudden flip, my rage toward Beth turned inward. Instead of outrage, all I felt was self-loathing. *You're a horrible person, Frank. You know what it's like to be treated this way. Your father's malignancy has infiltrated you. You and he are exactly the same.* Stunned by shame, all I could do was walk away.

Over a week went by, during which we hardly spoke to each other. For me, the silence was a two-way punishment, a combination of resentment toward her and anger toward myself for the way I treated her. We eventually reconciled without ever really addressing what happened between us that dreadful night. Instead, we put the incident behind us and moved forward with our busy lives.

Then Beth asked me to help her find a therapist. After just a few weeks of exploring herself, she realized that the stress of residency was taking a toll on her. Ready for a fresh start, she decided to take a year-long sabbatical from her program and, to mark this turning point, she changed the name she went by from Beth to Liz.

I was genuinely happy for her. Seeing both of us working on ourselves renewed my sense of hope for the future. I finished my residency and stayed on as an associate professor of psychiatry at Harvard Medical School while continuing part time at Bessel van der Kolk's Trauma Center in Boston. I was beginning to establish myself as a trauma specialist.

All these changes helped Liz and me navigate the struggles in our relationship. Our communication gradually improved. We continued going to aerobics together. We took day trips to explore more of New England. We even saved up for an international vacation and spent an idyllic week in the French countryside—Val de Loire, Auvergne-Rhône, the Alps, Burgundy, the Côte d'Azur.

We also began building our friend community in Boston. During my training at the Trauma Center, Liz and I had become close friends with a fellow psychiatric resident, Amy, and her partner, Lydia. Amy and Lydia were the first openly gay couple I had ever known, let alone hung out with. We were all surprised when, after completing her residency, Amy confessed that she had fallen in love with a colleague, an expert in the field of women's studies named Evelyn. It was more than a fling— both women were leaving their existing relationships to be together. In the immediate aftermath of their breakups, they had no place to stay, and since Liz and I both loved Amy, and Amy was in love with Evelyn, we naturally welcomed them to live with us until the dust settled for them. By then, we had moved from our apartment in Beacon Hill and bought a house in Newton, an upscale suburb of Boston. We had the extra space and enjoyed the company; we also welcomed the distraction from our own difficulties.

However, witnessing the love between Amy and Evelyn—their connection, their tenderness, the little moments of romance between them—activated something within me, something I'd been hiding even from myself. As it turned out, Liz wasn't the only one lying in our rela- tionship. Just a few months before our friends moved in with us, I had begun harboring a secret of my own.

It began on a night when Liz was on call, and I was home alone. I decided to go for a run along the Charles River. After about seven miles,

I was spent and sat down on a bench to enjoy some peace and quiet while looking at the Boston skyline.

My reverie was broken when a man, a complete stranger, walked over to me.

"Hey, how's it going?"

"Good," I responded. "How's it going with you?"

He sat down next to me, which was odd. My heart started racing, which was even more odd.

"It's beautiful out here at night, isn't it?"

"Yes, it is," I said, feeling scared and confused. *What in the hell is happening? Am I going to get mugged? Is he going to try and rob me? Can't he see that I'm in running gear and not carrying a wallet?*

He reached over and gently touched my leg. I froze. He then moved his hand under my tank top and started touching my nipple.

"Hey, you're really cute. Do you want to go over there behind those bushes with me?"

"No, thank you," I managed to say as I pulled away and got up off the bench. My heart was beating so fast, it felt like it was going to burst right out of my chest.

Terrified, I started running. My body was on fire, my mind spinning out of control. I felt the same way I'd felt back in college when that guy exposed himself to me in the bathroom. *Not this again. What in the hell is happening to me?* That night, I woke up from a wet dream and found myself entertaining a sexual fantasy starring the guy on the bench. It was the first time in my life I had experienced either one of them, let alone at the same time.

I couldn't ignore that something big had shifted within me. After that, anytime Liz was on call, I would secretly go out, find various cruising areas around Boston, and have anonymous sex with men. Naturally, this unsettling compulsion became the main topic of conversation in my therapy with Mike. He knew about my sordid habit but, thankfully, wasn't at all judgmental about it. Instead, he set out to help me under-stand why I was drawn to this behavior.

I kept telling myself I couldn't be gay—I was a Harvard man, I had a wife, I grew up in a conservative family in the Midwest, I was baptized Catholic. If a patient had come to me with these same objections, I'd have gently advised them that none of that had anything to do with their sexual orientation. But on a personal level, all my scientific training was useless against the cultural stigma I had internalized around homosex-uality. Between its decades-long classification as a mental disorder and the national AIDS crisis raging in the public health and political spheres, same-sex orientation was still largely confined to the closet. Added to this was my certainty that my family would disown me in a second if they ever found out. *Is this what they were trying to exorcise by putting me in therapy as a child?*

Maybe there was something else wrong with me. Perhaps I was sex-ually abused as a child. Perhaps I was enacting some desperate desire to be admired by men to make up for the fact that I never felt loved by my father. Mike and I even wondered if I had some form of split personality, something often provoked by severe childhood trauma. But after one meeting with a leading expert in the field, the answer was definitive: no, I didn't have any of the telltale signs of multiple personality disorder.

I was happy to cross that possibility off the list, but it didn't help resolve the growing conflict within me or my behavior. The more I pro-cessed my traumatic history, the more powerful the compulsion became. It was as if a leak had sprung in the concrete wall I'd been constructing since age six. I was driven, obsessed, chasing after something I couldn't fully comprehend or put into words.

Even after a lifetime of self-suppression, I was shocked at how good I was at keeping my secret life a secret. That is, until Liz requested that we go to couples therapy to work on our relationship. I can only imagine she sensed how distracted and distant I was; out of guilt, I agreed to go with her. Liz was in therapy, I was in therapy, and now we were in therapy together. Even as a psychiatrist, I couldn't help but wonder, *Isn't there such a thing as too much therapy?*

One night, following a particularly difficult couples' session and a silent car ride home, Liz and I agreed to make dinner with our new housemates. We all decided to make it "spaghetti night"—what better way to lighten the mood than with a family-style meal of homemade pasta? Liz got things started by pulling out the pasta maker, a wedding gift from her mother, still in its box. Amy and Evelyn joined in eagerly, opening jars and uncorking bottles, while I was delegated to fire up the bread machine (another classic nineties-era gift).

In just twenty minutes, our feast was ready. Across the table, I caught a glimpse of Amy reaching over and, with a wink, giving Evelyn's leg a squeeze. Evelyn smiled back at her with an emotion in her eyes that I had never felt before. Embarrassment at catching this intimate exchange mingled with a feeling I longed for and didn't quite comprehend. I looked down at my plate, feeling anything but hungry for the heap of machine-made pasta confronting me. Everything on the table seemed to come into focus at once: the jar of Classico marinara sauce, the plastic shaker of Kraft parmesan, the cube-shaped loaf of bread, even (adding insult to injury) the bottle of white Zinfandel. It was as though my heritage was shaking an accusing finger in my face.

Are you serious? This is not what you grew up with, Frank. My family was far from perfect, but one thing we did well was celebrate who we were. The best parts of my childhood were the times when we came together over traditions as old as the family name: canning our own tomatoes picked fresh from the garden, making our own bread and pasta from scratch, drinking wine we made from grapes that were imported from Italy. The love we had for each other was complicated, but it was authentic. It came from who we truly were.

That, I realized, was the life I wanted. Instead, I'd created a perfect life that was as fake as the meal in front of me. I was living a lie—cheating on my wife, for heaven's sake. That was not who I was. That was not the love I longed for. I wanted a relationship like Amy and Evelyn's. I wanted a life that felt natural and authentic. I'd demanded honesty from Beth, but I'd never been truly honest with her or, it seemed, with myself. That dinner opened my eyes to something I had never experienced before in my life, something as simple and sublime as homemade bread and wine: being who I truly was, and being loved for it.

* * *

That weekend, I was cutting the grass in our backyard with our push mower when R.E.M.'s "Losing My Religion" started playing on my Walkman. Though I'd heard the song a hundred times before, the lyrics stopped me in my tracks that day. The revelation of that faux Italian dinner had been looming over me, a dark cloud heavy with consequences I both craved and dreaded. But on this day, I felt clear, at peace with what I now knew about myself. As suddenly as the knowledge had come, it somehow felt as though I'd always known it. And though I was certain that following this path would blow up my life, I felt calm and content in a way I had never experienced before.

I talked to Mike about my revelation, and he was supportive and genuinely happy for me. After that, I sat with it for over a month before I said anything to Liz. This, too, was new for me: holding my truth consciously, without needing to express or deny it. I no longer felt the compulsion to keep moving forward or, for that matter, running away.

But when Amy and Evelyn announced that they were starting to look for an apartment of their own, panic momentarily returned. *It's time,* I thought to myself. *I can't keep living off the fumes of their love. I can't continue doing this to either Liz or myself. The lie must come to an end.*

In our next couples therapy session—what better place, after all?— for the first time ever, I said the words out loud: "I'm gay."

"What?" Liz was flabbergasted. "What do you mean?"

"I mean I am gay," I responded with a mixture of fear and clarity.

She looked from me to our therapist and back again. "How would you even know something like that?"

"I've been having sex with men," I confessed. "Anonymous sex. I have been very careful—I haven't done anything to put you or myself at risk. But I've been unfaithful."

I could see her putting the pieces together in her mind, her facial expression turning from shock to disbelief to rage. Finally, she blurted, "That explains why you've had so many mosquito bites on your back!"

Our therapist intervened. "Liz, I want you to know that even though this affects you deeply, this is about Frank. This is his truth. It's not for you to share. You need to respect and protect his privacy right now."

Now I was the one in shock. *Is that really true? I'm allowed to be in control of my story?*

"You mean," I ventured, "it's okay for me to tell people at my own pace, in a way that feels safe and comfortable to me?"

"Absolutely," the therapist assured me.

To my amazement and enduring gratitude, Liz agreed to hold my truth between the two of us. But that night, we drove home from our therapy session in separate cars and spent the night in separate beds. We never slept together again.

CHAPTER NINE

MOVING OUT

"Believe" | Cher

Finally falling in love was amazing. The experience of heartbreak was devastating. The question was, do I believe in life after love? Was it in the cards for me or was I destined to perpetually repeat my trauma?

* * *

In the next couples therapy session, Liz and I began the process of ending our marriage.

"I need to talk about how Frank's realization affects me with the people I most trust," Liz told our therapist. "I need to tell my personal therapist, my mother, my sister, and my best friend."

Before responding to Liz, our therapist looked directly at me. "Frank, is it okay with you if Liz talks to these four people, and only these four people, about your being gay?"

"Yes," I said, "that's totally fine. I want her to get the support she needs."

I didn't want to hurt Liz. She was my best friend, and for as long as I'd known her, I'd loved her as truly as I knew how. I hadn't understood before that being *in love* with someone was an emotionally complete experience, one that involved your mind, body, and spirit, like I'd witnessed with Amy and Evelyn. I didn't know until now that it's impossible to truly love someone else or receive their love in return until you truly know and love yourself. But now that I saw myself clearly, I could also see how deeply betrayed she felt by my actions. Having anonymous sex with someone outside the marriage was a different level of violation than the lies she had told me. I'd broken the vow I made to her on our wedding day, and for that I was deeply sorry.

By that point, living in the same house had proved too painful. Liz and I spent a month alternating between staying at home and staying with various friends while I looked for a place of my own. Once I found an apartment in Cambridge, we sold our home in Newton, filed for divorce, and went to a mediator to work out how we would divide our shared possessions and assets.

This process seemed to finally unleash Liz's anger: "I want the Jeep, the couch, the bread machine, the pots and pans we got from the wedding, and the cat."

I didn't blame her, and the last thing I wanted was to fight over our "stuff." Feeling at peace inside myself made it easy to let her take whatever she wanted. All I wanted was to finally be free.

Inevitably, the process of disentangling our shared lives led me to reflect on how we'd got there to begin with. In hindsight, it was clear that something wasn't quite right from early on in our relationship. Most couples talk and dream about starting a family together, planning their timeline, picking out names for their future children. But even though I loved kids, I'd never wanted to have children with Liz. On a subconscious level, I must have known that something wasn't right.

With Mike's help, I also understood another layer of why Liz's lying affected me so intensely. It wasn't only the echo of my mother's betrayal. It was the way her dishonesty mirrored my own. Since the day I stood beside my parents' bed that fateful morning when I was six years old, I'd been suppressing my own truth in order to be loved and accepted. While Liz brought her own baggage into our relationship, which manifested as passivity, lying, and insecurity, I had to acknowledge that this marriage failed because of my inability to live authentically.

At some point, while we were packing up the house together before it sold, Liz found the courage to ask me a painful question.

"Why did you need to get away from me so badly?" A single tear fell from the corner of her eye.

I looked into her eyes, my heart aching for her and all the pain I had caused. "Liz, sweetheart, honestly, I wasn't running away from you," I explained. "I was running toward me."

* * *

Coming from my traditional Italian family, I was aware that being divorced had stigma attached to it (from the Italian side), as did being gay (from the traditional side). Knowing this, I kept my coming out news to myself for a few years. It wasn't hard, as I was still out of contact with my parents. The only family member I told was my brother, Ross. It must have been challenging for him—he grew up in the same household as I did—but if so, he never showed it to me. He and I had moved beyond the fighting that marked our childhood and become each other's biggest supporters. While I was working my way through medical school, he had married Marla, had three beautiful children, and eventually moved to Mississippi. In many ways, Ross found his place in the world, too. He fits the stereotype of a Southerner—an avid hunter and proud gun owner, and he has even been known to vote Republican. I, on the other hand, live in Boston and check off many of the boxes for a liberal Northeasterner. But our differences didn't matter to us. His love for me prevailed over his preconceived notions about what it meant to be gay.

A year later, I decided to invite my sisters, Luna and Sophia, out for a visit. At that time, I had a cordial but superficial relationship with them, but I wanted to share the news in person. I brought them to Vermont, where we stayed at a quaint bed-and-breakfast for the weekend. They had never been to New England before, and we had a wonderful time together, eating, shopping, and seeing the local sights. Finally, on a hike in the Green Mountains, I told them everything—about Liz and me, about the divorce, about realizing I was gay. They hadn't been exposed to a gay person before; I imagine they weren't sure what it meant about me or how it would affect our relationship. But they were quietly accepting and understanding because they loved their big brother. Their visit bolstered my hope for coming out to my parents when I was ready.

However, my family has never been the best at respecting boundaries. When, about six months later, I reached out to my parents by phone, they told me that they had heard from my sisters about the changes in my life.

My dad surprised me by saying, "I had a feeling this would resurface at some point." He shared that, when I was a child, their marriage counselor had asked him how he would feel if his son decided to become a hairdresser someday. (It didn't take much to guess that "hairdresser" was code for gay back in the late sixties.) My dad said he had responded, "I guess I wouldn't care, as long as he's happy. That's what matters."

I was speechless. I thought of all the hours he made me work at the pharmacy, the tennis games where he'd resorted to cheating just to get a rise out of me, the way he'd shouted me down when I announced my plans to propose to Liz. It seemed highly unlikely that my happiness had been all that mattered to him; it felt more like one of his familiar platitudes, along the same lines as "As long as you're healthy, you have everything" or "Alla famiglia."

But even as I thought this, he said again, "It doesn't matter to me, Frank, if you're with a man or with a woman, as long as you're happy."

My mom also had an unexpected response. "Maybe you're gay because you and I were too close when you were growing up."

Hearing the unmistakable tone of guilt in her voice, I assured her that our relationship didn't make me gay. "It's just who I am," I told her, "and I'm finally happy."

The call left me with more questions than answers. On one hand, it seemed that the long period of disconnection had done its work, that having a relationship with me was more important than their expectations of me. On the other hand, those expectations had new meaning now that I understood who I was. I could see that my "special meetings" had, in fact, been a form of conversion therapy. The "normal" behavior they were hoping it would teach me had actually been "straight male" behavior.

Was that why Dad was so violent with me? I wondered. *Because I was more interested in playing with dolls and beads than hunting or fishing? Or was it because of his drinking and unstable mental health? Or did he simply hate me?*

All I knew was that I needed to figure out how to move forward with my family, now that they knew the real me.

* * *

On Wednesday, at eleven o'clock in the morning, I arrived at the Cambridge District Court for the finalization of my divorce. I went alone; Liz, thinking it would be too painful, decided not to attend. I had no idea what to expect or how I would feel. As it turned out, I didn't have time to feel much. After taking a moment to review the presented documents, the judge declared, "The case between Guastella and Guastella is uncontested, accepted, and final." That was it—our entire relationship dissolved in a total of twenty minutes.

I left the courtroom feeling a strange mixture of sadness and joy, of accomplishment and failure, of freedom and loneliness. Not quite knowing what to do, I wandered aimlessly around downtown Boston until something in a shop window made me pause. It was a tiny figurine of a gargoyle, hunched over in a posture more sheepish than menacing. He wore a serene, boyish smile that, I felt, evinced a gentle soul, even though on the surface he looked like a monster. It captured exactly how I was feeling that day. That little memento still sits on my desk, reminding me how, at the age of thirty-two, after hundreds of hours of therapy and six years of being married to a woman, I finally learned to love who I was on the inside.

* * *

Aside from Amy and Evelyn, with whom I remained extremely close after my divorce, I didn't have any gay friends. I had no frame of reference, no role models to help me get acclimated to being gay. After living in a straight world, my entire life as a respected Harvard-trained psychiatrist and up-and-coming trauma specialist, I was now a gay man, newly out and ready to embrace my sexual identity . . . and I had no idea what that meant. *How do I do this? What do gay people do? What is "normal" now?*

Every week, I drove into Boston to pick up a copy of *Bay Windows*, the local gay newspaper. It was exciting to learn about local LGBTQ events happening in and around the city and to see people who looked like me promoting their shops, products, and businesses. I had no idea that you could hire a gay lawyer, plumber, dentist, or insurance agent if you wanted to. One evening, I went to a free lecture on safe sex offered by Fenway Community Health Center, the local gay mental health clinic. There were more than a hundred in attendance. *Wow, all of these people are gay?* I thought as I looked around the auditorium. I walked down the streets of the South End—the "gay borough," as they called it—and watched people, much as I'd observed my uncles when I was a kid. *Do gay men look different? Do they act different? How do they talk?*

For someone setting out to create a gay life, there was no better place to begin than Provincetown, one of America's gay meccas and only a two-hour drive from Cambridge. I started going there on the weekends. My mind was blown by the sight of all these gay men out in the open, lying together at the beach, dancing together in nightclubs, kissing in public, even walking hand in hand down Commercial Street, the main street in town, fully dressed in drag. I felt simultaneously like an outsider and like a kid in a candy store, petrified and pumped up by possibilities I'd never imagined.

One of the guys I'd met while cruising asked me out on a date. That's not typical cruising behavior, to put it mildly. But I was excited and intrigued by the offer, and once Liz and I were separated, I ended up saying yes. I wanted—maybe needed—to go on a proper date with a man.

Despite my Italian heritage, I'm basically a white guy from the Midwest. Paulo, on the other hand, was full-blooded Colombian—dark and handsome, tempestuous and magnetic, with a thick accent, curly hair, and a murky past. He was a preacher, though clearly not the Catholic variety, because he certainly hadn't taken a vow of celibacy. In fact, he had a wife and child who lived back in Colombia. Eager to flee that life, he came to the Boston area, where he had relatives who were willing to sponsor him in opening a branch of his church in America. By day, he was a pastor, preaching rapture and redemption to the Spanish-speaking community in Cambridge. At night, he went cruising for men to hook up with.

Paulo was closeted yet passionate; I was newly out and wide open to exploring. I felt something powerful between us and wanted to see where it went. It turned out that where Paulo wanted to go, at least for our first date, was the International House of Pancakes.

"Sure, why not?" I said, trying to sound less taken aback than I was.

Since my college days, I'd never gone out on a weeknight. But this must be another example of the new set of rules I had to live by, as a gay man. "I'll meet you there this Wednesday night at 7:00. See you then."

As I drove to IHOP, my mind was all over the place. *What do I talk about? I hardly know this guy. What am I doing? This is crazy.* My body was freaking out, too—I couldn't believe how much I was sweating. I wondered if I should have worn something nicer than jeans and a T-shirt. *Are you kidding?* my unhelpful mind scoffed. *You're going to a damn pancake house.*

When I arrived, Paulo was there waiting for me, a warm yet coquettish grin on his face.

"Nice to see you again," I said, as I placed out my hand for a shake.

"It's great to see you too," he replied, as he got up and hugged me.

Okay, then, I thought. Whatever I'd been expecting, it wasn't a hug.

Dinner was fine—I opted for a burger and fries over pancakes—and the conversation was more interesting than I expected. Paulo insisted on paying the check, then hit me with another surprise. "Hey, what do you say we go and get a hotel room for the night?"

Are you serious? It's a Wednesday, and I have to work all day tomorrow. "Sure, why not?" I agreed. "Let's go for it."

We ended up at a Marriott and had sex all night long. We explored each other's bodies, took a shower together, did things I had only read about, and other things that were beyond my wildest dreams. It was spontaneous, indulgent, dare I say hedonistic—a totally new experience of sexuality for me. For the first time in my life, sex and emotions were combined. I couldn't even compare it to being with a woman. One experience was flat and monochromatic, the other in three-dimensional full color. I didn't feel constricted. I felt safe enough to fantasize. It was life-changing. I went to work the next morning a changed man.

After that first date, Paulo and I began a secretive relationship. I tried to laugh at the irony of it—I was finally out, basking in my authentic sexuality, having great sex for the first time in my life, all with a man who couldn't acknowledge me to his community. Paulo would periodically invite me to his church, where I would sit and listen to him preach in Spanish. I was mesmerized by his impassioned preaching and, being familiar with Italian, was able to pick up the gist of what he was saying. Often, the congregants would ask me how I knew the pastor, since it was obvious that I didn't know Spanish. "Oh, we're just friends," I'd answer, until Paulo moved into my apartment after a few months, when the answer shifted to "Oh, we're just roommates."

Our relationship was both wonderfully liberating and severely closeted. In a strange way, it was what I was comfortable with at the time. Given my past, having any amount of freedom within the confines of tight control felt new and exciting to me. If anything, too much freedom could have felt overwhelming—more bliss than I could handle—perhaps even frightening.

• • •

Much to my surprise, my past showed up in this relationship as well. But whereas I'd acted at times like my father with Liz, while she acted more like my mother, those roles were reversed in my relationship with Paulo. In the face of his volatile temper, demands, and verbal outbursts, I accommodated, acquiesced, and made excuses for his behavior. In many ways, my first relationship with a man was as troubled and emotionally draining as my failed marriage to a woman. As I often say, we either repeat, repress, or learn from our experiences in life. Apparently, I was in repeat mode.

The relationship with Paulo was also complicated by our cultural and social differences. I was an Italian American Harvard-trained psychiatrist, while he was a native-born Colombian and a charismatic man of the church. The more I learned about the deeply rooted cultural beliefs we each struggled to relinquish, the more I discovered that our differences were easier to embrace in theory than in reality. As good as it felt to be madly in love with someone for the first time, I couldn't ignore the fact that Paulo and I were not a couple in any enduring or meaningful way. I never thought, *I've met my soulmate. We're meant to be together. I want to spend the rest of my life with this man.* Still, I told myself that it was worth staying—I was exploring my sexuality, discovering my gay identity, and having fun (except when I wasn't). The truth is that I wasn't strong or confident enough to leave him. I was attached to Paulo much like my mother was attached to my father, to a man who frequently treated me in a way that was oppressive and, at times, abusive. I'd broken free from my inauthentic sexuality, but I wondered if I would ever be able to break free from repeating my abusive history in close relationships.

Our tumultuous connection lasted for too long—a total of three years. Before we broke up, I met Paulo's family in Colombia. He wanted to see his daughter and asked me to come with him. Since travel is a passion of mine, I said yes. Paulo's wife didn't speak any English; she simply smiled at me and nodded when she dropped off their daughter at our hotel room. She must have believed, as the church did, that her husband

and I were just friends. Or perhaps she was as passive and accommodating as I was.

Paulo's daughter, Bianca, was ten years old when I met her. Beautiful, with long, curly black hair, blue eyes, and a slender frame, she had the makings of a model. The three of us hopped on a plane, and Paulo and I treated Bianca to an amazing two-week adventure throughout Brazil. We explored the beautiful city of Recife. We went to Carnival in Fortaleza. We spent time at the beach and dunes in Genipabu near Natal. Then, at the end of one of our whirlwind days, Bianca unexpectedly asked me, "When we go to bed tonight, are you and my daddy going to have sex?"

I was dumbfounded. Throughout the trip, Paulo and I acted like nothing more than friends in front of her; we were never demonstrative in any way. But with a child's unerring sensitivity, she must have picked up on our energy.

Of course, I said, "No, your dad and I are not going to have sex." Of course, we did.

Six months after our trip to Brazil, my grandma Florida passed away. At the time, Paulo and I were living together in my apartment in Cambridge. I planned to fly to Chicago for the funeral and I wanted him to come with me.

"I'm not going," Paulo told me, firmly.

"But why? My grandmother is an important person in my life. I know her funeral is going to be difficult for me. I would love it if you would come."

"No, I don't want to go," Paulo stated.

"But why? Can you at least tell me why you don't want to go?" I pleaded.

"I just don't want to, that's all." He was losing patience.

"Paulo, it would really mean a lot to me if you came with me," I said, hoping against hope to change his mind.

"I'm not going. Don't ask me about it again."

Paulo stormed out of the house. In that moment, I felt a wall go up around my heart. *This is not a man I can trust,* I realized. *This is not a guy who will be there for me no matter what. I can't rely on him, so, why am I still with him?*

Shortly after I got home from Chicago, I broke up with Paulo. But ending a complicated relationship is, well, complicated. After three or four days apart, we were back in bed together. Unfortunately, I stayed with him for another six months before I was able to find the confidence to stand up to him, speak my truth, and sever our toxic connection. After our final breakup, I never saw him again.

Despite it all, I don't regret my relationship with Paulo. I believe that everyone, gay or straight, could benefit by being with a free-spir- ited, hot-blooded lover at some point in their life. With Paulo, I tapped into an emotional expansion I had never felt before. I also learned a lot about myself during my time spent with him—namely, the qualities I had internalized from my mother. I was insecure, I tolerated more than I should have, and I could be passive and overly attached. I was amazed at how emotional pain could be felt so profoundly in the body. My heart throbbed with a physical ache as I slowly got over Paulo and began to move on with my life. But I ultimately learned that I was strong enough to get out of something that wasn't healthy for me and could survive losing someone I was in love with. I was making progress, gradually feeling like a confident, independent person who is worthy of love. And that felt good.

CHAPTER TEN

FINDING MICHAEL

"Songbird" | Eva Cassidy

When a relationship is new, non-dysfunctional, not a reenactment of your trauma, the songbird sings. I am no longer crying, the sun is shining, and when I'm with you, I know it's right.

* * *

During our three years together, Paulo and I often spent time in Provincetown, the one place where our relationship wasn't closeted. One summer, we rented an apartment for the entire season. That was a summer I will never forget—full of friends, freedom, and true belonging. The day we moved out of our seasonal rental, I sat in the driveway and cried harder than I have ever cried in my life. Leaving that freedom behind felt intolerable. Fortunately, I had made lasting friends that summer: Bill and Brian, a couple Paulo and I got to know in Provincetown.

Not long after I ended things with Paulo, I bought a small cottage right next door to Bill and Brian's property, and they made it their mission to teach me how to look and act like a single gay guy. I went from shirts and ties and blazers, worn with a beard and glasses, to tight pants, form-fitting shirts, a Speedo bathing suit, and contacts. I looked (and felt) nothing like my former self.

Growing up, nobody had ever said I was attractive. My brother was the one who got all the attention; the family, the neighbors, and, of course, the girls in town all saw him as the devilishly handsome boy next door. After a lifetime of hiding who I was, being seen—as the cute new guy in town—felt like a shock to the system. I got free coffees from baristas. I got free T-shirts from souvenir vendors. I got catcalled on the street. At times I felt uncomfortable, even objectified *(So this is what my women friends are talking about)*, but I couldn't deny that the attention felt good too, especially now that I was single.

Bill and Brian knew how to work the bar scene much better than I did. I wasn't a big partier, but I was in the game now and excited to go out and play according to their rules.

"First," Brian instructed me, "you spend the day at Herring Cove, but make sure you walk all the way to the left, where the men's nude beach starts."

"Around three o'clock, everyone heads over to T-dance at the Boat Slip Hotel, where you stay until five o'clock," Bill added. "This is where you check out the 'merchandise' for the upcoming evening."

"Most people start drinking at T-dance and get tired, so they take a power nap before going out to dinner around eight thirty," Brian continued. "The main event starts at ten thirty or eleven o'clock, where everyone goes to the A House. That's where you dance, drink some more, and pick up your conquest for the night."

"Have sex, but never sleep over the first night," Bill stressed. "It's a good thing you just got contacts."

"What are you talking about?" I asked, confused.

Bill walked me through the protocol. "You go to the A House with your contacts in, but don't bring your contact case. You meet somebody on the dance floor, things get hot, and he invites you to go back to his place. You go, you hook up, and then you leave. 'Thanks for the great time, but I have to get home, I forgot to bring my contact case.' It's the perfect plan. You don't show too much interest, you don't look desperate—and he doesn't take it personally."

"It's not you, it's my eyes," added Brian. "Thanks for a great night, see you around, bye-bye!"

Impressed and disturbed, all I could say was, "I had no idea."

Despite being in Provincetown for almost a year, I had never taken part in the beach-bar-sex scene. But I was as eager a student of gay life as I had been in medical school and, on my very first Saturday as a single gay guy in P-town, I checked all the boxes: nude beach, T-dance, nap, dinner, then on to the A House as instructed—contacts in, contact case out.

Beers in hand, Bill and I stood at the edge of the dance floor, slowly moving to the music as we checked out the prospects we had previewed earlier that day. I was beginning to relax—I felt free and easy. Suddenly, across the dance floor, I saw someone. Handsome, brooding, sexy as hell. I couldn't stop staring.

"Holy cow, Bill," I said with excitement. "Look at that guy over there in the work boots and flannel shirt."

Bill went into coach mode. "Here's what you do. Act casual, keep drinking your beer, move onto the dance floor, and just start dancing next to him."

It sounded so calculated, and I felt conspicuously awkward . . . but what the hell? *Here goes nothing!*

I slowly headed toward the man who'd caught my eye and started dancing next to him. Eventually, he looked over at me and smiled. I smiled back.

"I'm Michael," he said.

"Hey, my name's Frank."

Michael and I danced and talked to each other for the rest of the night. After the bartender announced last call, the DJ put on "Last Dance" by Donna Summer and the whole place went wild. I looked directly at this sexy stranger as all the clubgoers sang along. I felt fantastic and free. *I'm actually doing this! I'm single and I'm playing the game.*

As the bar started clearing out, Michael surprised me with the question I'd been hoping for. "Hey, do you want to head over to my place for a while?"

"Yeah, sure," I said, hoping my nonchalant tone would hide how nervous and excited I felt.

We grabbed our jackets and headed out of the bar, back to his place. Just as I had anticipated, we spent what was left of the night having sex. Without a second thought, I ended up falling asleep, contacts still in.

I woke up in the middle of the night, confused and disoriented. Seeing Michael beside me in the bed, I realized with dismay that I'd broken protocol.

"Hey," I whispered, "I wear contacts, and I don't have a contact case."

"I've got you," Michael said. He got out of bed, went into his kitchen, and came back with two shot glasses. He filled them with water, I placed my contacts inside, and we fell back asleep in each other's arms. So much for the plan.

The next morning, Michael was in the kitchen making coffee when I woke up. I climbed down from his loft and found something waiting for me on the kitchen table: a container of contact lens solution and a contact case. Apparently, he woke up early that morning and went to the store to buy them for me before I got up. *Are you kidding me?* Deeply touched by this simple but important gesture, I realized, *This is a kind man with a huge heart.*

I thought of Bill and Brian. *They're going to kill me.* The morning after my first night as a single guy and I'd already screwed it up! *How can you get attached again, after one damn night?* Hoping to salvage myself as a player, I cleaned my contact lenses, finished my cup of coffee, and said to Michael, "Nice to meet you. I had a great time last night. Maybe I'll see you around sometime."

With that, I left. I didn't even ask for his phone number.

I spent the rest of the day working on my cottage renovations with the help of Bill and Brian. I was dreading my conversation with them. They were understanding, but I saw a twinge of disappointment in their eyes. I told them not to worry, I was gearing up for another round next Saturday. New weekend, new man, right?

To my surprise, who should show up at my place the following weekend but Michael?

I was excited to see him. *Wait, how did he know where I live? I guess P-town is smaller than I thought it was.* I was impressed by his detective skills and taken aback by his desire to find me.

"It's good to see you again, Frank. I had a great time with you last weekend. I'd love to get together with you again, if you're interested."

Michael took out a pen and wrote his phone number on one of the exposed beams in my cottage. He then asked for my number, which I gave him, and walked out the door.

A few days later, I got a voice mail message from him, inviting me to an art exhibit opening at one of the galleries in town. Apparently, as a side gig, he did some modeling for a sketch artist. The show was a series of nudes, and Michael was one of the subjects. I was being exposed to a whole new world, not to mention to an unexpected side of Michael. This hot guy was pursuing me, wanted to spend time with me, and was being showcased in a gallery. It was all so new and enticing. Despite my "training" from Bill and Brian, I was getting hooked.

• • •

Michael ended up being different from anyone I'd ever met. He brought together the best features of James Dean and Martha Stewart: brooding, mysterious, gorgeous but also domestic, nurturing, and an incredible cook. Meals at home with Michael were worlds apart from the machine-made dinners I had with Liz. Anchovy pasta from scratch was one of my favorites, usually featuring fresh heirloom tomatoes, breadcrumbs, sweet-smelling basil, and other aromatic herbs freshly picked from his garden.

Michael had moved down to the Cape from Connecticut seven years prior and now lived there year round. He earned a living from working with AIDS patients as a healthcare and hospice worker as well as a variety of creative ventures: landscaping, making stained glass sculptures, designing department store windows, doing hair and makeup. He even did my makeup for my introduction to "drag bingo," which we attended together during carnival week in Provincetown. But mostly, we hung out together, watched iconic Hollywood movies from the fifties and sixties (*Breakfast at Tiffany's, Singin' in the Rain, Rebel Without a Cause*), and spent hours talking and getting to know each other. During the week, while I was up in Boston, we talked on the phone and watched TV sitcoms together with the receivers to our ears.

I was enjoying myself so much that I hadn't seen a lot of Bill and Brian. At the same time, while I loved spending time with Michael, I wasn't overly attached to him. I wasn't clingy and needy and craving his approval. I wasn't volatile and controlling, either. Therapy was paying off. My way of relating with Michael was different from my past connections—with my parents, with Liz, with Paulo. It was balanced. It was *healthy*. I clearly remember when that realization hit me. One Saturday morning, Michael and I were working in his garden, and he was in a rare shitty mood.

"I don't think I want to hang out together today," Michael said, seemingly out of nowhere.

"That's fine with me," I replied. Much to my surprise, I meant it. *Wow, I'm not taking this personally, and I'm not feeling hurt or rejected.*

"I'm not in a great mood today—I think it's better if I spend some time by myself," Michael added.

That's new, I thought, *taking responsibility for his feelings instead of blaming me.*

"No worries. I think I'll go to the beach today; I haven't gone in a while. Take the time you need. Call me later, or not." I gathered my stuff and got ready to leave.

"Wait," said Michael. "Do you want to have a cup of tea before you go?"

"Sure, why not?"

We sat and sipped our drinks in a silence that felt calm, not at all uncomfortable.

After we finished, Michael said, "Do you want to watch a movie?" Before long, his mood lifted, and we ended up spending the day together.

This small interaction was a huge shift for me. As I soon learned, it was a huge shift for Michael, too. Like me, he was no stranger to volatility or drama, having recently ended a toxic relationship with a guy who had a drug habit. He appreciated my accepting, matter-of-fact reaction to his mood that day. In turn, I appreciated the way he took ownership of his feelings and worked through them one step at a time.

Intimate relationships are often about people unconsciously seeking someone to heal their past wounds. This one was different for both of us. We negotiated spending time together while we were in different places emotionally, and we didn't project our feelings onto the other person. For the first time in my adult life, I wasn't repeating my history by being controlling or yearning to be rescued. I knew that I was in new territory with Michael, and I wanted to keep exploring this foreign landscape with this man without reenacting the damage from my past. I wanted to be happy and stay balanced, and with Michael, I felt I had a good shot at achieving that.

Bill and Brian weren't exactly thrilled for me when I told them where I'd been for the past several weekends. In fact, they were downright pissed. Their next-door cottage neighbor wasn't fun anymore; he had turned into a homebody with a steady partner. Some of our friends even said we acted more like lesbian women than gay men: "Are you guys renting a U-Haul after your first date too?"

All told, between my passionate yet tumultuous relationship with Paulo and my loving and healthy relationship with Michael, I was single for less than three months. I guess I wasn't cut out to be the bar-bed-bye kind of gay, after all.

* * *

Every four months or so, I called my parents to offer a brief update on my life, careful not to share too much. But given how things were progressing with Michael and me, I decided to tell my parents about him and see how they responded.

"Hey, Mom. It's me, Frank. How's it going?"

"Oh hi, honey!" she answered enthusiastically. "We're good. Your dad is working a lot, as usual, and he and I are going golfing when he gets home. We'll be able to get in a quick nine before it gets dark."

"Well, that's good." I replied. "I wanted to tell you something. I met someone. His name is Michael, and he's a really nice guy."

A long pause. "That's nice. I want you to be happy." Another pause. "Will we ever meet him?"

Knowing that it was me she really wanted to see, I replied, "Someday." I ended the call feeling cautiously optimistic. *At least she didn't freak out when I told her I was dating a man.*

After that first summer, Michael and I were officially in a relationship. We spent every weekend together. We became fast friends with another couple, Nina (a colleague of mine) and her then-partner, Millie, who also had a second home in Provincetown. Our connection with them was effortless, a loving friendship that nurtured and supported our relationship with each other. We were the perfect foursome for going out to dinner, hanging out in P-town, and traveling to New York City to see Broadway plays. When gay marriage became legal in Massachusetts, Michael and I were the best men at their wedding.

For Michael and me, however, it took some time to take the leap of living together. For the next ten or so months after we made our relationship "official," I lived on my own in Boston from Monday through Thursday. Occasionally, I went out with friends or colleagues, but mostly I worked in my private practice and kept to myself. Michael, meanwhile, lived his Monday through Thursday life alone in Provincetown. After all, he was a brooding artist, and he liked his solitude.

We took the next big step forward when, near the end of our first year as a couple, the lease on his apartment was up. I tried my best to be laid back when I suggested it. "Why don't you move your stuff into my cottage?" To my delight, he said yes.

For the next several months, Michael and I lived together three days a week: Friday, Saturday, and Sunday. From Monday through Thursday, he stayed in P-town while I went back to see my clients in Boston. Things were going great between us, but I wanted more. Knowing that I was more social while Michael was more reserved, I was careful not to come across as pushy.

"At some point," I finally ventured, "I would love to live together full time, if you're interested?" Again to my surprise, he agreed and came to live with me in Boston, too. It was nice to be with someone who wanted to be with me as much as I wanted to be with them.

For the next several years, we moved back and forth as a unit—half the week in Boston, the other half in Provincetown. We had a strong, nurturing, passionate, joyful relationship. I was building my career as a trauma expert, so professionally, I was in a very good place as well. But it felt like there was still something missing in my life. I began to dream of starting a family with the man I truly loved.

In those days, the late 1990s, gay men with children were an anomaly. It was culturally accepted for lesbian women to have kids, but convention still held that two men shouldn't raise children together; all kids need a mother. Still, I was determined. I'd always had a goal in the back of my mind: *If I'm not in a committed relationship by the time I turn forty, I'll find a way to have children on my own.* I held the belief that my mom instilled in my head at a very young age: "Frankie, you can do anything you want in life." Michael and I were thirty-five when we met, so that goal wasn't that far off, and I was resolute about actualizing this desire in my life.

Early on in our relationship, during one of our late-night calls together, Michael asked me out of nowhere, "Do you want to have kids someday?"

Did I hear him correctly? I was stunned. *This is way too early in this relationship for the topic of kids to come up. Especially in a gay relationship.* But even though I was a bit stunned by the question, I decided to answer with my newfound honesty.

"Actually, yes. I do want to have kids one day. It's always been a dream of mine. What about you?"

After a long pause, Michael responded, "I've never really thought about having children before." *Damn.* "To be honest, I've always had a desire to have chickens someday."

Strange as that desire sounded to me, it made sense that Michael, the fabulous cook and gardener and homemaker, had always wanted a home with a chicken coop. But children *and* chickens? Was that what gay guys did? Certainly not Bill and Brian. But for Michael and me, kids and chickens just might work.

Even though he's sensitive and artistic, Michael is also grounded. In some ways, he's more pragmatic than I am. So he came up with a plan and a proposal. Before committing to kids and chickens, he needed to do some work on himself.

"I guess I'm open to the idea of having children in my life someday, but I would need time to get ready," Michael told me.

"Say more," I encouraged him, intrigued. *Maybe there's some hope here, after all.*

"First, would you agree to only one kid and no dogs? Dogs are a pain—they're dirty, and need a lot of care."

Yes to chickens, but no to dogs? "Sure, I'm down for that," I assured Michael. "I've never been a big dog lover."

"I also need to quit smoking and focus on my career. I want training and credentials in a field I can depend on. If you really want a kid, I'll need about five years to get myself ready," Michael stated.

Clearly, he's put some thought into this. "Okay, then," I said, elated. "It's a deal."

* * *

For the next three years, we continued to travel back and forth from Boston to P-Town. I worked with my clients, Michael worked on himself. We put my condo in Boston up for sale and began our search for a property somewhere outside the city.

First, we put an offer on a house in Maine, just outside of Portland, but got outbid. Then, realizing how difficult it would be to move my entire practice, we narrowed our search to suburban Massachusetts. Ultimately, we settled on Stow, a charming little town about an hour outside of Boston, in Middlesex County. We bought a big, beautiful colonial house with newly renovated interiors and two acres of land. It was a place where we could feel safe, put down roots, and begin our journey to building a family. But first, Michael got busy and built a chicken coop. Carpentry proved to be another one of his hidden talents, and this coop was a work of art: gray clapboard with white trim to match our house, complete with a porch, two windows with shutters, and an enclosed run so the chickens could roam outdoors. It looked like it belonged in Martha Stewart's backyard.

For a couple of gay men used to living in urban areas like Boston and Provincetown, small-town life was an adjustment. Actually, "awakening" might be a better word for it. Shortly after we moved in, a neighbor came to our door to welcome us to the neighborhood.

"Michael, come here for a minute," I called, excited by the hospitable gesture. "Someone's here to say hello, and he's brought us a plate of brownies."

The man looked at me, then at Michael. He looked at both of us again, paused for a moment, and with a confused look on his face, asked, "Are you two brothers?"

Speechless, Michael and I glanced at each other. We looked nothing alike—obviously, we were a couple. *How in the world do we answer that question?* All I could muster in response was, "Uh. No."

"Oh," said our neighbor. Apparently, he was speechless too. He handed us the plate of brownies, turned around, and walked away without uttering another word.

Michael and I exchanged another glance. *Toto, something tells me we're not in Kansas anymore.* The whole experience reactivated childhood memories of being different, feeling like an outcast, feeling unsafe in our own home.

Our introduction to the suburbs bestowed some important wisdom, albeit a bit too late: Before moving anywhere, do your homework. Scour the town's website. Hang out at a local coffee shop. Pay attention to the vibe of the town, not only the quality of the house. On the surface, Stow looked like a lovely, welcoming place to live. But from our experience, it wasn't the town for us. I would frequently go for a run and, finding myself in one of the neighboring towns, look at the various houses and fantasize about living in one of them someday, hoping it would feel more welcoming.

After the "brownie incident," our neighbors kept their distance. We barely got to know anyone, in fact, except for a lovely woman named Martha who lived up the hill from us. After three years in Stow, we moved to the neighboring town of Harvard where, word had it, several gay families lived. What a difference! Quaint streets lined with historic buildings, apple orchards, and horse farms scattered amid winding, tree-lined roads, and most importantly, a safe, welcoming atmosphere with accepting neighbors. As soon as we were moved in, Michael built another coop. The next few years ahead had a focus and a plan: a life together with chickens and children.

The only thing left was to tell our parents.

CHAPTER ELEVEN

CHICKENS AND CHILDREN

"Glitter in the Air" | Pink

It is here where I learned, for the first time in my life, that I was not in control. This was out of my hands; it was larger than me. I had to close my eyes, trust it, and let go—that's when things started happening.

✳ ✳ ✳

"Hey Mom, how's it going?"

"Good, honey! Let me get your father on the phone—he's working from home today."

After a moment, my dad got on the line.

"Hey Frank! Your mother told me that you met someone. I'm sure he's a nice fellow. I hope to meet him sometime."

"He's a really nice guy. I think you'll like him," I responded, feeling as though I was treading water, waiting for the right moment. *Why not dive in head first?* "He moved in with me, and believe it or not, we've been talking about having a child together, someday."

After an abnormally long silence, Mom piped in. "Having a child is a big commitment, honey."

"I know it is, Mom."

"Don't you think it would be hard for a kid to grow up without a mother?"

"Honestly, Mom, I think I'm more nurturing than many of the women I know," I responded. "Remember, you were the one who told me

151

I could do anything I wanted in this world. You know how much I love kids. Raising a child is one of the things I've always wanted to do in life."

More silence.

"Yes, I do know that." The resignation in her tone was unmistakable.

Baby steps, I thought to myself. As the firstborn son, I was aware that I'd always been pushing them to grow, from attending a private high school to refusing to work at the pharmacy. Now I was a firstborn gay son, living with his boyfriend, wanting to have a baby, I'd gone way beyond their comfort zone. Still, I could tell they were trying their best, and for that, I was grateful.

* * *

Michael and I had begun exploring the options available to gay men for having a child. We quickly found that the logistical challenges of being gay and having a child were just as fraught as the cultural challenges. No matter what approach we took, there would be mountains of paperwork, staggering expenses, and no way of predicting how long the process would take. During this time, I found myself often remembering the way my sister Sophia described her own approach to "family planning": "We went out to dinner for our anniversary, I had an extra margarita, and oops—I got pregnant!" *That's all it took?* I thought enviously. *A $6 margarita? If only we could be that lucky.*

Michael and I decided to go with a surrogate agency rather than the adoption route. As a psychiatrist with an awareness of my own attachment issues, it felt important to establish a bond with our child from the moment of their birth. I didn't care whether our child had my genetics or Michael's, but I wanted to be there the moment that baby was born. I also felt strongly that a child raised by two dads should have the chance to know their biological mother.

Even compared to private adoption, surrogacy is an expensive process. At the time, clients were expected to not only pay for the surrogate's health insurance and medical bills but also cover her costs of living for a full year. At that time, surrogacy was roughly a $150,000 investment for us. Without hesitation, we sold our house in Provincetown to cover the costs.

We were fortunate to find a surrogacy agency that specialized in working with gay couples and filled out an extensive profile with the qualities we were seeking in a surrogate. We spent our Saturdays at the kitchen table, drinking coffee and combing through profile pictures.

"This is so strange," I mused as we clicked through page after page of potential surrogates. "We're picking out the mother of our child from a list of random women on a website. It's just like being on Match.com, but instead of a girlfriend, we're choosing a birth mother."

"How about this one?" said Michael. "She has white teeth, high cheekbones, big breasts."

"Are you serious?" I was learning that Michael had a way of saying outrageous things, but I was still startled by his priorities and blunt response. "I want her to be intelligent and stable. I wish they listed IQs and a full psychological evaluation on their profile."

After a lot of laughter between us, we combined our wish lists in a way that satisfied us both. It made sense that looks mattered to Michael as much as brains mattered to me. Why not give our child the advantage of both brains and beauty?

Michael felt that I should be the sole sperm donor because kids were my passion. I was touched by his generosity and responded in kind. "Then our kid should have your last name. That way, they can have a piece of both of us."

In the end, we agreed to take turns at insemination, and I decided to change my name from Frank Louis Guastella to Frank Guastella Anderson. That way, we would become the Anderson family. I was surprised at how easy it was. Go to the courthouse, fill out a form, and pay fifty bucks—now you're legally someone else.

I was more surprised, however, at how hard the transition turned out to be for me. I went to Babies "R" Us to pick up a baby swing and a pack and play we had ordered, and stood at the customer service counter for fifteen minutes, waiting for them to call out my name, until I realized that the man was repeatedly saying, "Order for Anderson." By the end of the nine months it took me to internalize my new last name, not to mention all the agencies I had to contact and update, I had a newfound respect for all the women who have gone through a similar process in their lives.

The logistics of changing my name paled in comparison to telling my parents about it. Anticipating that it would be a tough conversation, I called during a time I knew my father was working.

"Hey, Mom, it's me. So we found an agency that works with gay couples, and we are moving forward with having a child."

"I'm sorry about our last call," my mom said. "Maybe your father and I are a bit old-fashioned. It will take us some time to get used to all of this, that's all. I do want you to be happy."

"Thanks, Mom, I appreciate that." *Brace yourself for the next bomb to drop, Mom,* I said to myself before I said it out loud. "I've been talking to a gay couple who already have two children, and they told us that it was a good idea for everyone in the family to have the same last name." I took a big breath. "So I've decided to change my name to Anderson."

A pause.

"Oh, that's interesting," was all my mom could muster in response.

Frank, why do you keep doing this to them? I thought as we hung up the phone. I felt so guilty. There was a raging battle inside of me between living the life I wanted and staying connected to my parents, knowing how they were struggling with all I kept throwing at them.

Not long after completing our profile, the agency found us a match. Charlotte was from rural Arkansas. She was definitely attractive—a tall blonde with a dazzling smile and, yes, large breasts. Intelligent? At least on paper. Grounded? Hell, no. Charlotte was unhinged, and that's putting it mildly. However, it took us a while to fully realize this—after we'd done six rounds of insemination with her, none successful, all stressful and bizarre.

For our first insemination date, Michael and I flew down to Arkansas. We took Charlotte and her husband out to a very nice restaurant to get to know them better. As we opened our menus, I looked across the table and thought, *My sperm will soon be inside your wife. You've reached a new level of crazy, Frank.*

As it turned out, the crazy was just beginning. In the middle of dinner, Charlotte blurted out, "We can't do the insemination tomorrow as planned; it'll have to be the following day. We have a memorial mass tomorrow. It's the one-year anniversary of our daughter's death."

Did I just hear that correctly? One year since the death of her daughter? You don't have to be a psychiatrist to know this is not the time for her have another baby, especially a baby for someone else. The agency never told us that the potential mother of our child had recently lost a child, and neither had Charlotte. Michael and I, being new to this process, weren't confident enough to speak up at that point; plus, we really wanted a baby. Despite the huge red flag for us, we continued working with her.

During another insemination session, Charlotte flew to Boston. She called me from the airport, frantic.

"Oh no, Frank. I'm in so much pain right now. I had some dental work done last week, and I think something's wrong."

"That's terrible. I'm so sorry," I said.

"Wait, you're a doctor!" Charlotte's voice brightened with this seemingly sudden remembrance. "Do you think you could call me in a prescription for Percocet? Just a few. Enough to get me through this next insemination."

"Why don't you call your dentist back home and see what they recommend?" I suggested.

"It's the weekend, and the office is closed," Charlotte told me. "Couldn't you call in a prescription for just a few pills?"

Absolutely not. That's totally illegal. I would never put my medical license at risk. Are you out of your mind?

As it turned out, the problem with Charlotte's teeth mysteriously went away when I refused to give her any pain medication. Michael and I should have spoken up at that point, but having grown up in families where substances were abused, we were programmed to be silent and not make waves.

The worst incident and final straw was when Charlotte faked being pregnant. A few weeks after an insemination session, Charlotte called us, elated.

"Oh my God, the test was positive. We're having a baby!"

Michael and I were thrilled beyond belief. *This is really happening!*

"Maybe I can come up there and have the delivery in Boston," Charlotte offered.

"We'll see," I said. "This is so exciting. Thank you from the bottom of my heart."

The very next day, Charlotte called back. "Maybe my test wasn't totally positive—it was more like a faint blue line. Or I could have had a miscarriage. I'm not sure if I'm pregnant or not."

At this, I finally called the surrogate agency and told them everything. They contacted Charlotte and suggested she go to the doctor and have an ultrasound to confirm one way or another. She refused.

My history made it hard for me to speak up and confront people, and in my desperation for a child, I'd kept accommodating and making excuses for Charlotte. But enough was enough. Michael and I decided that we couldn't work with this woman any longer. Between flying to Arkansas and paying Charlotte's medical and living expenses, we had spent nearly $80,000, not to mention so much time and energy, and we had no baby to show for it all.

I didn't share much about the details of the surrogacy process or of Charlotte's crazy antics with my parents. It was clear that they were struggling with the idea of two men—one being their son—raising a child. I didn't need them to be a part of the process, but it would have been nice to have love and parental support along the way.

With our family planning turning out to be incredibly stressful, we decided to take a break. Several months later, the agency reached out to us. They had found another woman who matched our profile. Amanda lived in Southern California. She had a fiancé, a stable job, and two kids of her own. She was attractive and intelligent, had a good sense of humor, and perhaps most important, was fertile and excited about working with us. We started up the insemination process again.

As we had done with Charlotte, Michael and I alternated insemination. For the first round, we flew out to California together, but Amanda didn't get pregnant. For the second round, Michael did the inseminating, but Amanda didn't get pregnant. She seemed to be doing everything right, and I was doing everything in my power to make it happen—monitoring her cycles, tracking her ovulation, sending her thermometers and ovulation test kits on a regular basis. At one point, Amanda called me to ask when she would be ovulating next. Why wasn't she getting pregnant, and why did I know her cycle better than she did?

In June of 2003, I had a turning point. All of a sudden, it dawned on me that the whole thing was out of my control. *I can't keep doing this like this.* With this realization, I did something unprecedented for me.

I let go.

I knew myself as determined and driven, a fighter, a person who gets shit done. I fought to get good grades in school. I fought to get into medical school. I fought to help Mateo. I fought through my abuse. I fought to set boundaries with my parents. I fought to fit in, first with "normal" people, then within the gay community. This was the first time in my life that I'd encountered something that was beyond my power to achieve.

In the center of our little town is a coffee shop flanked by two churches, one Congregational and one Unitarian. One Sunday morning, coffee finished and with nothing else to do, I found my way into the Unitarian church. To my own surprise, I found that the service invited me to self-reflect in a way utterly different from therapy. It was a whole new way of connecting with my inner world, different from psychology and science. Learning to love and accept a part of myself that wasn't focused on achievement, to trust something outside myself, empowered me to stop trying to control the surrogacy process. I even entertained the possibility that it might not happen. *Maybe kids weren't in our future?* Looking back, that decision was the beginning of my spiritual path. And as I'd find in the months and years to come, it made all the difference in my journey of creating a family.

Three weeks later, on the Fourth of July, Amanda called me in Boston.

"My kit just turned blue, Frank. I'm ovulating! Let's make a baby."

The confidence in her tone was unmistakable this time. It was my turn at bat for insemination, so I grabbed my packed suitcase and drove to the airport. As my flight took off that night, fireworks were just starting to light up the sky in Boston. California is three hours behind us, and the flight was roughly six hours. When I arrived in California, fireworks were still lighting up the sky. It was a such a surreal experience. It felt like the whole world was cheering us on.

On July 6, at six thirty in the morning, I got a call from Amanda's gynecologist.

"Frank, Dr. Gold here. How's it going?"

Great. I'm hoping you'll help me impregnate my surrogate Amanda today. How's it going with you?

"Good, Dr. Gold, and you?"

"Here's the plan for today," he began. "I want you and Amanda to meet me at my office before it opens, say around seven thirty this morning. My nurses will help prepare Amanda for the procedure. Right before you head over, I want you to produce a fresh sperm sample, wrap it in several towels, and put the sample in between your legs to keep it warm while you drive to the office. Sound good?"

Well, that won't be an awkward ride. I could only hope I wouldn't get pulled over by the police for speeding.

"That sounds great," I said. "I'll let Amanda know. We'll see you soon."

"Sounds like a plan," he said, calm and confident, and he hung up.

A feeling of gratitude swelled up inside me. *This has been such a long and exhausting journey. Maybe we're finally on the right path.*

We planned on doing an intrauterine insemination, which meant that rather than our usual turkey baster method, the gynecologist would wash and concentrate the sample and insert it directly into Amanda's uterus with a specialized catheter. This was the first time we were trying this procedure.

When I walked into the doctor's office, Amanda was there waiting for me. She looked directly into my eyes, smiled, and said, "Trust me, Frank. It's going to work this time."

And sure enough, she was right. On July 6, 2003, Amanda got pregnant. Two weeks later, the test was positive, and an ultrasound confirmed the pregnancy. We were going to be parents.

The next nine months certainly had its ups and downs. It was challenging to be on opposite coasts of the United States from the mother of our child. Some days, Amanda would call with exciting news.

"I heard the baby's heartbeat for the first time during my checkup today!"

"Oh my gosh, the baby was kicking like crazy today. I wish you were here to feel it."

Other days were less thrilling.

"I had some spotting today. I'm not sure what it means, or what I should do. Do you think I need to go in for a checkup?"

"I've been throwing up all weekend long. I think I got food poisoning from this new restaurant we ate at. I'm not a big fan of seafood."

The roller coaster of emotions made it feel like the longest pregnancy in history (not that I had anything to compare it to). Meanwhile, back in Boston, Michael and I read every baby book we could get our hands on: *What to Expect When You're Expecting*, *The Baby Whisperer*, *The Attachment Parenting Book*, and more. We signed up for emails describing how the fetus was developing each week: "Michael, the baby can hear now. They just grew fingernails. Their lungs can breathe air this week."

In between learning about stages of development and the essential needs of infants—eating, burping, sleeping, bathing, health, and safety—we both took up knitting. Michael and I created an impressive collection of blankets, booties, and scarves while waiting for our baby to arrive. I even made a big throw blanket for Amanda.

I was thankful it took forty weeks' gestation for a baby to enter the world—I needed the time to mentally prepare. I thought about my relationship with Michael and what kind of parents we would be. I processed our crazy path to pregnancy and wondered about a child growing up in an unconventional family with no mom and two gay dads. Mostly, however, I hoped that my child wouldn't feel they had to hide their authentic self in order to be loved.

Meditating on this brought me to another turning point: I felt it was time for me to reenter my family of origin. I had worked through a lot of my history, I had come out, I was in a stable relationship, and now I was in the process of having a child. All of this made me feel stronger and more confident to hold my own around my parents' beliefs and opinions. My mom had organized a surprise sixtieth birthday party for my dad at Palermo's, our family's favorite restaurant, and I decided to attend. It had been close to seven years since I had last seen them, and it would be the first time they met Michael.

We intentionally arrived a little late, after the surprise had already been revealed, hoping to be unobtrusive. But as soon as we entered the room, the first person to see us was my dad. He looked at me, burst into tears, and hugged me for what felt like hours.

"My firstborn son is here. Frankie has finally come home," he wailed.

It was overwhelming, but I understood. In the years since we'd seen each other, a lot had changed in me, and I imagined the same was true for them. I felt a sense of confirmation that being here was the right thing to do.

It was good to feel solid, independent, and in control around my family for the first time ever. Still, knowing my family's tendency toward loud drunken parties, we were prepared to flee to our hotel in case things got out of control.

We weren't quite as well prepared for the awkward turns of conversation. It was the first time many of my extended family had met a gay person (that they knew of, anyway). I'll never forget the moment when my cousin Jennifer asked me, "Frankie, what exactly is the difference between being gay and being a pedophile?"

I knew her question was in earnest—her worldview was extremely narrow—but I was mortified nonetheless. "Well, Jennifer," I answered, "the difference is that I'm not attracted to children. Are you?"

Thankfully, my parents didn't say anything outrageous, even though it must have been challenging for them, too. They were kind and welcoming to Michael as well. I knew it would take time for us to get to know the new versions of each other, but I was grateful to have reconnected.

* * *

Shortly after the trip, Michael and I flew out to California to be there for the twenty-week ultrasound, which would also be the gender reveal. We were convinced that we were having a girl. We'd even picked out the name: Maya. I think we wanted a girl because as boys, each of us had gone through a traumatic relationship with our fathers. As an expectant father of what I was sure was a girl, I set an intention: *I'm going to raise a strong, powerful girl.* We went to the ultrasound eager to get a first glimpse of Maya.

The ultrasound technician squirted some gel onto Amanda's lower abdomen and started moving the sensor back and forth to capture images of the baby. As a doctor, I've seen plenty of fetal ultrasounds, but it was incredible to see our baby moving around like that. After a few seconds, we were both surprised to hear, "Oh, look, there's the penis."

Wait, what? In a flash, I got another unexpected surprise: I instantly felt relieved. *Oh, thank goodness, now I don't have to worry about my daughter being violated.* I was shocked by my reflexive response and the unconscious assumption it included about gender differences. A moment later, I thought, *Wait, now we have to pick a name for our son.*

Michael and I returned home with this task. We were torn between two names and couldn't decide which one we liked better. A little over four months later, we returned to California for the birth of our son, whose name we had narrowed down to Mason or Logan.

When we registered at the front desk of the hospital, the nurses treated Michael and me like we were celebrities. Two gay men having a baby in their own hospital? They were so into it. After all, this was California. We got a private suite to ourselves, complete with our names on the door. When our baby arrived, the staff added the cutest sign: *New Dads—Please Do Not Disturb.*

But while we were being treated like royalty, Amanda was enduring an excruciating labor. She got induced but even so, the baby wasn't budging. Dr. Gold eventually suggested that she go home—"We can try this again in a couple of days." But as we were weighing our options, one of the nurses looked Amanda directly in the eyes and said, "Sweetheart, it's time to let go."

As I've said before, nurses know what they're doing. OB-GYN nurses definitely know the emotional components surrounding child-birth, especially with surrogacy or adoption. Just like that, Amanda let go and all of a sudden, the labor progressed.

The delivery came fast but with significant challenges. On his way out of the birth canal, our son got stuck due to shoulder dystocia—simply put, his shoulder bone got caught above Amanda's pubic bone. To avoid welcoming a newborn into the world with a clavicle fracture or worse, one of the nurses kept him from moving through the birth canal while another nurse pushed the emergency alarm button in our room.

"What's going on?" Michael asked me, a look of panic on his face.

"I have no idea," I responded. Red lights started flashing and about ten nurses rushed into our room.

"Call Dr. Gold, stat!" one of them said.

Another nurse called out, "He's in the locker room changing out of his scrubs."

"We can't wait," replied a different nurse as she performed some maneuver that looked like she was once again trying to keep our baby in Amanda's birth canal. Then, all of a sudden, he was there, followed by a big pool of blood that splattered all over the floor.

Michael and I were in the corner of the room, observing it all, when Dr. Gold finally rushed in. "What's happening?" he asked.

"Shoulder dystocia, but everything's fine," said the amazing nurse who ended up delivering our son. The instant we saw him, we knew he was Logan. On March 20, 2004, Logan Ross Anderson made his world debut and a dramatic, lasting impression on our lives.

As the pediatric nurse evaluated Logan, the doctor tended to Amanda. "Nice job, everyone," he said. Michael and I looked at each other and exhaled a sigh of relief. "Who wants to cut the cord?"

Michael, who was known to pass out from getting blood drawn, looked to me. But I was already volunteering: "I will!"

Eager yet apprehensive, we approached the baby warmer, where our little boy Logan was lying. His hands were over his face, trying to block out the intensity of the bright lights as he opened his eyes for the first time in his life. His skin was pink, his forehead was wrinkled like an old man, and his head was slightly misshapen, which I knew was normal from my medical training. He looked so innocent and vulnerable lying there. I felt in that moment that I was here to help this precious soul maneuver through this sometimes scary but also joyous world, and I was up for the task.

We had a bouquet of flowers delivered to Amanda and gave her time alone to hold our baby. I knew saying goodbye to Logan would be hard for her, and I wanted to be sure she knew how grateful we were for giving us such an incredible gift. The nurse then gave Michael a tiny bottle to feed Logan his first meal. I sat back in a rocking chair and cried as the surreal notion of having a child *someday* became a reality. I hadn't shed a tear in years, but the love and the joy I felt in that moment burst through the barrier I had built up for so long, just like it did when I came out. I was holding an opportunity to rewrite the injustices I experienced with my father, to offer support, guidance, and acceptance to this child in a way I hadn't experienced growing up. I was overwhelmed with emotion—gratitude, hope, and endless possibilities for love.

After being set up in our private room, we were left alone to get acquainted with our son. That first night was pretty daunting, not to mention really messy.

"Michael, wake up!" I exclaimed. "Can you help me?"

"Sure," he answered groggily. "What's going on?"

"Logan just shit all over the place!"

"Do you really need my help? Why can't you change him yourself?"

"Just come here and take a look at this." I wheeled the tiny clear crib over to his side of the bed.

"Holy shit is right! What in the world is that stuff?" Michael was now wide awake and thoroughly disgusted. Our precious baby was covered from head to toe in a black-green, sticky, tar-like substance.

"It's called meconium," I explained. "It's made up of all the waste products that accumulated in the placenta over the last nine months. You know—amniotic fluid, dead skin, hair, intestinal cells, and bile. Basically, it's fetal poop."

I knew what it was, but I had no idea how to clean it up. Despite all the books we had read, nothing prepared us for this first parental task. Because the nurses were committed to respecting our privacy, they didn't check in on us, and we didn't think to ask for their help. *A mother would probably know how to handle this,* I thought. Well, we were fathers, and we ended up figuring it out by ourselves. It took two grown men a full hour to clean up the mess from this tiny baby, as well as two full boxes of wipes and all the available towels in the room. We needed to change the sheets, change Logan's outfit, and wipe down the little mattress in the basinet. It was disgusting and hilarious. We were laughing at ourselves and freaked out by the mess and our incompetence. Welcome to parenthood—what have we gotten ourselves into?

• • •

Michael and I stayed in California for about a week after Logan was born to finalize all the documents. At the time, California was one of the few states in the country that allowed same-sex couples to be listed on the birth certificate as the legal parents. The six-hour plane ride back east proved uneventful. Logan slept most of the flight and, thankfully, didn't have any explosive diapers we needed to change on the plane.

When we returned home, we had a wonderful surprise waiting for us. It was a gift from my parents—a big, beautiful diaper bag with the name ANDERSON embroidered on the front flap. In that moment, I felt a big shift in my heart. I knew how hard it must have been for them to do that, and it felt so important for me and my new family to be acknowledged in that way. Michael and I looked at the bag, looked at each other, looked at our son, and kissed. *Alla famiglia,* I thought.

• • •

By the time of Logan's birth, same-sex marriage had just become legal in Massachusetts. Accordingly, when Logan was eighteen months old, Michael and I decided to make it official and tie the knot.

We had a small, intimate ceremony and reception at our house, with a total of twelve guests in attendance—ten dear friends and two relatives. Amy and Evelyn, the first gay couple whom I became friends with and who showed me what true love is, were there. In fact, Evelyn became a minister for the day in order to marry us. My brother and his wife, Marla, were there, too. I couldn't imagine getting married without Ross being by my side. However, we decided not to invite our parents to our wedding ceremony. Michael's family had struggled with his being gay for many years, and I had only recently reunited with my parents after several years of silence. Looking back, it was a decision I regret. I wish they were there with us to celebrate our love and commitment to each other. Nevertheless, it was a lovely, meaningful wedding and a wonderful start to our new life of domestic bliss, complete with a child and chickens.

Michael and I decided that our son would call us "Daddy" and "Papa," respectively—something all same-sex couples need to figure out. Because we were equally committed to raising Logan and didn't want to rely on childcare, we each worked three days per week—Monday through Wednesday for me, Thursday through Saturday for Michael. Sunday was our family day. This arrangement really worked for us. We had a lovely home in a beautiful town, Michael had his chickens, and I had the child I had longed for.

Logan hit all of his developmental milestones on schedule. At three years old, he was potty-trained, talking, and walking—running, actually—all over the place. He was a healthy, bright, adorable, active, and happy little boy. What more could I possibly want? Another kid, naturally.

Despite my childhood traumas, I had many fond memories of growing up alongside my siblings and cousins in our big Italian family. I wanted Logan to grow up with a brother or a sister. One child just didn't feel like a proper family to me; it felt more like three individuals living together. I wanted a version of what I grew up with—a group, a pack.

Michael was, to say the least, not receptive to the idea. He felt betrayed, in fact. I understood. After all, we had made an agreement: one kid, no dog. But I couldn't have anticipated how I would feel having only one child. Sharing my desire to have a second child activated Michael, and the tension shot us into couples therapy. During our sessions, Michael and I talked about our feelings, our childhoods, our relationship, and the importance of family.

In the meantime, my relationship with my parents was slowly improving, and everyone in Chicago was eager to get to meet Logan.

That included my father, who soon became a doting grandfather. This came into play during couples therapy; our second child-centered agreement included two possible solutions to satisfy my desire for more family in my life. We could move to Chicago with one child and live closer to my family, or we could stay in Harvard and try to have a second child. I felt it was important to let Michael decide, because I was the one who'd changed our original agreement.

After thinking it over, my husband said, "Let's have another kid." Above all, he wanted what was best for Logan, but he also worried that living near my boisterous family might be overwhelming for him. (He was probably right about the latter.)

We couldn't afford to do surrogacy again—it was just too expensive, not to mention draining—so as we embarked on the journey of having a second child, we started looking into adoption. We contacted several agencies, settled on one, completed a home study, filled out all the required forms, and consented to financial and legal background checks. As we waited to hear from the agency about a potential baby, something happened one day in October 2007 that we never could have anticipated.

"Hey, Frank, it's Amanda. How's it going?"

I hope nothing's wrong, I thought. Amanda rarely called, though we regularly kept her up to date on Logan and his milestones.

"Everything's great here. Logan is doing fantastic—he keeps us super busy—and work is going well too. How's it going with you?"

"Well, that's an interesting question," Amanda said, a sly tone in her voice that I knew well. "I know we haven't talked in a while, but have you and Michael ever thought about having another kid?" *What? Talk about timing!*

"Funny you should ask," I said. "We literally just finished filling out paperwork with an adoption agency. We do want another child but can't afford the surrogacy route again. It's too expensive."

"Well, I may have an interesting proposition for you. Noah and I went to Vegas to celebrate the Fourth of July—you know how I love that holiday. Well, Saturday night, one thing led to another, and I got pregnant."

I smiled, unable to help wondering if there had been one too many margaritas involved.

"We really can't afford to raise another child right now," Amanda continued, "and I immediately thought of you and Michael. Would you guys be interested in adopting this baby?"

"Are you serious, Amanda? Of course, we'd be interested. We would be honored. This is amazing. Wait . . ." Chills instantly ran throughout my body. "Did you say Saturday, July 6?"

"Yeah, why?"

"Three years ago on July 6, we were in Dr. Gold's office doing the insemination that brought us Logan."

"Are you serious? That's crazy," Amanda said. "I guess it was meant to be!"

I paused for a moment. *This is beyond rational; this is beyond a coincidence.* Once again, life had shown me how much is beyond my control—this time, in the best way possible.

"Yes, it is crazy," I agreed. "And yes, Michael and I would love to adopt this baby."

Once again, I flew to California for the ultrasound (Michael stayed home to take care of Logan), and once again, a penis showed up. Logan was going to have a baby brother by the same mother. There were forces at work larger than all of us helping to create this family. It was truly meant to be.

Michael, Logan, and I took a trip out west in late March. And on Logan's fourth birthday, March 20, we went to the hospital to be there for the birth of our second son. Once again, Amanda's labor was induced. While Michael took Logan to Toys "R" Us to buy his new baby brother a birthday present, I stayed with Amanda and waited up with her all night. The baby kept flipping. Breech, not breech. Breech, not breech. The nurses instructed me to keep watching the heart rate monitor to make sure there weren't any significant drops in the fetal heart rate. I was glued to that monitor all night long.

The following morning at six, Amanda let out a loud "Holy cow!" and that baby shot right out of her. He was ready to begin the journey, and there was no stopping him. There he was, lying on her bed, screaming and crying. I started screaming too, for someone to come and help. I am a doctor, but one who talks about what it feels like to have a baby, not one who delivers them. Luckily, it was the change of shift, and Dr. Gold and several nurses were gathered at the nurse's station. They heard my calls for help and rushed right in. They immediately got to work, cleaning him up, cutting the umbilical cord, checking for abnormalities.

On March 21, 2008, four years and one day after the birth of his brother, Brett Miles Anderson made his dramatic entrance into the world and our lives. He was a beautiful, blond-haired, blue-eyed baby with a long and lean build, a combination that was new and exciting coming from my ethnic background. I was thrilled and curious to get to know him and discover who this little boy was. *Welcome to our family, Brett.*

Every year, we celebrate two separate birthdays—cake, balloons, presents, a party, the works—one day apart, first for Logan and then for Brett. And each year—it's become a tradition—we pull out the photo albums and recite their birth stories, which they love to hear, because they were truly extraordinary.

CHAPTER TWELVE

FATHERS AND SONS

"Dream On" | Aerosmith

Parenting was one of the biggest challenges of my life. It brought me to my knees. I learned that I was imperfect, I was fallible, I could be a monster. It shot me into my next layer of healing. I paid my dues, the lines on my face got clearer, and my past was becoming a distant dream.

✳ ✳ ✳

Life has a way of showing us what we need to work on, what we need to heal. I created the life I wanted, and on the surface, it looked and felt wonderful. But having two high-energy boys was stressful, and I started losing myself as another layer of my unresolved history resurfaced—this time, in relation to my kids.

When we brought Brett home from the hospital, Michael and I thought, *This will be a piece of cake.* We already knew what it was like to have a baby in the house. With Logan, we had survived diapers and bottles, crying and crawling, tantrums and potty training. But from the beginning, Brett brought different challenges from his big brother. For starters, he had medical complications—trouble keeping food down, reflux, and persistent ear infections. He never slept through the night, so naturally, neither did we. It was nerve-racking and exhausting.

Brett was prescribed acid-suppressing medications to manage his reflux. When he was nine months old, he had ear tubes surgically inserted to prevent fluid buildup, which allowed him to sleep through the night for the first time in his life. He finally started eating food but then was diagnosed with food allergies to wheat and soy and placed on a food elimination diet. As an infant, he barely babbled; after he turned two, he still hadn't spoken a word. He had, however, begun to walk, and we couldn't keep up with him. We had to put chain locks up high beyond his reach on every door in our house, because when he started running he wouldn't stop for anything; he would run right outside if he had the opportunity and never return. He never displayed stranger anxiety; he would go off with anyone who showed the slightest bit of interest in him. This was a whole different level of stress for our family.

When Brett was three years old, we decided it was time to find some answers and got him a thorough neuropsychological evaluation. He was diagnosed with pervasive developmental disorder (PDD), which is characterized by delays in the development of multiple basic functions, including socialization and communication. Today, PDD is recognized as falling under the autism spectrum disorders. Shortly thereafter, he was also diagnosed with attention deficit disorder with hyperactivity (ADHD).

Brett is an amazing human being with a great sense of humor. He's tall for his age and has sandy blond hair, blue-green eyes, and a big smile that rarely shows up in pictures. He's observant, highly intelligent, extremely sensitive, and for the most part, a joy to be with. Michael and I wanted the best for him, and our whole life revolved around making sure he was getting the care and services he needed. By the time Brett started preschool, we engaged a speech therapist and an ABA (applied behavioral analysis) specialist, enrolled him in early intervention, and enlisted a cohort of providers and health aides to come to the house three to five days a week. Even with all this outside support, Michael and I rarely got a break. Playdates were difficult to manage. When we went to a friend's house, Brett would inevitably get overwhelmed, have a meltdown, break or throw something, or hit somebody. Socializing with friends was so stressful that we eventually stopped trying (and stopped getting invited). Our wonderful circle of friends got smaller and smaller.

Parenting Brett was not only overwhelming; it was expensive. Up to that point, Michael and I had each worked three days a week on alternate schedules so that one of us would always be home to take care of the kids. But to pay for all the services and specialists Brett required, I started taking on more work. As a result, we had to hire a babysitter with experience in managing special needs kids on the days we both worked.

At the time, Michael was working as a professional cake decorator; as I was a psychiatrist, my income was significantly higher. Knowing this, Michael said to me one day, "We pay the babysitter more than I make per hour. I think it's time for me to quit work and manage our home and the services Brett needs."

I couldn't have agreed more, and I was grateful that he was willing to do it, especially since I was the one who'd wanted the second child in the first place. When Brett was five and Logan was nine, Michael decided to quit work and become a full-time stay-at-home dad.

* * *

My motivation for working more hours was not purely financial. I knew I wasn't handling the stress of parenting very well. I lost my temper, became reactive, and periodically yelled at the boys for their behavior. I saw Michael as the calmer parent and was hard on myself whenever I lost it. I didn't want to negatively impact my children. More to the point, I didn't want to become my father. Somewhere deep down, I thought my kids were better off with less exposure to me.

One such occasion happened when I was driving home after one of our town-sponsored playgroups. Leaving was always a challenge because transitions were hard for my boys, and Brett was overdue for his nap. They were yelling and screaming at each other during the car ride home.

"Stop the fighting, you two," I ordered.

"He started it," said Logan.

"I don't care who started it, I'm telling you to end it *now*."

But it continued, until Brett threw his bottle at Logan and it cracked open, spilling everywhere. The fabric seats, the windows, the carpeting were covered in formula. I stopped the car in the middle of the road and started yelling.

"What in the hell's wrong with you two? How many times do I have to tell you to stop fighting? Get out of the car and walk home from here."

Even as I said it, I knew it was absurd. When I saw the look of panic on their faces, I immediately pivoted.

"When we get home, you're both grounded, and you're going to clean up every drop of milk . . . by yourselves."

Again, a ridiculous consequence. Did I really expect two kids to do a detail job on the car upholstery? The fact is that I was as out of control as they were. The problem was that I was the parent, while they were just kids being kids.

The last straw came when, while we were playing together in his bedroom, Logan bit me and I reflexively pushed him away. I saw the initial confusion in his eyes, followed by fear. He had no frame of reference for my being physical with him, yet he was frightened by my response. After I recovered, I apologized for my behavior and immediately got myself back into therapy.

Around that same time, while teaching at one of Bessel van der Kolk's trauma conferences, I sat in on a workshop by Richard C. Schwartz, founder of a promising new treatment approach called Internal Family Systems (IFS). His formulation of the psyche as "parts," each with their own unique value and function, offered an intuitive way to make sense of the internal conflicts that so often result from a person's trauma history. IFS was uniquely non-pathologizing; rather than seeing patients as "sick" or "abnormal" for their extreme and often destructive thoughts and behaviors, IFS viewed these patterns as simply the result of the patients' various parts trying to help them cope with their trauma. By helping patients connect with their parts, IFS empowered patients to bring those parts out of the past, release them from their burden of trauma, and regain their healthy functioning in the present.

I'd been working with the reigning experts on trauma for years, yet nobody had ever suggested something like this was possible. I saw IFS as a continuation of the work that the Trauma Center had begun. Just as I'd done after meeting Bessel, I dove headfirst into IFS, taking every training, attending every workshop, volunteering at events as often as I could. This naturally put me in the orbit of Richard Schwartz himself—Dick to his friends, as I soon became. Between my work at the Trauma Center and my increasing renown as a leading practitioner for trauma recovery, I was a natural candidate for becoming an IFS trainer. Dick even entrusted me with writing his organization's first curriculum, a five-day intensive trauma training course, as well as running his non-profit foundation for the advancement of IFS research.

Over the next several years of working alongside Dick, the hero worship I felt for him (much like I had for Bessel) developed into a relationship that felt more like the father-and-son relationship I'd yearned for. Where Bessel was a powerful, god-like figure among his staff, Dick's leadership was gentle and quiet, his manner warm and caring. Many of my conversations with Dick morphed into informal counseling sessions, helping me explore and make sense of my own parts. I felt that his influence could help me be the father I wanted to be to my sons.

Nevertheless, the stress-triggered outbursts didn't stop. Instead, I became even more critical and self-loathing whenever I lost control. I knew what healthy parenting looked like. I taught it for a living in my workshops and coached clients who were struggling with their children. Most important, I had vowed never to be like my father with my children. Despite the physical distance I'd created with my dad, he remained alive and active inside of me. I was capable of yelling at my kids just like he yelled at me.

Strangely, it was one of these difficult moments with Brett that ultimately helped me become the parent he needed me to be. It happened on a Saturday when I was home alone with the boys. The previous night had been rough for Brett, and I knew he was getting close to his mid-morning nap (and I was counting the minutes). I heard loud noises coming from our primary bathroom, which was not uncommon. At three and a half years old, Brett loved opening and closing doors—"stimming," as this self-stimulating behavior is known. As I entered the bathroom, I saw him repeatedly slamming the vanity doors. *Bang, bang, bang.* He smashed the doors so hard, one broke off the hinges.

The sight instantly took me back to being a little boy, watching the hinges of my bedroom door rattle as my father pounded on the door. The circumstances were different, but the feelings it evoked in me were exactly the same. I screamed, "What in the hell are you doing?"

Startled, Brett looked up at me, then launched into one of his infamous meltdowns. He proceeded to run into his and Logan's bathroom, where he started banging on the shower door. This time he knocked it so hard that it came off the track and almost fell on top of him.

I shouted out again, "Stop it right now, Brett! You're gonna kill yourself." Enraged by his behavior yet relieved that he didn't get hurt, I was at my wits' end, and I collapsed on the floor of the bathroom. *I can't take this anymore.*

Desperate for help, I called my neighbor and good friend, Joyce. As hard as it was to reach out this way, I knew she would get it, having been a sleep-deprived and overwhelmed parent herself. To my great relief, she came right over and immediately took charge. "I'll put Brett down for his nap and take Logan over to my house for a playdate with Caroline. You get some sleep while Brett naps."

This was exactly what we all needed. I was extremely grateful—first, for having the courage and humility to call for help, and second, for Joyce's willingness to respond and being so helpful.

That evening when Michael came home from work, he looked tired from his day, but he immediately recognized the kind of day I'd had. I gave him the look we both knew so well: eyes rolled up and back, a facial expression that said, *I've been to hell and back today.*

"Frank, why don't you go to the gym? I'll make dinner and take care of the kids," he generously offered. "Just go! We'll be fine."

Relieved, I got dressed, drove to the gym, found an open machine, and hopped on the Stairmaster. *Relax and let it go,* I said to myself, as I closed my eyes and turned up the volume on my headphones. *You know exercise always helps you.*

Suddenly, behind my closed eyes, I saw a bright white light. Next, I heard a clear and strong voice say, "You know, he is here to teach you as much as you are here to teach him."

It stopped me in my tracks. I opened my eyes, but there was no one there.

This was another important spiritual moment in my life, one that shifted my perspective on Brett. Why was I trying so hard to make him fit into this world? Why not let Brett be Brett? Maybe the world and I needed to fit him, instead of him fitting us. I thought of his sweet, beautiful little face, the pure, loving innocence within his eyes. *It's not his fault; he's trying his best to manage an overwhelming brain. He's my son, and I love him more than life itself, and I'll do anything in my power to protect him.*

* * *

Michael and I got in the habit of visiting our respective families at least once a year so our boys would maintain a connection with their extended families. It was clear that our parents loved our kids, but it was also clear that it was challenging for them to see us struggle with parenting Brett. My dad had developed a strong connection with Logan. Whenever we visited, he would frequently take Logan aside and slip him some money or give him a rare coin from his coin collection. As strained as my relationship was with my dad, I loved watching him interact with my son. I saw how loving my father could be, and I saw the way Logan felt special to him, just the way I did with my grandfather.

It was different with Brett, for both my parents. Out of the corner of my eye, I would see the look of judgment on their faces whenever Michael and I parented him with the hands-off techniques we'd been taught by his ABA specialists. It wasn't hard to read between the lines of comments they expressed.

"In our day, parents were in charge, not the kids," said my dad. "I was taught that kids are not your friend; it's your job to teach them right from wrong. To give them consequences for their behavior, not to get them to like you. They need to know who's boss."

A part of me thought, *Are you kidding? You're the last person in the world I would take parenting advice from.* Another part thought, *I know he doesn't have any experience with special needs kids. He just needs to spend more time with Brett; then he'll understand.* A third part thought, *Parenting is so hard. I have no clue if we're messing up our kids or doing right by them. Please, somebody help us!*

Things started to settle down for Brett when he reached ten years old. Our town's school system decided to transfer him to a therapeutic school that specialized in kids on the spectrum. I'd like to say that it was smooth sailing from that point forward, but it was only the next important step in my journey to finding myself and loving myself, as a parent and as a person.

I knew there were two underlying motivations that drove me deeper into my career. The first was to keep a safe distance between my kids and the part of me that got reactive toward them. It was definitely improving, but I was still prone to volatility, and I was committed to fully eradicating it. Second, my focus on success was also an attempt to gain the approval and validation I never got from my father. I was becoming a trauma specialist at a time when the world was desperate to learn how best to treat PTSD and dissociation. I began accepting offers to host workshops and speak at conferences, helping professionals work with people who suffered from trauma. This pattern of protecting my boys from my anger and searching for love through success continued until the next wake-up call presented itself—this time, related to my relationship with Logan.

With so much of our time, attention, and energy in taking care of Brett, it was a blessing that we didn't have to worry about Logan in the same way. Aside from the challenge of Logan being diagnosed with ADHD when he was around seven years old, he was a normal, well-adjusted, high-energy kid. He had friends, he fit in at school, and for the most part, he could take care of himself. At least, that's what Michael and I believed.

When Logan was age twelve, in the seventh grade, I had plans to speak at a conference in Sacramento. It was a major event, with about 250 participants in attendance to hear me teach on the topic of relational trauma (or C-PTSD). Shortly after I boarded the plane, I powered down my cell phone as usual. Six hours later, as soon as I landed, I turned it on and was stunned by a string of text messages from Michael.

"Call me as soon as you get this... Mary called an ambulance... Logan's in the hospital... He's unconscious. I'm heading over to the hospital now... They think it might be a suicide attempt... Call me as soon as you land."

I got off the plane, frantic. "Oh my God, can someone please help me? I have to get home."

A flight attendant came over to me and asked, "What's wrong?"

"I'm not sure exactly," I answered truthfully, my tone panicked. "My son is in the hospital; he may have killed himself. I got a bunch of messages from my husband but I can't get hold of him. I think they're at the hospital right now. I need to get home as soon as possible. What do I do?" I was out of my mind, engulfed by fear.

The flight attendant, who might have been an angel, firmly grabbed my elbow and turned me around. "Get back on that plane. I'll get your luggage." She walked me to a seat in first class. "This plane is going back to Boston. It's a red eye. You'll be home in the morning."

Dazed and overwhelmed, I thanked the flight attendant profusely. While the passengers were boarding the plane, Michael called me back.

"Logan is alive," he told me, "but he's still unconscious. I don't know much at this point. Apparently, he drank a lot of alcohol. Joyce is at the house; she'll sleep over and take care of Brett. I'm going to stay here with Logan overnight."

I burst into tears. *Thank God, he's alive. What in the world happened? I can't believe Michael has to do this all by himself.* It was intolerable to be out of town and away from my family, unable to do anything for them. I felt like jumping out of my skin. *Please let Logan be okay.*

Pulling myself together, I managed to let Michael know that I was back on the plane and it was scheduled to land in Boston at six o'clock in the morning. "I'll head right to the hospital from the airport," I assured him. "I love you, honey."

"I love you too."

It was the longest plane ride of my life. I didn't sleep a wink. The man sitting next to me, another total stranger, proved to be another godsend. He listened to my worries and fears and supported me with a positive outlook throughout the flight. He kept saying what I so desperately needed to hear and believe: "Everything will be fine. Don't worry, you've got this. You can handle it."

When I arrived at the hospital, Logan was conscious but far from coherent. He had been admitted with a dangerously high level of alcohol in his system and had his stomach pumped. Was it a suicide attempt? That's something we couldn't really determine at the time. Michael and I were beside ourselves. We were committed to doing everything in our power to help him get better . . . but from what?

We learned later that Logan and his friends had discovered alcohol during some of their sleepovers, sneaking sips of liquor at each other's houses. The afternoon of my flight, Michael had taken Brett to see a movie, leaving Logan home alone. On an impulse, he ventured into our liquor stash and started drinking tequila, until eventually he stopped drinking and started vomiting. Fortunately, he called his friend Cody for help, and even more fortunately, Cody told his mother, Mary. The two of them drove over to our house, found the door unlocked, and walked in to find Logan passed out in his bed in a pool of vomit. Mary called an ambulance, then called Michael.

Michael and I were not big drinkers, having both grown up with family members whose alcohol use made them volatile and violent. However, when Michael and I had parties with neighborhood friends, he often made a themed cocktail, so we had a basement full of half-used liquor bottles. But after the event with Logan, we agreed that we would be a completely sober household and got rid of every bottle of liquor we owned. Going forward, if friends came over to our house and wanted a drink, they knew to bring their own alcohol and take any unused portion home with them when they left. For our part, Michael and I gave up drinking almost entirely. Occasionally we have a drink when we go out to dinner, but we rarely drink at home.

At the hospital's suggestion, Logan spent a week in an inpatient psychiatric ward. They determined that he was depressed, and upon discharge, he was placed on antidepressants and instructed to start therapy. His birth mother, Amanda, suffers with occasional depressive episodes, so genetics may have played a role in his actions that day. But by Logan's report, it wasn't an attempt at ending his life, simply a dangerously impulsive act. At the time, though, I saw the whole thing as being my failure, as a parent and as a psychiatrist.

Why didn't I see this coming? I should have known better. How did I miss this? I asked myself.

While Logan was in the hospital, I connected with a young, desperate part of me that got in the way of being the parent he needed. Visiting hours were coming to an end, and Logan didn't want me to leave.

"Please, Papa, don't go. I don't want to stay here anymore. I hate it here. I don't belong with these people."

"I know, honey. I did everything I could to see if they would let me stay with you overnight, and they said no."

"It was just a mistake, Papa. I promise I won't do it again. Really, I promise. Please don't leave me."

Hearing Logan pleading with me was heart-wrenching. As I searched for words to comfort him, the nurse came into the room and politely said, "Visiting hours are over, Dad. It's time to for you to leave."

I wrapped Logan in a tight, desperate hug. "I promise I'll see you tomorrow morning." I assured him.

On the ride home, I got a call from my longtime mentor Dick Schwartz. "How's it going with Logan, Frank?"

I immediately burst into tears. "It's absolutely horrible," I answered, distraught. "It kills me to leave him there all alone."

"Pull over," Dick commanded.

"What?" I asked, confused by his request.

"Pull over," Dick repeated, "and let's take a look at the part of you that's feeling so desperate right now."

Are you fucking kidding me? My kid's in the hospital—he almost killed himself! Of course I'm feeling desperate. More than a bit incensed, I nevertheless pulled off the highway into the breakdown lane.

After I took a deep breath, Dick and I talked. Much to my surprise, he helped me get in touch with the part of me that felt hopeless, abandoned, and all alone as a child. That little boy inside me was activated by Logan's desperate request for someone to be with him and his pain. This momentarily eclipsed the parental love and compassion I was feeling for Logan. As I comforted the little boy within me, letting him know I loved and cared about him, I was able to differentiate Logan's experience from my own. Logan naturally felt overwhelmed by what he was going through and by being away from home and in the hospital for the first time. My extreme feelings of distress, on the other hand, had as much to do with my own history of abuse and neglect as they did with present-day concern for my son's safety.

When I returned to the hospital the next day, I was noticeably calmer and more stable, and thus able to be fully present with Logan as his parent, without any childhood feelings from my past resurfacing. I told him I knew what it felt like to be scared and alone, that I was fully committed and available to help him manage those same feelings in himself. He instantly felt the shift in me and began to settle down, trusting that I knew what to do and had his best interest at heart. He started talking to his doctors about what transpired for him over the past several days leading up to the alcohol poisoning event. Healing finally began.

It was a humbling experience, but not the kind that left me with guilt or shame. I didn't care about how it looked to others that I was a psychiatrist with a son who struggled with mental health issues. I was solely focused on Logan's well-being. We gradually learned that he wasn't happy at school. The community of Harvard boasts one of the top school systems in the state, focused on rigorous academics and college preparation. For Logan, this environment was a horrible fit. Even though he had an individualized education plan, the school district didn't provide him the services or support he needed to be successful in such a competitive environment. Not surprisingly, he got poor grades and felt like a failure. Social pressures also played a role. Logan had two close friends, but he was often teased because of his ADHD-related behavior and didn't feel accepted by the kids in his class.

Even though Logan never explicitly stated it, I suspect he wasn't happy at home, either. He spent more time alone in his room, which we attributed to normal adolescent behavior. However, when Logan was little, Michael and I arranged our work schedules so we could take turns being home with him and focus all our attention on him. When Brett arrived, it would have been natural for Logan to experience some bumps in the road as he learned how to share our attention. However, the learning curve was much more extreme due to the level of care Brett needed. Logan went from having two devoted dads all to himself to, I suspect, feeling neglected by us and resentful toward his younger brother.

Add in the increasing frequency that I was away from home, traveling for work, and it all added up to a perfect storm for Logan.

The day Logan almost died was the most traumatic day of his life and of mine. Yet, as I've learned personally and often tell my patients, trauma can lead to transformation when you take advantage of the situation and learn from your experience. Thanks to Logan's crisis, our family situation dramatically changed. After the incident, I tried to work less and stay home more, returning to coparent more equally with Michael. I also made it a priority to spend more time alone with Logan. We both enjoy outdoor activities, so I started there. In the winter, I took him and his friends skiing. In warmer weather, we frequently went up to New Hampshire for mountain biking trips together.

Looking back, it became clear to me how an attempt to fix one unwanted behavior unconsciously recreated another. I dove into work to shelter my kids from my reactive behavior, afraid of turning into my dad. In turn though, my withdrawal inadvertently replicated another one of my dad's mistakes: frequently being away from home. This resulted in my kids not feeling like a priority to me, just like I felt with my father. I ended up creating what I was trying to avoid.

Michael and I also realized that we were both too passive and permissive as parents. We resisted being angry and controlling like our fathers, but we went too far in the opposite direction. Logan's substance use and depression expressed itself as anger and isolation, and we let it go on far too long. We tolerated his outbursts and attacks instead of setting limits and providing the structure he needed and was desperately asking for through his actions. I remember the moment the tide changed, and we stood up and claimed our parental power.

Six months after Logan's hospitalization, he stumbled into the house, mumbling something incoherent. His clothes were disheveled, his eyes half open, and he looked confused and sounded . . .

Wasted.

"Logan, what did you take?" I asked, a hint of urgency in my voice. "You're not making any sense right now."

"Nothing, leave me alone," he said. "I'm just tired." Leaving the front door wide open, he dropped his backpack and headed straight for his room.

Michael combed through his backpack and found a dab pen and a half-eaten brownie wrapped in white paper. For us, this was the last straw. We wouldn't repeat the passivity we enacted with our first surrogate, Charlotte, and we were committed to not reliving our own childhoods in which substances governed the family.

"Logan, we need to talk," Michael said, calmly but firmly. We had learned by then that talking to Logan together, as a united front, was a more effective way to stand up to his strong adolescent personality.

"Leave me alone!" he yelled from inside his room.

"Now!" Michael and I responded in unison. With a courtesy knock on the door, we entered his room. Logan was still fully dressed, lying on his bed.

"We found all of this in your backpack," Michael said as he showed Logan the drug paraphernalia and the laced brownie.

"You're grounded until further notice," I said. "And you've lost phone privileges."

With that, Logan exploded. He got up and lunged toward us, screaming, "You have no right to go through my stuff. What the fuck! You can't take away my phone." He started throwing things around the room.

"Stop it, right now," I told him. "We will not tolerate any more drug use in this family, period. We own the phone, this is our house, and we are your parents. Like it or not, we're in charge here."

In response, Logan punched a hole in his bedroom wall.

"You'll fix anything and everything you decide to break," Michael stated. "And if you try to hurt any of us, we'll call the police." With that, we walked out of his room and pulled his door shut, knowing it was time to give Logan some time to sober up and think.

Taking a stand like this was scary—terrifying, actually—for Michael and me. Confronting Logan brought back frightening images from our childhoods. However, it was also empowering. For the first time ever, we were clear and calm, united and in charge. Firm in our determination not to ever again live in a family that was violent and destructive, we had the power now to create a safe, drug-free household where we were in control in a non-abusive way.

This shift in our parenting helped our family dynamic change for the better. Our kids needed strong parents, so we needed to be stronger than our kids. Up until that point, Michael's and my histories got in the way. As we all learned from and maneuvered through the challenging times we encountered together as a family, we slowly began having more moments of levity at home. I remember those years as a montage of carving pumpkins, having family Nerf gun fights, jumping on the trampoline, going on hikes, swimming in the pool, or playing together in the bouncy house. Vacations continued to be special times for our family, much like the ones I remembered as a child. Family dinners were also more enjoyable, not stressful and overwhelming as they once were.

"This steak tartare is incredible. I didn't think I'd like it, but I'm glad we tried it," Logan said as we finished up dinner at the steakhouse Michael chose for his birthday celebration.

"Does anyone want dessert?" I asked, already knowing what Brett wanted: his "usual."

"Yes, Papa," Brett responded, right on cue. "Vanilla ice cream with whipped cream on top. No cherries and no chocolate sauce."

"Anyone else? What about you, Birthday Boy?"

Michael chimed in. "I'm full, but why don't we share a piece of carrot cake? And please, no singing and no candles."

"Okay, fine," I said begrudgingly, knowing how much he hated to be the center of attention. "It is your day."

I smiled, reached over, and gave his hand a squeeze, remembering as I did it how I envied Amy and Evelyn for this same gesture a decade earlier. *I've come a long way from where I once was.*

On the way home, Brett had a request.

"Papa! Daddy! Let's do 'Pick a Song!'" That was our name for a family game where everyone gets to choose their favorite song to play.

"Okay, I'm first," chimed in Logan, in typical big-brother fashion. "I want Bon Jovi."

Anticipating his pick, I cranked up "It's My Life." When the song finished, Brett picked one from his favorite group, Fall Out Boy, and said, "And don't sing, Papa. Your voice is terrible."

"Thanks, Brett," I said with a grin.

For my turn, I picked an Aerosmith classic, "Dream On." I quietly sang along, finding new resonance in the lyrics I'd known by heart since I was a teenager. The lines on my face were undoubtedly getting clearer; the past (thankfully) was indeed gone; the dusk of my childhood's fear and pain had at last given way to a beautiful dawn, my life alight with the loving family I had hardly dared to dream of.

Suddenly, we hit a bumpy patch on the highway. It momentarily felt like we were on a roller coaster ride. In unison, the whole family screamed "Wheee!" as I maneuvered the car and recovered.

Inevitably, the experience made me flash back to when my father drove us home from my cousin's house that one snowy Christmas Eve. But with everyone reacting this time with laughter and delight, there was no emotional trigger. I knew this moment was totally different. *No one's drunk, no one's head hit the ceiling of the car, no one's afraid, and there's no need to deny reality.*

As the game continued, I was filled with pride and sadness simultaneously. Pride for what Michael and I had created in this family, even while knowing that it hadn't been an easy ride and we'd certainly made a lot of mistakes along the way. At least, we took advantage of our moments and learned from the hardships that arose in our family. We all risked changing—and we're all the better for it. I felt sadness for that younger version of me in the car that night, for the terror, the anger, the need to disavow reality in the service of survival. But I knew in my heart that I wasn't repeating my history. We weren't throwing fresh-baked pies against the wall or bringing hoses and buckets of water into the house, but we were having a great time together as a family. As we neared home, I felt happy, successful, fully present, at peace. I wanted this moment to last forever and, at the same time, I wanted to create more memories, just like this one, for my kids to take with them into their futures.

* * *

Having children, I've come to realize that we don't get what we want, but we get what we need. Logan and Brett have challenged and pushed me in ways I could never have imagined. From one year to the next, I have increasingly felt the redemptive value of parenting amid those challenges.

Still, I wasn't sure that Amanda would feel the same way. For the longest time, I didn't tell her about Brett's diagnosis or Logan's struggles with depression and drug use. Knowing how sensitive she is, I was afraid she would feel guilty or responsible in some way. When I eventually shared some of it with her, I was taken aback by her response, "Oh my gosh, Frank. You and Michael are the perfect parents for those boys. Logan and Brett are so lucky to have you. I would've never been able to handle things the way you guys do. You two are amazing."

I wanted to be a stronger, calmer, more confident father than my dad was. At times, I've accomplished that. At other times, I've fallen short and mimicked his worst behavior. Logan and Brett have helped me become the parent I needed and wanted to be. Through the process, they've helped me, more than anyone else, find myself and transcend my trauma. But I knew I still had work to do.

CHAPTER THIRTEEN

LET IT GO

"Closer to Fine" | Indigo Girls

The third time's a charm? On a constant quest for seeking relief, I went to doctors, to the mountains, had children, drank from the fountain. I was seeing and feeling progress; things were changing inside and out. I was finally feeling closer to fine.

* * *

When it comes to stress relief, there's the healthy stuff, such as clean eating, meditation, and exercise, and the less healthy stuff, like ice cream, drinking, or shopping. Most people have visited both sides of that equation at some point in their lives. What works for me are two things I've been doing since childhood, two things that started as ways to avoid external conflicts but are now intentional ways of dealing with internal dilemmas: running and therapy.

As a child, running was about keeping a distance between my father and from myself; as a teen, it was about getting out of the house, although I wasn't conscious of the latter at the time. Today, running serves to clear my mind, calm my nerves, and help me process what's going on in my life so that I can be my best authentic self in my relationships. Running in nature is a religious experience for me; it's where I connect with God and all things spiritual.

My self-care regimen also includes therapy. While the version I experienced at six years old was hardly voluntary and brought as much stress as it relieved, today I readily turn to therapy for the same reasons as running: to learn how to be with intense emotions, to know what I need, to connect with my inner wisdom.

I finished my second round of therapy with Mike shortly after I met Michael. After all, my symptoms of PTSD had resolved and things were pretty good in my life at that point. But the last thing I expected was that starting a family would bring up a different dimension of my trauma. Since I was committed to being the best parent I could be, I knew there was more to heal. A piece of my dad still resided in me, and raising my children brought it to the surface. There is no worse feeling for the trauma survivor than connecting with the perpetrator within them. Whenever I lost it with my boys, I was filled with disgust and self-hatred; it was the only time in my life I ever felt suicidal. *I would rather kill myself than inflict the same pain on my kids that my father bestowed upon me.*

When you don't know what to do, pain and distress have a way of deciding for you. Once I realized the corner I was in, I unambiguously chose once again to go back into therapy. They say the third time's a charm, right? This time, though, I did something unexpected: I chose a woman therapist.

Natalie Billings was exceptionally smart, highly intuitive, and genuinely empathetic. Trained in IFS, she held a remarkable capacity to honor and be with feelings, which helped me uncover a deeper layer of trauma buried within my body. With her guidance, I went back into my childhood and allowed myself to fully embrace how I felt as a kid. I was able to feel the fear, helplessness, and pain I experienced as a child. I went back to being screamed and cursed at, chased around the house, slapped and hit. This time, though, it was not about me telling the story. I was able to be with that kid and all of his pain in a loving way. In my mind's eye, Natalie directed my adult self to compassionately be with my child part as he shared all the confusing beliefs, overwhelming emotions, and physical sensations he held on to from my past. That younger part of me was finally able to release what never belonged to him but what he was forced to carry. He saw that I was strong enough now to be with his pain, that I fully understood his experience.

"My brother and I used to frequently have ice cream at night and stir it until it became liquid. We would scoop a spoonful and say, 'It's time to take your medicine,' and we would feed it to each other."

"That's a strange game to play," Natalie said, a puzzled look on her face.

"Remember, my dad was a pharmacist," I reminded her. "He always had tons of medicine around the house that he brought home from the pharmacy. You should've seen our medicine cabinet. I think we picked up this game because he used to give my sisters 'special' cough medicine at night. It was called Phenergan with Codeine."

"Were your sisters sick?" Natalie asked.

"No, not at all," I told her. "It was to help them sleep through the night . . . or maybe more accurately, to help my parents sleep through the night. My sisters are just eleven months apart and shared a bedroom, so if one of them was restless and up at night, so was the other one. And having two crying babies was more than my parents could—or wanted—to manage."

After a pause, another memory showed up in my mind. "My parents also gave us our immunizations at night."

"What do you mean?" Natalie asked, even more perplexed.

"We didn't go to the pediatrician's office for our shots," I reflected. "I'm not sure why. I just remember my dad would bring home a vial of whatever immunization was needed at the time, and my parents would give us shots at night while we were sleeping."

"Could you check in with that little boy, Frank, and see what it was like for him to get those shots at night?"

I closed my eyes and tried to internally connect to that younger part of me. "I can see him lying in bed. He's curled up in a fetal position, and he's terrified. He doesn't want to go to sleep because he knows what's coming. I can see my brother in his bed too. We're trying our best to stay awake, but we can't. We're too tired. So, eventually, we fall asleep. All of a sudden, out of the blue, the boy wakes up screaming when the pain from the needle enters his butt. He's petrified. He says, 'It's just like all the nightmares, but the pain is real, not only in my mind.'"

"Let him share the whole experience with you," Natalie gently encouraged me, "and let him see that you're an adult now. That you're able to be with him today in the way he needs you to be."

I close my eyes. *I'm sitting beside the little boy. I'm holding him and stroking his hair as he cries. My heart is full and I feel sad for him and what he is going through. Our eyes meet as he looks up to me.*

"He really likes that," I said, "and I can truly feel love for him." After a pause, I responded, "He felt alone—he needed someone to be with him back then, the way I'm being with him now."

"Yes, he did."

We sat quietly as I stayed with him. After a few moments, Natalie continued, her voice soft and caring. "Let him know that he can let go of what he's carrying connected to that experience."

"He hated them for doing that. He thought he should have been tougher. The sting from the needle came out of nowhere and it really hurt. I can feel the pain he felt back then."

"It all makes sense," Natalie said. "When he's ready, tell him that he doesn't have to hold it anymore. Now that you get it, he can let it go, and be safe with you."

After a few moments of being with that little boy in a loving and caring way, I began to see red flames shooting from his body. They slowly dissipated as they floated up into the sky. His body relaxed. "I can finally rest now, for real," he said as he gently fell asleep.

Natalie and I went through this process, over and over, with the various memories I had carried—or, more accurately, buried—throughout my life. Using this approach gave me a fresh perspective on my attachment to my mother, my toxic relationship with my father, and my ongoing need for love and approval. Through our sessions together,

Natalie helped me heal the part of myself that was Frankie, the trauma-tized, insecure, needy kid, while also helping me to claim and embrace Frank, the man, who was not only successful but healthy, whole, and well-loved.

It was a life-changing experience. Each time I revisited and released more of my history in this way, I began to feel calmer, more confident, more myself. Natalie also encouraged me to vocalize what I needed and believed in, to set better boundaries with people, to say "no" with con-viction. It was challenging, but being with my trauma this way allowed me to feel powerful, more in control, and more adult in a way that all my external achievements never had. I began to show up differently with colleagues at work, with my husband, and with my kids. It was like a new kind of coming out. Instead of shedding the clothes and affect of an inau-thentic sexuality, I was shedding the pain and fear that had colored my perspective and influenced my choices. I was coming out of a life defined by trauma.

* * *

My work in therapy also improved my relationship with my parents. It allowed me to separate what happened to me in the past from who my parents are in the present. As a result, I felt more receptive to having a relationship with them. My parents changed, too. I believe the period of separation, hard as it was on them, influenced them. They were less defensive, better able to hear me when I spoke up. My dad no longer tried to control me, and my mom could better acknowledge the strain between my dad and me. Now when I called home, my mom no lon-ger rushed to get my dad to join the conversation, hoping that he and I would repair the chasm that lay between us.

My dad always valued family and was thrilled to have us on speaking terms again. In fact, because my family was at its best on vacation, he generously offered to pay for the entire family—his kids, their partners, and all his grandchildren—to go for a week to Turks and Caicos at an all-inclusive resort. We had a wonderful time together. We ate meals at the various themed restaurants (and enjoyed Logan's first reaction to sushi), drank piña coladas (virgin and regular) at the swim-up bar, played beach volleyball, and cheered as my seventy-eight-year-old mom, to everyone's amazement, went down the big slide at the waterpark. It felt like a huge step forward for my family in resolving the problems from our past.

The newfound strength and confidence I gained in therapy also began to affect my professional life. After my breakthroughs with Natalie, things gradually began to change in healthy, empowering, and deeply fulfilling ways. I'm less performance-driven when I teach. I'm more authentic and self-connected and feel so much joy when I interact with people who resonate with my mission. My career no longer feels like work. It's less about success and proving my worth, more about con-nection and bringing trauma healing to the world. It went from a career to a calling, from a paycheck to a higher purpose.

As a result, I became more committed than ever to learn as much as I could and to help those who suffered from trauma like I had. I started speaking and teaching, not only from the perspective of a Harvard-trained psychiatrist but also from the perspective of someone who had a firsthand experience with both trauma and the healing process. I dove into writing and published two books about IFS and trauma. The first one was coauthored and called the *Internal Family Systems Skills Training Manual*; the second, *Transcending Trauma,* I wrote on my own. On the strength of these two books, I began teaching workshops all throughout the world.

I also showed up differently with friends and colleagues. In the past, I was always nice and kind to a fault. I was accommodating, never confronted anyone, and rarely shared my true feelings with them. As a result, people liked me but didn't really know me. Working with IFS, both on myself and with patients, empowered me to develop a different level of intimacy. The result was profound, particularly with two long-time colleagues, Libby and Wayne. For years, our working relationship was pleasant and cordial, with very little conflict. But ever since I began showing up differently, our connection deepened into an incredibly healing friendship. We can be totally honest and vulnerable with each other. I share the bad, shameful stuff about me as well as the thrills, joys, and excitements I've encountered, and never feel judged, or that I'm "too much." These friendships have changed the template I had with both men and women in my life. With Wayne, I've experienced a man as gentle, kind, and accepting, unlike my dad. With Libby, I've learned that women can be loving and trustworthy and maintain boundaries at the same time.

My relationship with my past mentors, Bessel van der Kolk and Dick Schwartz, changed as well. I projected my feelings toward my father onto both these relationships—I became fearful of Bessel and desperate for Dick's approval. I devoted decades of my life toward the advancement of their work, until I found that my own professional growth had hit a wall. To fulfill my own purpose, I had to follow my own path, even when it diverged from theirs—not an easy realization but a healthy one. Today, I see them both as colleagues and equals. I can speak up, be honest, even disagree with them, without fearing retribution or the loss of our connection. Rather than relating as father and son or mentor and protégé, we relate as adults, with respect for each other's unique role in bringing trauma healing to the world.

A version of this dynamic played out in my relationship with Michael. For the most part, Michael and I have a great marriage, despite the fact that we are very different people. I'm an extrovert, while he's an introvert. I'm passionate, he's reserved. I'm career-focused, he's domestic. I'm more logical, he's more sensitive. We also have a lot in common and enjoy spending time together. I feel extremely lucky, because after our many years together—twenty-four, to be exact—I'm still in love with him.

Michael and I rarely fight, mostly because our beliefs and values are aligned but also because of our history with our parents. Our primary role models for intimacy were uncannily similar, as were the dynamics that played out between our fathers and mothers. When we would visit

Michael's family, I felt like I was right back at home with my parents. This resulted in Michael and I having similar tendencies toward being passive and accommodating with each other. We resisted speaking up and avoided conflict to prevent an argument. While there were certainly benefits to this way of relating, especially compared to constantly yelling and fighting with each other, there was a downside: we both had trouble asking for what we wanted and getting our needs met.

For example, it's common for couples in committed relationships to have different sex drives. I work with partners all the time to help them navigate those uneven waters. It's amazing that after twenty years of therapy, both teaching and receiving it, I still struggle with bringing up things that bother me. I remember how, after a few weeks with little or no intimacy, I would start my usual pattern of obsessing over how long it had been since Michael and I made love.

When will he be ready again? I don't see any sign that he's interested. The complaint was immediately followed by a reprimand. *Don't say anything. Look at all he does for you. Look at what he does for this family. He gives you so much—be grateful for all that he contributes. Sex isn't the most important thing in a relationship, anyway. Let it go.*

A few more days passed. *Why am I the one who always has to initiate sex? Just wait a few more days. It's no big deal. Stop being so needy.*

The next day, I started to get pissed. *He clearly doesn't want me. Am I really not desirable anymore? People used to pursue me all the time. Maybe we're growing apart—maybe that's just what happens when you're married for over twenty years.*

A day later, I shut down and disconnected. *Just take care of yourself. Get over it. He just doesn't care anymore.*

The following day, Michael showed interest. We were intimate, and it was amazing. All the struggle, all the anxiety, and all the self-doubt went away . . . until it came back the next time.

This pattern would intermittently surface throughout our entire relationship. It was only after the work I'd done in therapy that I was finally able to "come out" about it.

On a cold and snowy winter evening, Michael and I were sitting on the oversized couch in our rec room. Logan was at his girlfriend's house, and Brett was playing video games on his iPad in his bedroom. A fire was blazing in the fireplace. I realized that, for once, we were talking instead of watching something on TV. The moment felt right, so, with all the courage I could muster, I decided to take the plunge.

"I would like us to be intimate more often," I said to Michael. Saying it aloud, I felt instant relief, even while simultaneously bracing myself for his response.

"I know—I can tell," he said, with a note of exasperation in his voice. "Why aren't you ever satisfied in our relationship? I'm happy. I feel like it's never enough for you."

Oh no, he took it personally and got defensive—my worst fear. Michael was a people-pleaser, and my open expression of my needs made him feel inadequate. *See, Frank, I told you so. You should've never brought this up. It only causes trouble.*

Fortunately, we got over that initial hurdle. I stayed present instead of caving, and Michael shifted away from taking it personally—growth for both of us. Finally, we were able to settle into a discussion and address this long-standing issue between us.

"Why don't you just ask me or say something? I can't read your mind," Michael said.

I was taken aback by the simplicity of his response. Of course, he was right.

"I know, but it's so hard for me to speak up. It's crazy. I'm aware that I can talk a lot, but when it comes to vocalizing my desires, forget it. The fear of rejection and the belief that my needs don't matter usually dominates," I explained.

"I'm open to being more sexual," he responded. "Just because I may not feel the need to have sex as often as you do, doesn't mean that I don't want you."

On one hand, I wasn't surprised at how well the conversation went. I knew how loving, willing, and reasonable Michael is. On the other hand, I was surprised by the contrast to what parts of me had feared: coldness, shame, total rejection. Mostly, I was struck by how influential my childhood history continued to be in my life. *Is healing ever complete?* The answer was clearly no. Life has a way of bringing up different dimensions of our trauma, offering us the opportunity to heal at a deeper layer.

Suddenly, I flashed back to the kitchen table in my parents' house, when I would speak up as a kid and get cracked across the face by my father. My awareness of how prevalent Little Frankie has been in my life—how his views, his feelings, and his fears have had a significant impact on my present-day relationships. Thankfully, I'm acquiring a greater ability to live my life through Adult Frank's lens now. Therapy has helped me to be less consumed by the fears of my past, change my old habits of avoidance, take risks, and express my needs more directly.

* * *

I'm a firm believer in rational thinking and the scientific method. Through IFS, I came to validate the equal importance of emotions. As a trauma therapist, I combine neuroscientific data with empathy, compassion, and the impact of the body in the healing process. As my trauma recovery journey has evolved, it's also expanded my belief in the power of spirituality.

My first spiritual experience was letting go and trusting that a child would enter my life someday during our surrogacy journey with Amanda. The second was on the treadmill at the gym, when a voice spoke to me about Brett: *Your son is here to teach you as much as you are teaching him.* Growing up, however, I never gave matters of faith or spirituality much thought.

I was baptized Catholic and made my first Holy Communion, went to confession, and was confirmed as a young teen. But my parents were not very religious, so going to Mass on Sunday wasn't something my family regularly did. In fact, my dad was a more of a religious skeptic when I was younger.

He would often say, "Every time I set foot in the church, something bad happens in my life. I'm better off without it." I've often suspected that something untoward happened to him in church.

My husband was raised in a Catholic, Baptist, and Pentecostal environment. Even though he currently rejects organized religion, partly due to it rejecting him, Michael never stopped believing in a Higher Power and forces beyond our earthly realm. Just as I rely on therapy for self-care, Michael regularly reads and incorporates spiritual practices into his daily life. It's one of the qualities that drew me to him.

Around the time Michael and I started couples counseling, he, in turn, encouraged me to consult with an energy healer. He believed it could help me balance out the high-achieving intellectual drive that so often consumed me. *Fair is fair*, I thought. *Why not try it? What harm could it do?*

Upon his recommendation, with an open mind and heart, I met with Ellen Sirois. Like Natalie, Ellen is highly intuitive and empathetic. However, instead of focusing on the body and past experiences, her focus is on the soul and unseen possibilities.

"They are saying you're ready for a change," she told me. "It's time to bring your gifts to the masses. People need the messages you have to share with them. I'm hearing things are better now at home, the kids are settling down, and Michael and you are calmer parents."

Through our sessions, Ellen confirmed what I knew to be true but hadn't fully acknowledged, and she helped me understand my calling and purpose in life. Thanks to my work with these two amazing, gifted healers, I was able to release a significant portion of my past trauma. I began to see my future as being filled with endless opportunities and felt renewed belief in my ability to have a significant impact on my relationships and on the world.

What's more, I gained confidence in my knowledge and strengths as a psychiatrist, therapist, teacher, and trauma specialist. I began mentoring two bright, rising stars in the field, Mastin Kipp and Matthias J. Barker. I am committed to teaching the next generation what I've learned over the years, while recognizing their unique abilities and supporting their journeys independent of mine. Just as I've tried to parent differently than the way I was parented, I'm mindful of the successes and failures I've experienced with my mentors and I'm trying to navigate from a different place.

After what felt like a lifetime of tumult and transformation, my life felt calm, balanced, centered, and focused. I thought I had finally made it, that all my hard work had paid off, that my trauma was finally behind me.

That was when I got the news that my dad was dying.

Me at eighteen months old. Dad was in pharmacy school and Mom worked the night shift as a nurse.

The summer of 1966. Ross and me—in matching outfits—with Mom.

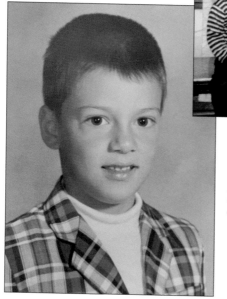

My first-grade school picture. The year I started therapy, 1969.

Grandpa Ross and
Grandma Katie's
wedding photo.

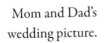

Mom and Dad's
wedding picture.

©Cadillac Studios

Uncle Tony, Ross, and
me in our Easter outfits.

Grandma Katie in her pointy
rhinestone glasses and
impeccable clothing.

The cousins playing outside after Sunday dinner at Grandma and Grandpa's house.

The grape mash in oak barrels before being put through the press.

Me, Ross, Luna, and Sophia on our family vacation to Florida, after the grueling car ride from Chicago, summer of 1976.

Me on vacation, after my
choice of a special activity—
a private tennis lesson.

The Guastellas all
dressed up—we presented
as the perfect family.

My Grandpa Ross and
me after he picked me
up from college and told
me about his jail time.

Grandma Florida, in one
of her "house dresses."

Our big Italian family.

Graduation milestones: needlepoint when I finished therapy in sixth grade and a diploma from Rush University Medical School in 1989.

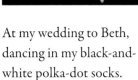

At my wedding to Beth, dancing in my black-and-white polka-dot socks.

The gargoyle I bought after the court date to finalize my divorce. A real turning point in my life.

The great reunion between my father and me after seven years of no physical contact.

Drag bingo.

Michael and me in front of my cottage in Provincetown, 1999.

Wedding number two, 2005. Michael and me engaging in the tradition of feeding each other cake.

The start of a new
life with Logan.

And then there were
four. The birth of Brett.

Thanksgiving dinner
with dear friends
Nina and Millie.

Brett resisting a photo of my
version of the "perfect" family.

My dad in his wheelchair,
at the kitchen table of
my childhood home.

Logan's high school
graduation cap, the day
after my father's funeral.

My mom and me at
my nephew's wedding.
Trying to move forward
after my dad's passing.

My family making
memories on vacation
in Los Angeles, 2022.

CHAPTER FOURTEEN

FORGIVENESS, FINALLY

"Both Sides Now" | Joni Mitchell

The layers began peeling away, the complexity softened, the dark clouds were clearing, the love was slowly emerging. Things were feeling different in the home of my childhood. I was seeing life from both sides now, for the first time in my life, and it felt good.

* * *

As a child, my father was sickly. He suffered from rheumatic fever and went to a special school. As an adult, he had a chronic inflammatory condition, which manifested as psoriasis and rheumatoid arthritis. Over the years, it had taken a toll on his body; moreover, he'd developed life-threatening side effects due to the self-prescribed medications he used to treat his condition. Chronic steroid use had led to bone deterioration, requiring multiple back surgeries. He developed a dependency on narcotic pain medications. On top of it all, he'd been recently diagnosed with pulmonary fibrosis. At the time, it was uncertain whether he might hang on for another few weeks, months, or even years. The only thing we could be sure of was that he would not likely go out peacefully.

It was clear that there was a part of my father that wanted to die; he had intermittently stopped eating and drinking, resulting in weight loss of more than forty pounds. But another part of him wanted to stay alive to take care of my mother and, as he constantly said, "just to see my grandchildren for one more day."

In the eyes of Frankie, my dad was a monster. He flew into rages. He bullied, berated, and beat me. I was terrified of him, and I hated him for decades. Fifty-plus years (and many hours of therapy) later, though, I could see my father for who he had become: a tiny, frail, elderly man with a body that betrayed him and a mind that no longer served him. Hunched over, unable to walk up the stairs, forgetful and easily confused. Seeing my dad like this broke my heart, just as any human being's suffering would, regardless of my relationship to them. I truly felt sorry for him. What's more, I largely forgave him for what he did to me and how he treated me as a child. Still, I didn't expect to be too broken up when he died.

By the time restrictions from the COVID-19 pandemic had eased, it had been nearly two years since I had seen my parents at my childhood home in Oak Lawn. Through regular phone conversations and the occasional Zoom call with my mother and my youngest sister, Sophia, I knew it was time to say goodbye to my dad. I planned to visit over a long weekend with my husband, our kids, and our little dog, Maya. Yes, Michael eventually caved on the dog issue. One day, out of the blue, he surprised the family with a tiny, eight-pound, all-white Havanese. She's become an integral part of our family—as Brett says, "The only girl living in our house."

Before we left for Chicago, I warned the boys, "I don't think we're going to see Grandpa Louis again. This will probably be your last visit with him." The night before our trip, I didn't sleep well. I couldn't stop thinking, *Please let this visit be different. No fighting. No tension. No drama. This is the last time I'm going to see my dad.*

Things didn't exactly start out smoothly. Our flight from Boston to Chicago was delayed due to a snowstorm. Then, as we were approaching Chicago, the pilot announced that too much snow had accumulated on the runway for the plane to safely land. *That's a new one*, I thought, as my stress level hit a new height. The plane had to turn around and wait until the runway was cleared. Accordingly, we flew east—as Logan commented, "We're back in friggin' Ohio!"—which added an additional thirty minutes to our flight. Naturally, when we finally got cleared for landing, it took yet another thirty minutes to return to Chicago.

I'd never been so happy to hit the ground in my hometown, or to see Luna's mile-wide smile at the arrivals area. Now in her early fifties, she works full time as a healthcare advocate, has a supportive husband and two beautiful boys, and still lights up a room—or in this case, her minivan—with her contagious charm.

"Hi, everyone! It's so great to see you," Luna exclaimed. "Logan and Brett, you've gotten so big since I saw you last. How's school? What's new? Michael, how are you doing?"

No one knew who should answer first, so I jumped in. "We're all good. Logan and Brett are both looking forward to graduating this year and Michael's busy with school himself. He's decided to go back to college and get a degree in psychology."

"That's wonderful, Michael. I can't wait to hear more about it." As we pulled onto the freeway, Luna's tone suddenly changed. "I just want to prepare everyone: Dad looks pretty weak, sleeps most of the day, and constantly complains of being in pain."

It was close to midnight when we finally pulled into my parents' driveway. Maya jumped out of the vehicle with Brett and Logan right behind her. Waiting for us in the entryway, as usual at the head of the kitchen table, was my father. This time, however, he was sitting in a wheelchair. His neck and shoulders were hunched forward, and his back was curved. His hair was visibly thinner and grayer, and his skin tone looked ashen. When he turned around to greet us, his smile revealed three missing teeth. He was wearing black sweatpants, a white T-shirt, and a thick black V-neck sweater that made him look smaller than he already was. All this presented a stark contrast to the image of my father still embedded in my mind.

Upon seeing his grandsons and our dog, my dad's face instantly lit up. He engaged the brakes on the wheelchair and slowly pulled himself up to stand.

"Hey, Grandpa," said Logan as he hugged him.

"Hey, my boy, look how tall and handsome you are! My goodness. I bet the girls can't keep their hands off you."

"Thanks, Grandpa."

"You've got good genes, you know," my dad, once tall, dark, and handsome himself, reminded my son.

"Yeah, I know, Grandpa," Logan said with a smile. I smiled too. It was like looking straight into the past—me and Grandpa Ross sitting at the kitchen table together.

"Hi Grandpa," said Brett. "This is Maya."

"I know, honey, I've met her before," said my dad. He always struggled with how to engage Brett.

Fortunately, his awkwardness never seemed to faze Brett, who commanded, "Come and pet her. She loves to be petted."

"Okay, I will, but how about you give me a hug first?" my dad requested.

This was a well-practiced pattern. My dad had been trying to get a hug from Brett for years, but Brett doesn't hug. True to form, Brett declared, "No hugs, only high-fives."

Oh no, I thought, fearful that a high-five would knock my dad right off his feet. "Careful, Brett. Go gentle."

"I know, I know, Papa." They high-fived and everyone was still standing. *Phew!*

"Hey, Dad, how ya doing?" Leaning down to hug him, I was jarred by the feeling of his bones through his clothing. *It's like hugging a concentration camp survivor.*

"Hey, Frank, how's it going?"

"Good," I said.

I knew he was happy to see me; I was happy to see him too. As always, though, there was a lack of warmth or ease between us. Even though I had done significant work around my history, I still struggled to fully integrate the changes I'd made in my life with him directly, and carried around a nagging fear that our complicated bond would never be fully mended. In that moment, though, reality hit me like a Mack truck: *My dad is no longer threatening or dangerous to me—or to anyone, for that matter. He is a fragile old man, and he's dying.* The last layer of anger, resentment, and hatred I had been carrying around for decades suddenly began melting away and my heart began to soften. For the first time, when I looked at Louis Guastella, I felt compassion.

Michael, the boys, and I had made a practice of visiting my parents once a year, usually tied into a holiday. Every visit had the same atmosphere I remembered from my childhood and young adulthood: big, loud, frenetic parties where we saw everybody—my three siblings as well as aunts, uncles, cousins, and their assorted significant others—and talked in quick, superficial sound bites. This visit was different. It was simply about spending time together. No parties. No tension. No drama from the past. Instead, to my great surprise, it was relaxing. Again and again, I caught myself thinking, *Wow, this is really nice.*

A similar surprise awaited me when the doorbell rang the next afternoon. It was my parents' longtime neighbor, Albert O'Connor—father of my childhood friend Mateo, impersonator of the Miller Babe, teller of the fudge-packer joke. I hadn't spoken to him in ages; the last I'd heard of him from my parents was that he'd been boasting around the neighborhood about attending the January 6 insurrection at the Capitol in Washington, DC. He'd heard I was in town and had stopped by to say hello.

Grateful to be spared the awkwardness of introducing my husband and children to the man who introduced me to the reality of homophobia (Michael had taken the boys out for lunch), I gamely chatted with Albert while my dad slept on the couch. I was looking for a way to ask him about how Mateo was doing when, to my surprise, he began asking me questions about my book, *Transcending Trauma*. "How long did it take you to write? Who did you write it for? What were you trying to accomplish?"

Before I could fully answer, Albert surprised me further by opening up about his own childhood trauma. How he and his siblings were regularly hit by his father. How he thought it was normal. How he believed that he deserved it because he was a bad kid. My therapist training kicked in, maintaining an attentive presence that mercifully masked my state of shock. This man, whom I'd feared and resented for most of my childhood, had spent his life carrying around the same profound hurt as me?

Standing up, Albert asked if he could give me a hug. As we embraced, he continued, in a husky half-whisper, "Frank, you're a better person than me. You want to help people. Would you be willing to sign a copy of your book for me sometime? I would really appreciate it."

My heart, already stretched wide, opened yet further for Mr. O'Connor. Instead of the carrier of my first experience of shame around my sexuality, I saw him as a little boy like me—afraid, confused, trying to figure out who we had to be in order to earn the love we needed. We looked nothing alike, we had different views, we came from different worlds, but underneath it all, we were connected, both by our traumas and by doing our best to survive in a complicated world. I signed his book and wished him well as he left.

* * *

For much of the visit, I sat back and basked in watching my parents enjoying my kids, chatting, and laughing together. Brett even convinced my mom to try playing his virtual reality game. (I couldn't resist taking a video of that—my mom is such a trooper.) We sat around the kitchen table playing Uno and 31, two of our favorite card games. We had bought my parents an air fryer, and the boys helped Grandma get the hang of making their favorite snacks. To my surprise, though, that was the extent of the cooking. After decades of stressful family visits revolving around food and drinks that took hours to prepare, my mom was happy to let us order takeout every night. Besides, eating solid food had become an ordeal for my dad. He struggled to eat just two pieces of sushi; it took him three days to finish one hot dog.

Along with enjoying my kids, my father engaged in conversation with my husband. During one of their cordial chats, when I overheard my father, it was clear that the narcotic pain medications he had been taking—some prescribed by a doctor, some not—were affecting his cognitive functioning.

"Michael, it's so nice to finally get to know you. You're my kind of person."

What a relief—Michael fell into the "good people" category.

"Thank you, Louis," said Michael, not mentioning the fact that they'd known each other for over twenty-two years by that time.

"You know, I've saved a lot of money over the years in my career as a pharmacist," my dad continued. "I've been thinking that it makes sense to leave more money to my girls. They've been so good to me. They're always coming over, constantly bringing me things to eat, and doing stuff for me around the house. It's the only logical thing to do."

"Well, Louis, it is your money, after all," Michael said. "You can do whatever you want with it."

Overhearing this, I bit my tongue. *You son of a bitch! You still want to try and control us from the grave. You're just like your father—cutting his son out of the will for getting divorced.* Once again, he was showing favoritism in the family, just like he'd done when we were kids.

But then, much to my surprise, my mindset shifted and a sense of calm took over my body. *I'm not going to let this consume me and ruin our trip. Let my sisters have the money—they do so much for my parents. I'm happy for them.*

The work in therapy was really paying off. I was done carrying around anger and resentment toward my father. It was important to momentarily acknowledge what I felt, but it was even better to not hold on to it. The freedom of letting go is intoxicating.

During our visit, my husband and I slept in my childhood bedroom. The room remained remarkably unchanged—the red, white and blue soldier wallpaper, the dressers and bookshelves crowded with trophies and pictures from our childhood, even the hinges and the pushbutton lock on the door. The only difference was that the twin beds had been replaced by a king and Grandma Florida's favorite rocking chair sat in the center of the room. But during this visit, I didn't have any flashbacks or nightmares, I didn't wet the bed, and I didn't feel hatred toward my father. Instead, after Michael and I reviewed the events of the day, I cuddled up next to him and peacefully drifted off to sleep.

On the last day of our time together, my dad said, "This was the best visit we've ever had, Frank."

My mom looked on, a big smile on her face.

"I totally agree, Dad," I said, with a similar smile. For me, the visit had been unexpectedly refreshing, even heart-opening.

Still, I was surprised to hear my dad ask, in a soft and vulnerable voice, "Could you stay longer? I wish you guys could stay for a few more days."

I started to tear up. "I feel the same way, Dad. It's been great seeing you, and I wish we could stay longer too. But unfortunately, we have to go."

As I walked down the driveway, it crossed my mind that this could well be the last time I would ever see my father. The sadness of that thought was mingled with an entirely new emotion: For the first time, I felt hope in my relationship with my father. *This visit is different. My dad is different. I am different.*

Luna was waiting in her minivan to take us to the airport. I was just about to get in when another thought struck me.

I should say I love him. It's the right thing to do.

I turned around and went back into the house. "Love you, Dad."

"I love you too, Frank."

I gave him one last hug, shut the door, and left.

* * *

I'm learning that forgiveness is complicated, much easier said than done. It's something that some religious institutions thrust upon many prematurely. Saying the words "I'm sorry" or "I forgive you" isn't that hard to do. What's hard is fully feeling it in your heart.

Have I truly forgiven my father for how he treated me when I was a little boy? Have I totally let go of the emotional pain and psychological torment I've carried for all these years? To be honest, I am not sure. Sometimes I suspect that I'm wishing forgiveness upon myself, wanting to be done with it all when I'm really not. But something is definitely changing inside of me. I truly care about my father and I feel empathy for his suffering.

But do I love him? Again, I'm not sure. Even though I said the words before we left that last family visit, they felt hollow to me. I know what love feels like. I love my husband, and I love our sons. I love my mother, flaws and all, and know she loves me. But I'm not sure I feel that kind of love for my father. While I no longer hate him and my heart breaks for him, I wonder if, given our history, this is as far as it can go.

After fifty years and countless hours of therapy, I've visited many of the painful memories I experienced at the hands of my father. I've released a lot of the negative energy I unwittingly absorbed through the way I was treated as a child. Thanks to my newfound confidence and self-love, I've been able to let go of much of what I've carried for so long. I see now that forgiving my father is a gift I'm gradually giving to myself.

As for my dad's feelings about me and the way he treated me, those are his to sort out. My journey is to learn from my experiences and unload what no longer serves me. I am well on my way; I hope he is, too.

I left my childhood home with a strong and clear feeling—a premonition of sorts—that I would be the one to oversee and arrange my father's funeral. I would take care of all the details, be there to greet the mourners, and comfort my mother. I would plan a wonderful memorial for Louis Dominic Guastella, for his grieving widow who loved him dearly, and for his family and friends, who knew him differently than I did. My father spent a portion of his childhood sick and in need of care, and most of his adult life helping sick people get better through his work as a pharmacist. I believe that helping others was his calling in life, and I know he truly loved his job. We have both those qualities in common—I've inherited them from him and can feel proud of that.

* * *

After the last visit with my parents, my heart was open. I felt reconnected to them and wanted to do whatever I could to help. My mom was working nonstop, and my sisters were working full time at their jobs while taking care of their own families and doing whatever possible to help care for my father. Knowing all this, I tried to arrange a caretaker to lighten their load at home. Through various family connections, I arranged for two healthcare workers to come to the house for an initial interview. Ross suggested that he and I pay for their services, which I immediately agreed to. It was the least we could do.

However, upon meeting each of the women, my father straightaway rejected them. When I called to check in on how the visits went, he flatly informed me, "We don't need any help, Frank. This is just a little setback."

My mom chimed in, her tone supplicating. "But Louis, I could use some help. Don't you think? Maybe for a few hours, just a couple times per week, so I can get some bookwork done and go to the grocery store."

"No, Butch, we're fine. Dr. G. says he has a good pulmonologist I can see. We'll get some answers soon. This is just temporary."

"Okay, Louis, if you say so."

He's always in control, and she always accommodates, I thought. *Oh well, at least I tried.* Even in thinking this, though, I noticed with gratitude that I wasn't holding on to anger or resentment.

The next day, I called my parents' house early in the morning to check in. Luna was visiting and picked up the phone.

"Frank, how did it go yesterday?"

"Well, he rejected them both. There comes a point with aging parents when you need to step in and take over. I think we've reached that point, Luna. We shouldn't be asking for his permission anymore. He's not eating, and he's taking way too many pain meds again. He's physically and cognitively impaired. It's not fair to you, Sophia, or Mom to be managing all of this without additional help. Ross and I will take care of all the costs. We've moved into a new phase now. Hiring a health aide is in everyone's best interest, including Dad's."

"I know you're right," responded Luna. "It's been really hard to manage everything, and it's only getting worse."

"Who in the hell are you talking to, Luna?" my dad barked from his bedroom. Apparently, he'd been secretly listening in on our conversation.

"Oh no, I've got to go." Luna hung up the phone in a panic.

After that phone call, my dad didn't talk to me for over two weeks—the familiar pattern of anger followed by disengagement. He heard the whole conversation, and his pride had taken a big hit. "No one's going to tell me what to do," he said to Luna.

Ever since the seven years of no contact with my parents, I'd learned how to set boundaries with them, to live my own life, to let them live theirs. However, after seeing my dad in such a weak and vulnerable state, I'd let down my guard and tried to help again. Unfortunately, the same dynamic still existed. Dad needed to be in charge and in control. I felt bad about him overhearing two of his children talking about his inability to care for himself, but all I did was name reality. Once again, I got shot down for speaking the truth and trying my best to help solve a problem my father was invested in ignoring. *This is why I've been so conflict-avoidant most of my life,* I reflected.

In addition to being conflict-avoidant, I've struggled with staying present and working through tough moments with someone. It's been hard to tolerate another's anger and to apologize when I've made a mistake or hurt someone's feelings. In Frankie's world, doing something wrong meant getting verbally assassinated or physically smacked because of it. Being perfect and achieving success was the solution I came up with as a kid. Do well, be perfect, and no one will ever get mad at you—end of story.

I'm finally learning that it's okay to slip up, to do or say the wrong thing. It comes with being human. Furthermore, it's okay to allow someone else to have their feelings, to stay in the conversation, to take responsibility for your actions, to feel bad about what you did, and to do your best to repair the breach that was created. More than okay, it's a sign of strength. I'm less critical now of myself and others; it no longer feels dire or relationship-ending when something goes awry or someone gets upset.

This was all new territory for me at that time. Despite my misgivings, I couldn't help but wonder, *Should I try it out with my dad?* I decided to take a bold step and give him a call.

"Hey, Dad. I'm sorry you heard the conversation between Luna and me. I didn't mean to hurt you. I'm sorry."

"I know, Frank. I understand your intentions were good," my dad said, to my overwhelming relief. "But I really don't need help," he continued. "This is a short-term problem. I'll be up and around soon enough."

The apology was successful, but the denial was still impenetrable. *Well, 50-50's not bad,* I said to myself. *Baby steps, Frank, baby steps.*

CHAPTER FIFTEEN

FULL CIRCLE

"To Be Loved" | Adele

The moment finally came, the one I had been waiting for, wanting, striving, and working toward my entire life. It caught me off-guard, it was different than I had imagined—to be loved and love at the highest count.

* * *

The text showed up the day after I had returned from yet another business trip. I'd recently had an uptick in travel for work; the previous six weeks had taken me to four different speaking commitments in four different parts of the country. I was exhausted, and the last thing I wanted to do was take another trip, especially to Chicago. But the message from Sophia, directed to both my brother and me, was impossible to ignore.

"Is anyone available to come in and help? Anytime would be great. Dad is failing and Mom is completely overwhelmed."

Ross couldn't get off work, so I booked a flight that day. Two days later, I got up at two thirty in the morning to catch a five o'clock flight; two and a half hours later, I was back in my childhood home.

My parents were still asleep when I arrived, so I had some time alone in the house to look around. There was a quiet stillness that was unfamiliar to me as I walked from room to room. *This is where it all happened*, I thought to myself. *The scene of the crime, as they say.* However, it all looked smaller now, felt less ominous compared to my childhood perspective. Wandering amidst the memories in that house, I felt stronger, more confident, more in control.

My mom came downstairs. She looked exhausted. With a smile and a big hug, she brought me upstairs to see my dad. Still asleep, he looked like a corpse lying on his back with tubes in his nose and his mouth wide open while the oxygen tank next to him made a loud rhythmic noise. The image was shocking, but I felt very little inside. I had already said my goodbyes. I was here strictly to help my mom and sisters get a break from taking care of him. Or so I thought.

Eventually, Dad woke up, and I reentered his bedroom to say good morning. He was disoriented and speechless as he looked up at me.

"What are you doing here?" he asked, his voice weak and shallow.

"I'm here to help." I gently hugged him.

"It's so good to see you, Frankie, but I don't need any help."

"Well, I'm here to help Mom, then." I smiled at her out of the corner of my eye. *Okay,* I said to myself, *let's do this.*

With prompts from my mom, I helped him get out of bed. Transferring him to the chair placed next to his nightstand, I proceeded to take off his pajamas, followed by an adult diaper soaked with urine. *I had no idea he was at the diaper stage.*

Mom handed me a pile of clothes, and I started dressing him. First, I put on a fresh diaper. Next came his socks and sweatpants. Last, I helped him put on a fresh white T-shirt. (Apparently, he was out of the "dago T" phase.) It all felt unreal. I said nothing and simply did what Mom asked of me.

I then tied a thick black belt around his waist, and he held on to me as I slowly helped him down the stairs. It was a technique taught to my mom by a physical therapist who came to the house a few years prior, when my dad was in rehab after his back surgeries. At this point in his life, it had become the new normal. He could no longer safely get out of bed, get dressed, walk to the bathroom, or go up and down stairs without significant assistance. It was yet another confirmation of what I already knew: there would be no recovery.

I managed to get my dad safely to the kitchen table and transferred him to his wheelchair. As Mom made breakfast, he repeated, "I can't believe you're here, Frankie. I just can't believe it."

"It's really me, Dad, live and in the flesh," I said, trying to keep things light while thinking, *I can't believe I'm here, either.*

Over the next forty-five minutes, my dad ate two small bites of a peanut butter and jelly sandwich. He was down to about 125 pounds now, much thinner than the last time I saw him three months earlier. As he kept repeating, "I can't believe you're here," I looked at his small, frail frame and thought to myself, *This is not the same person who used to chase me around the house screaming, "You cocksucking motherfucking son of a bitch."* It was next to impossible for me to integrate the father of my past with the person sitting next to me.

After breakfast, it was time to move him from the kitchen to the couch in the living room. His daily routine consisted of resting on his vibrating massage pad, which I'd bought him for Christmas a few years back. As my mom and Luna told me, he often said it was the best gift he's ever received; he spent several hours a day on this pad because it was one of the few things, other than pain medications, that helped the joint pain from his rheumatoid arthritis and the back pain from all the drugs he'd taken over the years to treat the arthritis. As I sat next to him, he moved in and out of consciousness, intermittently sleeping and snoring.

My mom looked totally depleted. A nurse by training, she was spending her golden years on private duty 24-7. Understandably, she was grateful to see me and taught me the ins and outs of caring for my dad, hoping I would be able to provide her some relief since she had so much to catch up on. For years, she had handled all the bookwork for the pharmacies they owned, and now she was adding inventory, order fulfillment, and other duties my dad could no longer manage. She was afraid to leave him unattended because one afternoon a few weeks prior, when she had left him alone in the house for a couple of hours to go to the beauty shop, he took too many pain pills, fell, and suffered a small stroke. Consequently, she hadn't been out of the house in more than three weeks.

"First things first," I said to my mom. "Call up your hairdresser and make an appointment for this afternoon. See if they can squeeze you in."

"Oh, Frankie, I can't leave him."

"Go, Mom," I reassured her. "That's why I'm here."

I'm still helping her with her hair, I thought as she left. *Some things never change.* However, some things had. How bizarre to reflect that now I was the one chasing my dad around the house—in this version, though, I wasn't threatening or swearing at him but instead holding his oxygen tank and making sure the tubes didn't get caught in the spokes of his wheelchair.

As soon as Mom left the house, Dad started talking. He started reviewing his life, looking back at all the good times he remembered from his past. That's when it hit me: *I'm here to help him die.* The realization honestly felt comfortable for me. As a psychiatrist, I was used to sitting with people, listening to them, and validating their feelings and experiences as they talked about their lives. It was clear to me that this was what my father needed to do, and I was happy to help. We spent two beautiful hours together, me listening, him talking.

"All and all, I've had a good life, Frank. Remember the time we went to California on vacation? That was a wonderful trip, wasn't it?"

"Yes, it sure was, Dad," I agreed.

"We've had a lot of great vacations over the years," he reflected. "When you were younger, we used to go up to Spooner, Wisconsin, on fishing trips. We didn't have a lot of money back then, but we still had a lot of fun. Do you remember those trips?"

"I do. Remember the time I caught that largemouth bass and it won the biggest catch of the week? They placed it in a freezer in the town center for everyone to see."

He's also helping me remember some of the good times we shared together. In return, I reminded him of the day I got two hits in baseball and he was there to watch it unfold.

"Oh, yeah, that's right. I remember that too," he said with a smile. "I've also been so fortunate to have such a great career. Have I ever told you that if you love what you do, you'll never have to work a day in your life?"

"Yes, you've told me that, Dad." I reassured him. "I feel lucky because I do love my work."

"I know you do. I'm so proud of you and all you've accomplished. You are at the top of your field, just like I said you'd be. We are both lucky, Frank."

"Yes, you're right. We're so fortunate to love what we do," I confirmed. It was profound to see how, with his defenses down, he could actually say he was proud of me. Just as profound was the fact that I could feel it was true. It wasn't love, but maybe it meant the same thing for him.

"I'm worried about your mother, Frank," Dad confided. "She needs me. God love her, but she's so damn insecure sometimes."

"I know she is, but I want you to know that all of us kids will help her. I promise you I will always look out for her," I said, and I meant it.

"I know you will," Dad responded. "I appreciate that."

How strange, I thought to myself, *the object of his rage becomes his saving grace.* My mom couldn't help him review his life in this way because she was too desperate to keep him alive. I was grateful to assist him in starting to let go, and even more grateful that he was at last able to receive my help. I also felt good about not needing to challenge any of his perceptions or share my views that differed from his. The conversation was about him and all that he needed to sort through and make right before dying.

"Frankie, it's amazing!" my mom told me the following day. "Ever since you've arrived, he's been better than he's been in months."

"He usually sleeps all day and hardly eats or drinks anything," Sophia chimed in.

My simply being there with my dad, caring for him, sitting together to eat or talk, seemed to breathe new life into his fragile mind and body. Was my presence important to him? Did he actually like having me around? Or did he just need someone to come in and take charge instead of letting him run the show, as my mom and sisters were accustomed to doing? It didn't matter—it was working.

That said, it wasn't all easy for me.

"Come on, Dad. It's time to drink something. Just a few sips," I encouraged him. "No more Diet Pepsi. Caffeine-free Pepsi is much better for you. It has more calories, and it doesn't have any caffeine, which is dehydrating." *What he really needs to drink is a protein shake, not soda,* I thought, *but we'll address that tomorrow.*

"Okay, if you say so, Frank." He managed to take two sips, then shook his head and sat back.

Since my father hadn't bathed since he was released from the hospital three weeks earlier, my mom asked me to help him take a shower. Putting the strap around his waist, I helped him walk back up the stairs and led him into the bathroom.

"Come on, Dad. It's time to take a shower," I said. "I'll help you take your clothes off."

"Okay, Frank," he complied.

The image of this tiny old man, hunched over, with multiple scars down the entire length of his back, his shrunken butt and sagging skin, will forever be etched in my mind. I helped him get into the shower as he sat in the plastic hospital chair that my mom purchased a few months prior. He proceeded to give me instructions on how to bathe him.

"The shampoo needs to go on first," he said. "Then we need to wash from the top down, face first, then the body, and last the legs. This way, we won't get any dirt on the areas that are already clean."

"Okay, Dad," I said calmly. "We can wash in whatever order you want to."

"We need more soap on that washcloth—it needs to be really soapy," he instructed. "And make sure you wash in between each one of my toes when you get to my feet."

"I sure will." As I washed my dad, images of Little Frankie flashed through my mind. *A full-circle moment*, I thought. I used to spend hours in this very bathroom with my mom—who would sometimes be just in a bra and underwear—helping with her hair, makeup, and outfit choices. Now I was back here, some fifty years later, helping my dad undress and take a shower. I didn't want to be there back then and I didn't want to be here now. But, for entirely different reasons, I couldn't say no to either of them.

That night, I had a familiar dream, one that had frequently recurred throughout my adult life. In the dream, it was the last day of college, and my friends and I were having a big celebration. Everyone was hugging each other and saying goodbye as this chapter in our life came to an end. I hugged my friend Amy and told her that the last four years had been great. Then I proceeded to pack up my dorm room to head back home.

This time, however, the dream felt different. Usually, it was filled with sorrow and a sense of loss; I typically woke up crying. But this time, I wasn't sad at all. Instead, I felt serene when I woke. I then realized that the past few days were not only helpful for my father; they were helpful for me, too. *Endings can be peaceful*. It was a new insight for me.

As I zipped up my suitcase and headed downstairs to the kitchen, I was greeted by an envelope with "For Logan" written on it. Beside it was a travel coffee mug with a note attached: "For Frankie." I burst into tears. I knew the coffee cup was my mom's doing—she is so sweet and thoughtful in those small but significant ways. I took a tentative sip and was grateful to find that she'd filled it with coffee, not Linco.

The envelope for my son was from my dad. Peeking inside, I found three fifty-dollar bills and two small pieces of paper with my parents' handwritten names and initials. During my visit, Logan had texted me a request: "Can you get Grandma and Grandpa's signature or something memorable of them to bring home? I see a tattoo in the near future ☹." I started crying all over again.

Just as I was about to leave to catch my flight, my mom came down the stairs.

"Oh, I'm glad I caught you," she said. "Your dad wanted to make sure you woke him up and said goodbye before you left."

I walked back up the stairs and stood beside his king-size bed, the very same spot where I stood as a six-year-old boy when my dad told me, "You're not going to school today, Frankie." I paused for a moment, thinking about all that had transpired in my life from age six to now, like watching a movie on fast-forward. Then I leaned over and kissed my dad on his forehead. He woke up with a start and looked me in the eyes.

"Frank, I may not have been the father you needed or wanted, but I have always loved you."

Overcome by his words, I burst into tears for the third time and held my father close.

As I pulled out my laptop to write this chapter on the plane ride home, I was still crying. It felt as if the dam finally and fully broke. I'd never cried so much in my entire life—not when I came out, not during my wedding to Michael, not for the birth of my two boys. *I must look like a complete fool to the passengers sitting around me,* I thought. Oddly, I didn't care. I really couldn't help myself, anyway. I had finally connected to the huge, deep well of sorrow inside me. Sorrow for all that I went through growing up—the hurt and pain my dad inflicted on me, and how much I hated him for it. Sorrow about the anger and resentment I carried around with me toward him for the vast majority of my life.

Sorrow about how my mother kept choosing her connection with my father over my safety and well-being as a child. Sorrow about enduring so many shitty moments in my childhood home and needing to repress my feelings and disconnect from my authentic self in order to survive. Sorrow that my main coping mechanism was to keep busy, keep moving forward, and continually achieve with the hope to be loved. Sorrow over all the years of missed opportunity for love and connection, not only with my parents but also with other people in my life.

But alongside the sorrow, I felt incredibly thankful and fortunate that I was finally able to feel it all now. In the past, I couldn't leave any room or space for feelings; there were too many, and they were too devastating. But now, while the sadness was profound, it didn't overwhelm me. At long last, I was strong enough to feel it.

Feeling the sadness slowly allowed me to feel more love. It opened the door for acceptance, and gratitude too. I felt love and gratitude for my husband, for my boys, and for the life we were building together. I felt gratitude for my work, the success I've achieved, and the people I've been able to help throughout the world. I felt love and acceptance toward my parents—love for their intentions, acceptance for their limitations. I no longer felt anger toward my parents, myself, or anyone. I was able to forgive myself for tolerating too much and staying too long in relationships that weren't good for me, and for having a hard time speaking my truth and expressing my desires. In a way that was profound and personal, I felt the truth of what I had long embraced and practiced as a therapist: trauma blocks love, but love heals trauma.

I was also crying because, after more than fifty years of continually seeking his affection and approval, I finally felt loved by my father. The time I spent with him over those few days was truly the first time in my life I felt his love, complete and unencumbered by his history or mine. It was something I had been wanting, searching for, my whole life. As he reviewed his life and prepared to die, my dad's defenses melted away and he was finally able to be vulnerable with me. After months of denial, he accepted the fact that he needed help, and he welcomed my support. At last, my dad was able to express his love for me, his firstborn son, which apparently was always inside him. And I was finally able to receive it.

Today, I feel calm. I feel settled. I feel at peace. I feel my dad's love for me, and I feel my love for him.

CHAPTER SIXTEEN

THE FUNERAL

"Kiss from a Rose" | Seal

Who knew that so much growth and healing could happen at the end of a life? The pieces of the puzzle were finally fitting into place, the path forward was filled with love and forgiveness. Your rose is in bloom and your light hits the darkness within.

* * *

As I write this, I once again sit on a plane—this time, coming home from my father's funeral. The funeral I planned, as I knew I would. This final trip was filled with suffering, sorrow, and dysfunction. All of that, however, was overshadowed by the healing that took place for me and for my family.

I had flown out to Chicago just a few weeks ago and had a remarkable, rare moment of shared love with my father. This trip, about three and a half weeks after the last one, was primarily about making it to my dad's bedside before he died. The hospice nurse—the one my parents finally let me arrange for my dad—had communicated to my brother, who arrived the prior day, that my dad was most likely in his final hours. Ross called me to deliver the news, and I once again booked a last-minute flight to Chicago. As I boarded the plane, I knew that my siblings, and, of course, my mom, were already by his bedside. I would be the last to arrive. Would I make it in time? Did I really want or need to be there as he took his final breath? It is often said that people near death will wait for their loved ones to arrive before they leave. *Was he waiting for me? Was I worth waiting for?* These questions kept swirling around my mind.

Perhaps my dad truly was waiting for me. When I arrived at his bedside, he was still with us. He was in the living room, lying in a hospital bed surrounded by boxes of syringes for his morphine, suction equipment to help remove the excess saliva from his mouth, a stack of hospital bed pads, a blood pressure cuff, and the ever-present oxygen tank. He was breathing sporadically, gasping for air every thirty seconds or so, and each breath looked and sounded like it could be his last. He was even thinner than he had been a few weeks earlier, which seemed unviable, and he appeared to be in constant agony. It was heartbreaking to see him this way.

The living room was full of people. Along with my mom, Ross, and myself, Sophia and Luna were there with their husbands and children. My dad's sister, Auntie Mia, was also there. Despite the crowd, the room was quiet, as if a church service was in progress. One by one, I looked around the room and made eye contact. There was a range of facial expressions: exhaustion, desperation, pleading for relief, gratitude for my presence. It was typical for our Italian family to sit in observance when someone was gravely ill—a far cry from our holiday celebrations but a coming together nonetheless.

Everyone there thought he would pass shortly after my arrival. My mom, looking utterly lost and frantically devoted, spent each night in a chair next to his hospital bed. She never let go of his hand, even when she intermittently dozed off for a few moments. I was on "morphine duty" that night, giving my brother and sisters a break from the job. Every two hours, I gave my dad a syringe full of liquid morphine in the corner of his open mouth to keep him comfortable. Having spent many a sleepless night taking care of patients during my medical training, this was familiar territory, so I quickly snapped into doctor mode. Would I be the one who pronounced him when he passed, like I had done previously? Technically, I was qualified for the job, but I didn't want that responsibility. Yes, I was a doctor, but I was also a son, and as my father approached his final moments here on earth, I wanted to stay in the role of his son.

Against all expectation, my father made it through another night. As the morning arrived, we were faced with yet another day of watching him gasp for each breath of air. At this point, I just wanted him to transition peacefully.

Thankfully, my mom's denial had softened. No longer hoping for a miracle cure, she began whispering into his ear, "You can go now, sweetheart, it's okay. I'll be okay. You don't have to suffer any longer." Seeing my mom so drained, fragile, and heartbroken was excruciating.

The day dragged on as we witnessed my dad's labored breathing and saw the coloring in his face change from ashen gray to a color that I had never seen before on a human being—a harrowing combination of dark gray, pale green, and light brown with a hint of purple. I had no idea how long he could sustain being in this condition.

Around seven o'clock that night, it seemed as if something collectively and unconsciously came over us all. My siblings, mom, and I looked at each other and gathered around his bedside. No one spoke a word—we just knew it was time for him to go. We surrounded him, holding his and each other's hands, and gently whispered, "It's okay, Dad. It's time to go. No more suffering. You can go now."

Somehow, we all knew that he needed our help to die. Michael, who is highly empathic and deeply intuitive, later told me that he sensed my dad stayed around so long because he was finally out of pain due to the morphine and enjoyed feeling peaceful for a change. He also affirmed what I had always known: my dad loved being around his family and didn't want to leave us.

After thirty minutes or so of holding vigil around his bedside, I closed my eyes, raised my hands up, and silently asked God to help my father transition. I had never done anything like that before. I've certainly had experiences of letting go and trusting, but never to this degree. As I fully relinquished control and asked for help, I felt a golden presence appear within me and slowly fill up the room. When I opened my eyes, I witnessed my dad peacefully take his last breath. We all looked at each other, and I said what we all knew: "He's gone."

Embedded in the silence was a palpable feeling of relief throughout the room. Dad was no longer suffering. We huddled together, hugged each other, and cried. I sensed that for each of us, the tears expressed different emotions. For me, they blended sadness and relief. I was sad for the suffering my father had endured. I was sad for my mom, who seemed adrift and brokenhearted. I was sad for all that had transpired between us over the years. At the same time, I was relieved that my dad was no longer tormented by the physical pain of illness, by the addiction that developed in his attempt to self-medicate, and by the emotional instability that plagued him throughout his life. I was relieved that he was finally at peace and I was finally free from our complicated relationship. My father's death was an exquisitely poignant moment, stripped of everything but love and connection. I will remember it for the rest of my life.

My mom sat with her husband for a few hours before she was ready for me to call the funeral home to take his body away. During that time, an aura of calm filled the house, somber and peaceful at the same time. That night, she slept through the night for the first time in months.

* * *

As we gathered around the kitchen table the next morning, I knew I had a lot of work ahead of me. My parents hadn't made any plans for my dad's passing; instead, they had focused single-mindedly on him getting better. Consequently, I took on the role of making all the arrangements, as I'd known I would. While I knew there was an unspoken expectation that it was my responsibility as the firstborn Italian son, I did it because I wanted to. I did it for my mom, to ease her burden; she seemed so lost and helpless. I did it for my dad because I wanted to give him a respectable send-off. And I did it for myself. It felt good to rise above the years of anger and resentment I carried toward him for most of my life. Still, it wasn't easy to get to this newfound place of open-hearted forgiveness and acceptance.

A few days prior, as I packed my suitcase to be with my father for the very last time, Michael gently approached me. "Hey, Frank, I know this is going to be a difficult trip, but you seem really out of sorts. Before you finish packing, how about you and I go into the hot tub?"

This was a ritual we had created of late. When anyone in our family needed to process something that was bothering us, we would go outside in the backyard and talk it through in the hot tub.

His suggestion stopped me in my tracks, making me aware for the first time of my state of mind and energy: frenetic, intense, bordering on frantic. *God, I love this man.* Donning our robes and our Crocs, we ventured outside into the beautiful spring evening. It was just before dusk, and the rhythmic song of male peepers filled the air. As the warm, bubbling water enveloped our bodies, I found myself able to sort through the range of feelings I'd been experiencing. First and foremost, I was pissed at the whole dysfunctional bunch of Guastellas.

"Why am I the only competent person in this family? Why does it always fall on my shoulders to take care of everything?" I vented to Michael. "Growing up, I was the only one who ever spoke up to my father when he said something outrageous and untrue. I constantly babysat for my sisters, way too young and way too often. When Mateo went missing, I was the one to arrange the search party."

"Frank, I know," Michael said. "But if you stay angry and in the role of the caretaker—the one who jumps in and does everything—you'll lose out on the opportunity to process your own feelings about your dad's death."

His words landed as an unvarnished truth, helping me shift out of a victim mindset. My whole body instantly relaxed. "You're so right, honey. What's wrong with me? Taking care of everyone and everything is a pattern I've worked hard to break out of. I'm bummed at how easily

I can slip back into that role, especially when it comes to my family." A feeling of disappointment settled heavily in my gut.

"I know," said Michael, "but you have a choice to do it differently this time. It's up to you, and how you show up with them."

"You're absolutely right," I responded. *Who's the therapist here, anyway?*

I took a moment, closed my eyes, and got in touch with Little Frankie. I began to feel guilt and shame for what was rising up inside me, so much that I hesitated to say aloud what I was feeling, even to my husband. But after a pause, I confided, "I hate to admit this, but there's a part of me that's actually excited about my dad dying. I can feel it. It's almost like there's this little boy inside, jumping around, shouting 'Yay!' Like he can't wait for this to happen. I feel repentant for feeling this, but it's true."

Michael simply nodded, so I continued. "It's the same feeling I had when I stood up to my dad for the first time, and at my wedding with Liz, when I was dancing on the tables like a wild man. It feels exhilarating—an anticipatory freedom."

"I totally get why some part of you would feel that way, with your history," Michael acknowledged. "But you're so different now with the people in your life. You teach about it in your workshops," he pointed out, "and you live your life with so much kindness and acceptance of others and their differences."

Once I connected to the range of feelings just below the surface and named them to Michael, the frenetic energy inside of me felt acknowledged and settled down. My husband was right: *This time, I can choose to do it differently.* I wanted to be with my family in the way I was with my friends and colleagues.

By then, the sun was setting. I looked up above the tree line and saw shades of orange, red, blue, even a splash of green paint the sky. I felt a calm presence come over me, and once again was able to surrender to it. A sense of release and relaxation moved throughout my body. *Why do I keep forgetting this?* I thought. *Trust and let go of what no longer serves you.*

These old patterns are like a well-worn path I've traveled on many times before. The grooves are deep, but I'm grateful that I can shift out of them more easily now. As a result, I *was* able to be with my family differently. I didn't show up from a place of duty or obligation; I didn't fall back into my old childhood role of the family caretaker. Instead, I took on the funeral arrangements from a place of love and compassion. I felt strong, clear, and in my power. I was capable, and I genuinely wanted to help. I did, however, need to move into high-efficiency mode due to the amount of work that needed to get done in the time allotted. But that was something I was good at, thanks to my medical school training and experiences as a resident. I could get shit done! And that's exactly what I did.

As the preparations unfolded, I felt fortunate that at fifty-nine years old, this was the first time I had to arrange a burial for someone close to me. I found a funeral home and managed the myriad details required to put together a Catholic wake and funeral: picking out a casket, writing an obituary, choosing the flowers, picking out the clothes Dad would wear for the open-casket viewing, contacting the cemetery, buying the plots, picking out the vault, finding the headstone, contacting the church, and arranging the Mass, complete with choosing the readings, the hymns, and the singers. It was an enormous feat to pull off in two days, but I did it. I was even able to ask for help when I needed it, and people were more than willing to pitch in.

It turned out to be a lovely affair, a true celebration of my father's life. The casket was ornate and there were red roses everywhere—it was very Italian, very Louis. I was struck by how many people showed up at the funeral home to honor my father. As several hundred guests crowded the room to pay their respects, it was clear that my dad had made a positive impact on many people throughout his life.

An elderly gentleman wearing a black fedora and tweed topcoat came over to say hello. "I'm Luigi, your father's barber. He was so kind to me and my family. I loved when your father brought his grandsons in for a haircut. He was always so proud of them. When he couldn't drive anymore, I would go over to his house and cut his hair. He was a great man. I was happy to do that for him."

Next, a short, stocky man in blue-green workwear came up to me. "I'm Benny, and I own a car wash. Your father used to come and get his car cleaned every week. Once, when I was strapped for cash, he lent me $25,000 to help me buy new equipment for my shop. He trusted me to pay him back—he never pressured me. My business is a success because of your dad."

I later learned that Benny wrote a promissory note on a bar napkin and paid my dad back every penny. *Four children and ten grandchildren, and you gave $25,000 to your car wash buddy? Without a contract or a lawyer?* All I could do was shake my head. Even at his funeral, there were new things to learn about my dad's impulsive nature and his need to help people.

In addition to many strangers who were close to my dad and thought highly of him, his wake gave me the opportunity to meet relatives who had been the stuff of family legend.

I was approached by two pleasant and polite middle-aged women, dressed in matching brown pantsuits, standing arm in arm: "I don't think we've ever met, Frank. We're Uncle Nino's granddaughters."

Wait—that *Uncle Nino?*

"Our grandfather always spoke so highly of your father," they said.

"Thank you," I responded. "So nice to meet you." After a pause, I gave into my curiosity. "I have a strange question to ask you. Did your grandfather's gas station blow up when you were kids?"

"No, not that I'm aware of," one answered.

"My grandparents did have a small house fire at one point, but I never heard about a gas station explosion," the other chimed in as she pulled out her phone and showed me a photo of Uncle Nino in front of his gas station with a big smile on his face.

"Wow, that's remarkable. What a big impact that story had on me and my siblings growing up." I wondered why my dad kept telling us that story. Was he trying to teach us a lesson or was it just his bombastic style?

"Hey Ross, apparently Uncle Nino's gas station never did blow up. Come and meet his granddaughters."

Next came a tiny old Italian lady in a cream-colored dress and black high heels with matching red earrings, brooch, and necklace. "Hi Frankie, I'm Nona Valente."

I took her hand while scanning my memory. *Is she a relative?*

"I've heard so much about you from your father," she went on. "He was so proud of you. My father was Angelo, your grandma Katie's cousin."

Does she mean the infamous Ut Angelo?

"The one with the dog?" I blurted out, a surprised look on my face.

"Yes, my father always had dogs," said Nona, smiling.

I couldn't believe my ears or my eyes. *Ut Angelo was a real person, and I'm having a conversation with his daughter.* I couldn't bring myself to ask her if her father had ever forced his dog to eat coal.

"My father, Angelo, loved your grandpa Ross so much. Ross was the only person to ever get my father's famous recipe for making wine. He also gave your grandpa all his winemaking equipment before he died."

The wine we made when I was a kid growing up was all thanks to Ut Angelo? Talk about connecting the dots. Even at my father's funeral, I was still putting the pieces of my history together.

"Honey, your father was so kind to me," Nona continued. "He gave me a discount on all my prescriptions and had them delivered right to my front door, free of charge. Once, the insurance company wanted me to start using Walgreens, and I got on the phone and had a big fight with the supervisor. I told him, 'I'm ninety-four years old, and my great-nephew Louis Guastella has given me my prescriptions for over thirty years. I'm not going to change that for nobody.' Do you know what he said? 'Fine, ma'am.' And I kept getting my pills from your father, and that insurance company kept paying for them."

Boy, don't mess with Nona, I thought. *She's as tough as her father.*

I was taken aback by all the wonderful stories about my father. Until the wake, I hadn't fully grasped the discrepancy between the way my dad treated me and the way other people perceived him. But it was clear that he was loved by many. Thankfully, I had finally reached a place in my life where I could hold the paradox with an open heart. My childhood experiences were true, and so were the experiences of the people who came to pay their respects.

To cap off the whole event, I coordinated the menu for the luncheon following the funeral services at my dad's favorite Italian restaurant, Palermo's, the same place my dad and I had our reunion after my seven-year hiatus. The owner, Lorenzo Pellegrini, refused to accept a dime. At his insistence, seventy-five people enjoyed a generous meal on the house, in return for my dad having taken care of all his family's prescriptions gratis. Over appetizers, salad, pizza, pasta, chicken, sausage, and unlimited wine and cocktails, we passed around a microphone so that folks could take turns sharing their memories of Louis. We heard stories of everything from family reunions to games of pinochle, from tattoos to skinny-dipping. Many of those gathered knew that my parents hadn't made any funeral preparations in advance, and everyone, friends and family alike, was appreciative of my hard work. I had created an event that allowed people to say goodbye to my dad and pay respect to my mom and our family. As ever, the Guastella family presented well. But this time was different from my childhood. What we showed to the outside world reflected what was going on inside the home.

• • •

While my dad was still living, my siblings and I had some difficult discussions about the division of labor. Sophia, always the closest to my dad and appointed to take over the family business, held a lot of understandable resentment about the inequity in my father's care—she did the lion's share of the work. However, despite a few tears and challenging moments, we were all able to honor each other's perspective while coming together for the common good. There was no yelling, no swearing, no denial of reality. We were honest and able to tolerate opposing views and feelings. As we sat together at my sister's kitchen table preparing the eulogy, each of my siblings began sharing wonderful memories about our dad: what a great grandfather he was to their kids, how much he loved our mom, how generous he was to his customers at work.

My siblings initially elected me to speak on their behalf, not only because I was the firstborn son but also because I routinely spoke in front of large crowds for my job. The assignment made me uneasy; after all, their experience of him didn't fully match mine. Knowing it wouldn't come across as genuine if I didn't feel what I was saying, I took the risk of speaking up.

"Hey, everyone. I'm sorry, but I really don't feel comfortable doing the eulogy for Dad's funeral on Wednesday," I told my siblings.

Even as I said it, I felt remorseful. *What's wrong with me? Why can't I just forget about the past, and only focus on what's good about him? Or are they just focusing on the positive, like most people do when someone dies?* I wasn't sure, but at least I had the courage to be honest.

Much to my surprise, my brother instantly understood. "I totally get it, Frank. Your relationship with Dad was complicated. Don't worry about it. I'll do the eulogy. I've got this."

What a relief! I took a chance, and my brother responded beautifully.

"I love you, Ross. Thanks so much."

"I love you too," Ross said as he hugged me. "I've got your back."

I flashed back to those nights in our childhood bedroom when he had my back during the repetitive nightmares I had as a kid. Some things really don't change, and sometimes that can be a good thing.

As it turned out, my siblings' response to my wishes paved the way for the most honest discussion I've ever had with my mother.

"Mom, we all talked yesterday and decided that Ross would do the eulogy instead of me," I told her.

Immediately, she pushed back. "No, I want both of you to speak at the funeral."

It wasn't like her to be so assertive. *Do I once again ignore my feelings and defer to her wishes? Or do I speak up with her, too?* The tension between these two impulses caused a different emotion to well up inside of me. Tearing up, I took a deep breath and asked what I'd inquired about so many times before.

"Mom, why did Dad treat me so badly growing up? Why was he always so mean to me? What was so horrible about me? I just don't understand it."

To my surprise, she started crying too. It was the first time I'd seen her shed a tear since the day my father died.

"Oh, Frankie, there was nothing wrong with you. Your dad and I weren't ready to be parents. To be honest, we shouldn't have had kids— we were too young and immature. Your father was a full-time student in pharmacy school in addition to working part time. He was perpetually stressed out. He would hit you when you cried, even as a little baby in the crib." She swallowed, shamefaced. "I don't know why—I guess he thought you needed to be disciplined or something. And I didn't say anything or stand up to him. On some level, I knew it was wrong, but I never grew up with a father and didn't know how a father should act."

I was stunned. My mind instantly started putting the pieces together. *So that's what the nightmares were about.* The recurrent dreams I'd had with a big dark figure looming over a baby in the crib weren't just dreams, after all—that had really happened. I was the baby. My father was the dark figure. My fear of him was real, not imagined.

"When you were older," Mom said, "I would always tell you that your father loved you, and I really meant it. He did love you, but he wasn't very good at expressing his feelings."

Well, he was good at expressing rage, I thought.

Mom continued. "He was under an enormous amount of pressure; I guess he was always out for the buck and wanted to be successful. He was different with his grandchildren—you know how great he was with Logan. He learned better and always felt bad about being absent for so much of your childhood."

"So, it wasn't my fault? It wasn't about being gay?" I said shakily, surprised by how young my voice sounded. "You mean it was about him, not about me?"

"Oh, honey, absolutely," my mom reassured me with a hug. As we stood there embracing, she repeated, "It was never about you, Frankie. It was about us not being good parents back then."

We continued to hold each other and cry for what felt like forever to the younger part of me. I was drained from all the practical and emotional labor I'd gone through over the previous few days. But beneath the exhaustion, I was strong and solid. I felt a new layer of tranquility and stillness within. I had received the gift of a lifetime a few weeks back when my dad said, "I wasn't the father you needed or wanted, but I always loved you."

Now I'd received a second gift, this time from my mom, with her acknowledgment that there wasn't anything wrong with me. It was extraordinary. I had come to this realization on my own during my many years of therapy, but to hear my mother validate it was a totally different experience. Kids take responsibility for what parents don't acknowledge or take ownership of, 100 percent of the time. Her words directly reached that little boy inside me, the part of me who always thought it was his fault, who always felt unlovable, who truly believed there was something terribly wrong with him.

I also felt my mother's love in a way that felt new and pure, no longer linked to her desperate need to stay connected to my dad. When I was a child, my mom's devotion to my dad made it impossible for me to trust her love. Moreover, her love for me had inflamed my father's insecurity and activated a jealousy toward me. Now, I felt a profound sense of peace and a new level of acceptance for my history and all the complexities in our relationships. It was as if a waterfall had emerged inside of me and my whole nervous system was being washed clean and returned to its natural state, the way it was meant to be from the beginning. I was finally becoming the me before my trauma. I could never have predicted that this level of healing would happen in my lifetime.

In the end, I decided to speak at my father's funeral after all. Empowered to speak from a place of love, not from a place of wanting to be loved, I talked about how life was made up of moments, some big and some seemingly small, all of which can turn out to be pivotal in our lives. I encouraged everyone in attendance to reflect on the moments they had with my father and shared that I wouldn't be the man I was today without the collection of moments I had with him, the good as well as the bad. I also talked about the importance of love, acceptance, and forgiveness. In closing, I expressed that I looked forward to the moments my dad and I will share together in this new phase of our relationship—him in spirit form, me in human form.

That evening, Ross and I sat with my mom at her kitchen table, reflecting on the events of the day. Uncharacteristically, my brother shared with us the perception he had of himself growing up.

"I was such a bad person," he reflected. "I was constantly getting in trouble. I was always so mean to kids and destructive of property growing up. What was wrong with me?"

In unison, we offered a rebuttal. "Nothing. You weren't a bad kid, at all. That was your way of dealing with the dysfunction in our family."

"Really?" he asked in disbelief.

It was clear Ross hadn't examined the impact our family had on him growing up in the same way I had—*not surprising,* I thought to myself, *with all the focus on me and my struggles.* Thankfully, Ross was able to take in our perspective and felt relieved by it. It was nice to give him some comfort and peace of mind after all he had given me throughout the years.

• • •

As a result of my father's passing, I've experienced a new dimension of forgiveness, one that comes after healing the wounds you carry: offering love and compassion to your abuser. Thanks to years of therapy and some hard conversations with my parents, I was truly able to rise above all the pain that my father inflicted upon me. I let go of the hurt, the anger, and the resentment that I held toward him for so many years of my life.

I have come to believe that forgiveness is more about the person doing the forgiving than it is about the person who is being forgiven. I was surprised to learn that it was only after truly forgiving my father that I could forgive myself. For putting up with too much for too long, fearing retaliation; for sacrificing myself in the service of others, concerned about losing the connection; for enacting a version of my father's behavior with my sons. It's when you see the humanity in those who have hurt you that you're able to have self-compassion for what you've done—to yourself and others. This, I believe, is the full cycle of healing.

During the last six months of my father's life, during his transition, and throughout the process of planning his funeral, I was kind and loving to him. I felt empowered by my actions and connected to the goodness that I knew existed in me. I was able to be my true self with more confidence, with more love, and with more compassion than ever before in my life.

After the funeral, Michael and I rushed our family back home to Harvard—Logan was graduating from high school the following day. Talk about an impactful week! Logan took a single red rose from the flower arrangements displayed at the wake to carry at his graduation ceremony. He had my husband glue it to the top of his cap, along with a picture of my dad from the funeral program. As Logan walked across the football field that day to receive his diploma, I began to cry yet again, this time for my son and how far he had come from the challenges earlier in his life. I cried for how proud I was of Logan, and that he had the special connection he had with his grandpa. Lastly, I cried with tears of gratitude for all the healing that had occurred over the past few days.

Shortly after graduation, Logan got his tattoo, the one my father gave him money for during our last visit together, when he told me he loved me. Emblazoned on my son's forearm is a red rose with my dad's signature connected to it.

Thinking back on that week of multilayered emotions, I believe more than ever what I said in my eulogy: Life is precious and comprised of many moments. Some are spectacular, and some are heartbreaking. Relationships can be wonderful and truly amazing, and they can also be extraordinarily complicated and devastatingly hopeless. We can sometimes show up as beautiful souls and at other times as horrific monsters. Holding the complexities of life is one of our biggest challenges, but it's also the sweet spot for our greatest growth if we choose to take advantage of the opportunity with an open mind and heart.

LET ME BE FRANK

"Rise Up" | Andra Day

Life moves forward with a different rhythm now. No more running; the silence is safe and calm. I live with strength, confidence, clarity. I am unburdened. I have risen from the day, unafraid, and would do it a thousand times again to feel the wisdom and freedom I've gained from my history.

* * *

After all these twists and turns, Frankie is at peace now. His truth and tenacious spirit proved to be stronger than his pain, anger, and grief. He learned through experience that trauma blocks love and connection and that, in turn, it is love that heals trauma. He no longer needs to be the one in charge, the one making decisions in my life. Nevertheless, he holds a special place in my heart. Because of Frankie, I—the adult Frank—live a fulfilling, aligned, and rewarding life today, full of love and gratitude. I'm able to connect with my emotions and trust my instincts. I'm more honest, no longer needing to overaccommodate others for fear of losing connection. I'm better at speaking up, having difficult conversations, and taking responsibility for my own actions. I'm not as conflict-avoidant or terrified of anger; I can hold tension and tolerate uncertainty. I'm embracing my confidence, my intelligence, my kindness, my power, and my ability to love freely. I believe that I will have a significant impact on the world by teaching people and showing by example that it is possible to heal from overwhelming life experiences.

Is everything in my life all wrapped up in a nice package with a pretty bow on top? Certainly not. I still struggle with hard times and challenges like everyone else. I have learned that evil does exist; I believe it's created when people are misaligned with their truth and out of touch with love. I'm also learning that anger has value, especially when it comes from the right place: a wish to protect, uphold boundaries, and prevent violence. I know that everyone is not united with my mission and purpose, and I'm okay with that. I'm learning how to be with their pushback and negativity when it presents itself. And while forgiveness still doesn't come easily for me, it's a choice I find myself increasingly drawn to. I'm more capable and better equipped to move through tough moments with less resistance and more trust. I recover more quickly and let go more easily.

• • •

If I've learned anything over the last fifty years, it's that relationships can withstand more than I gave them credit for. There are people who can work through difficult moments if I'm willing to show up and speak up. For much of my life, I remained loyal out of fear of either retribution or simply being left all alone. "Loyalty" often looked like being whatever the other person needed me to be—from an early age, I thought this was the way to be loved. But life has taught me that releasing my trauma and loving the person I truly am is what opens the door to receiving authentic love from others. As challenging as authenticity can be, I now know how to be in connection without reliving unhealthy dynamics or trauma responses from the past. I'm also capable of walking away from people who are no longer aligned with my values or the way I want to conduct my life. Letting go is no longer dominated by feelings of loss or loneliness; it's become more about acceptance and allowing the other person the freedom to be who they truly are. It's loving them the way I always wanted to be loved—a way that is honest, natural, free. And, to my great surprise, letting go doesn't always mean the end of the journey.

Thanks to a combination of therapy, the right medication, family support, and his own determination, my childhood friend Mateo has gone on to live a remarkably "normal" life. He eventually graduated from college, came out as gay, married an incredibly supportive husband, and now works full time at an agency that supports LGBTQIA+ youth. He has an amazing disposition and a unique appreciation for life, much like a cancer survivor who learns what's truly important by living through and thriving beyond adversity. I'm grateful to have helped him and know that I've had a positive influence over his life and made his path easier to navigate; I know this because he tells me so whenever we connect. He also knows about the impact he's had on my life: giving me the first glimpse of what would become my purpose.

Even though we don't stay in touch, I've heard through mutual friends that Liz eventually remarried, had two children, and works in a thriving practice in an upscale suburb in the Midwest. I'm genuinely happy for her and only wish her the best. We were young and naive when we met; I'm glad she was able to move beyond our relationship and find success and happiness in her life. She deserves it.

I have no information about Paulo or his whereabouts, but I wish him the best, too. Time and space helped me gain perspective on our connection and appreciate what we shared together. With Paulo, I discovered more than just my sexuality; I learned that I was strong enough to leave something that wasn't good for me.

Ross, Luna, Sophia, and I are all bonded by the experiences we shared growing up, some of them wonderful, others overwhelming. We each developed our own unique way of coping with the challenges: I dove into studying the science of trauma, Ross turned to hunting in the great outdoors, Luna leaned into her gifts as a consummate caretaker, and Sophia kept the wheels of the family business turning with her unflagging loyalty. Are our differences an adaptation to our family history, or a matter of personal interest or temperament? It's impossible to know for sure. But what I do believe is that our souls chose this family for a reason and that we were brought together and are bonded to each other for life. We're all in stable relationships and have done a remarkable job raising our children.

We planned a trip to Italy to celebrate the one-year anniversary of our father's death, and Ross and I paid for the lodging in continuance of my father's tradition. We all felt his presence throughout the trip, especially when we raised our glasses and toasted, "*Alla famiglia.*"

My marriage to Michael continues to be the most healing relationship I've ever experienced. I feel blessed to have found someone who is gentle, kind, and willing to do his own work. There's a familiarity and comfort between us that feels like we've known each other for several lifetimes. Sometimes, however, a strange realization takes over and makes me pause. *I can't believe I have fallen in love with a man! I'm a man who loves men, and we are raising children together and living as a family unit.* This utterly unexpected life we share feels weird and wonderful at the same time. No other person in my life has ever given me the space and freedom to be my true self the way Michael has. I'm so grateful that we found each other.

The biggest challenge, and the greatest place of growth in my life, continues to be with my children. They constantly push me beyond my current awareness. They help me expand beyond my present capacity. They drive me to love and accept beyond what I ever thought possible.

A recent interaction with Logan demonstrates this point. Shortly after my dad died, Logan started working at an upscale restaurant to kick off his gap year from high school. At first, he seemed to be thriving in his transition to adult life. Then, out of the blue, he became angry with me—needing to leave the room when I entered, rolling his eyes whenever I dared to speak. I had no idea what it was related to, and he wasn't forthcoming with any information. This went on for quite some time, and I became increasingly activated by the way it seemed to continue the family legacy: *He's treating me like my father used to—mean and vindictive. He's also responding to me the same way I did with* my *dad—distant and dismissive, not allowing any room for connection.* I felt stuck in the middle. On one hand, I relived being the son feeling hated by his father, and on the other hand, I experienced being the father who was abandoned by his son. Seeing how similar Logan and I were—tenacious, strong-willed, and determined—I felt new compassion for my father. *Was this the way my father felt when I cut him out of my life?* In addition, Logan wanted a motorcycle, and talked about joining the navy—nothing I could relate to or wanted to support. Again I wondered, *Did my dad struggle to relate to me, the same way I struggle to relate to Logan and his interests and desires?* This is about the capacity to love in the midst of difference. *How long will these lessons go on for?*

It was painful and illuminating to be on both sides of this familiar father-son dynamic. If I showed up as harsh or judgmental, I could push him away; if I stayed passive, I would allow him to treat me badly and engage in potentially dangerous activities. Neither extreme felt like a solution. Instead, I decided to wait it out, all the while sending him love and compassion. I even put a favorite picture of him on every device I owned so that when I picked it up, I was reminded of his warm smile, his sensitivity, his big heart.

This pattern continued until one day, out of the blue, Logan hugged me.

"I'm mad at you," he said. "You're controlling me, you always think you're right, and you're afraid of letting me grow up. But I'm really hurting right now and can use a hug."

As we embraced, I told him, "I hear you. I'm here for you. I love you, and I'm sorry. I'm open to listening to whatever else you have to say."

I remind myself, *You're not your father, and Logan isn't you. Stay present, love him, accept him, prioritize him, and hope for the best.* I can feel how different this approach is from what I grew up with, and it's the best I can do in the moment.

Much to our delight, Brett is doing remarkably well. He attends a therapeutic high school for high-functioning students on the spectrum and has matured beyond our wildest expectations. No longer smashing or throwing things, he is insightful and his humor and intelligence shine through like a beacon of light through a dark storm. In a turn no one would have predicted, he's the easy one to parent right now, needing far less than his older brother does.

I know there will be many more challenging times ahead with Logan and Brett. Some I will do a great job with and some I will mess up miserably. I know my trauma history affected my children. I know that PTSD gets passed down through genetic material. Did my lack of feeling loved by my dad make it harder for me to fully love my children the way they needed me to? I know they lost their safe parent each time I reacted from my past. I know my fear got in the way of allowing them to be independent and make their own mistakes. When they're older and self-aware enough to share with me all the ways I fell short of being the father they needed and always wanted, I will do my best to fully listen and validate their experience.

I live by an unspoken promise I've made to my kids: *I will show up, I will support you, I will love you unconditionally, I will work through difficult moments with you, I will do my best to take responsibility for my actions, I will try my best to apologize, I will teach you, and I will help you grow to live your best life.* I don't know how it will all unfold. I don't know how my intentions will land for them. All I know is that I'm giving it my best shot.

• • •

Three months after my dad died, I flew out to Chicago once again—this time, to visit with my mom and take her to my nephew's wedding. As I entered my childhood home, I wondered how it would feel with my dad no longer there.

However, I needn't have wondered. Louis Guastella remained as present as ever. There were pictures of him in every room of the house, framed on coffee tables, kitchen counters, and bedside tables, even taped to the wall in the hallways, bathrooms, and basement. The pictures showed him at various stages of his life that reflected how vibrant and energetic he was before his health started failing. All his belongings were still in place, too. Nothing had been touched. His toothbrush, comb, deodorant, and rinsing cup were still in the upstairs bathroom, as if he used them yesterday. Even his medicine bottles remained on top of the refrigerator and next to his bedside table. It felt abnormal, yet totally familiar. I knew my mom needed it that way, and I had no need to move her grieving process along.

Mom and I instantly settled into our comfort zone. There, too, it was like nothing and everything had changed, all at the same time. It felt natural and good to spend time with her. We fell into our familiar pattern, talking about this and that as she got ready for the wedding. The difference was that now the triangle between my mom, my dad, and me no longer existed. The house was quiet, and the tension had dissipated. In a way, we were closer and freer than ever before.

I decided to go for a run. I got my gear and set out on the same route I took the last time I was here to help my dad die and plan his funeral. However, this time it felt different. *I* felt different. It was as if my whole body was relaxed and reorganized after a lifetime of holding stress and unpleasant memories. Not only was the fear gone but so was the anger. I ran with a lightness and a pleasant sense of my dad's presence as I jogged through the neighborhood of my youth. It was strange to be back at the scene where all those horrific things happened to me, and to experience it in a totally new way, with a feeling of love all around me. I had been through a lot, and it was hard, but it was over. My dad was gone. My mom will never be the same. I had changed, too. Life had moved on, and I felt at peace.

• • •

Mom recently spent Thanksgiving with my family in Boston. It was hard for her to make the decision, especially because it was the first time she would travel by herself, but she did it—she was growing while grieving.

We had a wonderful time together. Brett loved spending time with her and was amazed at how similar my mom and I were.

"You both say 'reeeally' the exact same way," he pointed out. "You both are super loud when you chew your food. You have the same laugh, and it sounds weird. *Ha-ha-ha-ha-ha.* Gram-Gram, why didn't you teach your son better manners?"

We burst into laughter each time he pointed out a similarity. It was clear that my mom and Brett have a special relationship, much like Logan and my dad did, and it was beautiful to watch.

My mom had come a long way since my dad passed, yet we still had issues to work through. A few months after her trip, she got upset with me after she watched one of my workshops in which I shared sensitive details about my childhood with the participants. Teaching about trauma through my own experiences is a common practice for me, and I hadn't thought to warn her about it.

"When you talk about your history, it disrespects your father," she told me.

Her criticism stung, spurring a real conflict within me. *Do I stop sharing my story in the service of helping others?* I had no desire to hurt my mom (or my dad, for that matter) and I knew she was still in so much pain at that time. *But wait . . . What about what's important to me?* I feel drawn to let people know through personal examples that healing is possible. *Am I being selfish?*

Then it dawned on me. *This isn't really about putting her needs over mine. It's about Frankie's needs. His needs took a back seat to hers for years.* As I remembered how it felt to prioritize his/my needs when I came out twenty-seven years ago, I could see that I was being faced with the same dilemma yet again: whether to honor our story over my mother's pain or to protect her at our expense.

In my heart, I knew what was right. I, Frank the adult, need to prioritize that little boy now in a way my mother couldn't back then. I know he deserves to be loved by me. You're reading this book because I chose to honor him.

I know it's part of my mom's healing journey to navigate a new life without the man she loved dearly, while also coming to terms with the fact that this same man was harmful to the children she also loves. I will do my best to support and help her find her way through this complexity. I love my mom, I love myself, and I love that little boy whom I exiled for years. I will no longer sacrifice him in the service of another. Can my mother love my father while also acknowledging what he did to me in the past? That is out of my hands. It's up to her.

Shortly after my dad's death, I had a session with Ellen, my spiritual healer. She had never met or spoken with my father while he was alive, and he rarely came up during our sessions. That day, however, was different.

"Has your dad recently passed?" Ellen asked me.

"Yes, about a month ago," I told her.

"I have a message from him," she said. "This is what he wants you to know: He's sorry he didn't treat you well. He is saying that he wasn't strong enough. He's proud of you, and he's asking for your forgiveness. And he's sending you love. It's like there are stars coming from the sky, and he is sending them to you. His childhood was traumatic, bad things happened to him, and it affected his relationship with you. It was difficult and confusing for him, and he pushed you away. He wasn't there for you as a child, but he is here for you now. He loves you and he wants you to succeed. He wants you to go forward."

I was stunned by the message. Chills ran throughout my entire body. *Did I just hear what I thought I heard?* I started crying.

As Ellen talked, I strongly felt my dad's presence; her words felt as if they were coming directly from him. It felt like a continuation of the last conversation my dad and I had together, when I was at his bedside and he told me he always loved me. It was confirming and healing. Once again, I felt my dad's loving presence surrounding me.

It's ironic and wonderful that Frankie, the little terrified kid who hid in the crawlspace to ward off the horrors of his childhood and worked so hard to be what he was told he should be, is now happy, safe, and peaceful inside of me, the adult Frank. It's also ironic that I could feel grateful for all the pain and maltreatment bestowed upon that little boy; they helped shape me to be the man I am today. My trauma helped me become a loving healer. I teach workshops throughout the world and run two organizations that are dedicated to bringing trauma healing to the public. I have an amazing husband and two incredible children. I'm grateful that I can feel love for and from the people in my life that matter the most. I have learned that anything is possible with hope, love, forgiveness, and healing.

My wish for you is that you, too, can let go of your overwhelming life experiences, that you embrace the good and bad in everyone, that you forgive yourself and those who have hurt you, and that you're able to give and receive love, find your purpose, and live your most authentic life.

With boundless love and gratitude,
Frank

TO BE LOVED PLAYLIST

CHAPTER ONE: *"YOU'RE NOT GOING TO SCHOOL TODAY"*
"KID FEARS" · INDIGO GIRLS

CHAPTER TWO: *MOM AND DAD*
"BLOWN AWAY" · CARRIE UNDERWOOD

CHAPTER THREE: *THE KIDS*
"BOHEMIAN RHAPSODY" · QUEEN

CHAPTER FOUR: *ALLA FAMIGLIA*
"SPEAK SOFTLY LOVE" (LOVE THEME FROM *THE GODFATHER*)
ANDY WILLIAMS

CHAPTER FIVE: *MADE IT TO "NORMAL"*
"ROLL WITH THE CHANGES" · REO SPEEDWAGON

CHAPTER SIX: *FOR THE LOVE OF DOCTOR*
"LOSE YOURSELF" · EMINEM

CHAPTER SEVEN: *HAPPILY EVER AFTER?*
"NEVER DIE YOUNG" · JAMES TAYLOR

CHAPTER EIGHT: *HARVARD, REVEALED*
"LOSING MY RELIGION" · R.E.M.

CHAPTER NINE: *MOVING OUT*
"BELIEVE" · CHER

CHAPTER TEN: *FINDING MICHAEL*
"SONGBIRD" · EVA CASSIDY

TO BE LOVED

ACKNOWLEDGMENTS

This book would not have been possible without the myriad of people who have supported me throughout this journey. It truly does take a village. First and foremost, thank you to Linda Jackson and Karsyn Morse at PESI Publishing, who trusted me with the audacious idea to write a memoir. To the initial team, Justin Loeber and Mysia Haight, who interviewed me, helped me flesh out my story, and transformed it to words on the page. To the first round of editing support, Jeff Ourvan and Leslie Wells, who fine-tuned character development, finessed sentence structure, and pulled together the arc of the story. Next, to my writing copilot, Chelsea Thompson, who instantly "got me," was passionate about this project, and helped me turn a good book into a (in my opinion) great one. To G. Panzer, who dotted the i's and crossed the t's with their amazing copyediting support. And, lastly, to the team at Krupp Agency, who believed in me and saw the reach and impact this memoir and my message of healing could have on the world.

I would also like to thank Alexandra Ryan and Seanne Winslow, my initial readers, who offered honest feedback and helped explore the possibility of a movie adaptation of this memoir. To Bessel van der Kolk and Dick Schwartz, who mentored me and helped me claim my power. To my friends Libby, Wayne, Rich, Joyce, Chris, Bart, Janina, Amy, Mastin, and Matthias, who were and continue to be steadfast supporters of me as well as this book. To my brother, Ross, and sister-in-law, Marla, who have listened, encouraged, offered suggestions, and shared family memories with me. To Jim Frosch, Michele Bograd, and Ellen Sirois, my guides and advocates through the healing journey of my heart. To Michele Bruce, my partner in crime and co-creator of the mission. My life would not be possible without your organizational skills and endless support. You have my back, even when I don't.

To my incredible husband, Michael, who more than anyone else in my life has been there for me throughout the entirety of this process. When we went to bed, and you listened to the newest idea swirling around in my head. When I woke up at three o'clock in the morning to write another section of the book. You've been there for me through every chapter, every phrase, every word, and I am eternally grateful for the undying love and support you offer to every project I choose to embrace. To my boys, Logan and Brett, who put up with me when I sat on the couch in the living room or at the kitchen table for hours at a time, not fully present because I was totally immersed in the writing process. Thank you, and I am sorry. Lastly, to my parents, whom I've challenged and stretched beyond their wildest imagination. I'm grateful that you have constantly risen to the occasion, grown beyond your limits, and loved me every step of the way.

For all those named above, and for the countless others who have supported me throughout my life, I give thanks from the bottom of my heart.

ABOUT THE AUTHOR

FRANK ANDERSON, MD, is a world-renowned trauma expert, Harvard-trained psychiatrist, global speaker, acclaimed bestselling author of *Transcending Trauma*, and coauthor of the *Internal Family Systems Skills Training Manual*. Dr. Anderson has a long affiliation with Bessel van der Kolk at the Trauma Research Foundation and is a lead trainer at the IFS Institute under Richard Schwartz. He is passionate about teaching brain-based psychotherapy and integrating current neuroscience knowledge with cutting-edge models of therapy.

Dr. Anderson believes that traumatic events can have a lasting effect on the health and well-being of individuals and that addressing these events will help lead people down a path of hope, love, and forgiveness. He is the director and cofounder of the Trauma Institute (traumainstitute.com) and Trauma-Informed Media (trauma-informedmedia.com), organizations that provide educational resources and promote trauma awareness. As a result of his early childhood experiences and personal journey of transformation, he is dedicated to bringing more compassion, unity, and trauma healing to the world.

He splits his time between Boston and Los Angeles, where he lives with his husband and two sons. Follow him at FrankAndersonMD.com and on Instagram @frank_andersonmd.